D1457569

EXPERTS IN ACTION

EXPERTS IN ACTION

TRANSNATIONAL
HONG KONG–STYLE
STUNT WORK AND
PERFORMANCE

LAUREN STEIMER

DUKE UNIVERSITY PRESS · DURHAM AND LONDON · 2021

© 2021 Duke University Press

All rights reserved

Printed in the United States of America on acid-free paper ∞

Designed by Matthew Tauch

Typeset in Arno Pro and Bahnschrift by

Copperline Book Services

Library of Congress Cataloging-in-Publication Data

Names: Steimer, Lauren, [date] author.

Title: Experts in action : transnational Hong Kong-style stunt work and performance / Lauren Steimer.

Description: Durham : Duke University Press, 2021. | Includes bibliographical references and index.

Identifiers: LCCN 2020027523 (print) | LCCN 2020027524 (ebook)

ISBN 9781478010579 (hardcover)

ISBN 9781478011705 (paperback)

ISBN 9781478021261 (ebook)

Subjects: LCSH: Stunt performers—China—Hong Kong. | Martial arts films—China—Hong Kong. | Motion picture actors and actresses—China—Hong Kong.

Classification: LCC PN1995.9. S7S745 2021 (print) | LCC PN1995.9.S7 (ebook) | DDC 791.4302/8095125—dc23

LC record available at https://lccn.loc.gov/2020027523

LC ebook record available at https://lccn.loc.gov/2020027524

Cover art: Jackie Chan. Still from *Police Story* (1985, Hong Kong). Cinema Group / Photofest. © Cinema Group.

Duke University Press gratefully acknowledges College of Arts and Sciences Book Manuscript Finalization Support at University of South Carolina, which provided funds toward the publication of this book.

For the sixth floor of 721 Broadway.

CONTENTS

ACKNOWLEDGMENTS

If writing this book has taught me anything, it is that I have no right to call myself the author of this manuscript. While writing often seems like a solitary task, it is not. Work, in all its forms, requires the labor of others—others who all too often go uncredited for their contributions. I am bound to fail in this enterprise of acknowledgment. The task at hand is impossible, that of thanking all of the others who helped to make this book a reality through their own work—scholarly, emotional, physical, or otherwise. I'm going to try anyway. First, let me make something clear—my name may be on the front of this book, but my editor at Duke University Press, Elizabeth Ault, was my stunt double. She covered for me when my timing was off, she taught me the moves, and she made me look like a professional. She's the spectacular performer. I'm just the face that gets superimposed on all of her expert labor. Elizabeth, it was an honor and a privilege to work with you. I also want to extend my deepest gratitude to the entire team at Duke University Press. Thank you and I'm sorry, Kimberly Miller. You have, through your craft and artistry, tricked people into thinking I can write clear and grammatically correct sentences. Kimberly Miller is the fire-retardant gel that kept this stunt of a book from being a fiery mess. Thank you, Annie Lubinsky. Duke University Press may list you as a Project Editor, but I think of you as my Stunt Coordinator. You kept me on target and showed me the ropes. Karen Tongson read an early version of this manuscript, and if not for her support, this book would not be in print today. The international ethnographic research for this book project would have been impossible if not for the funding provided by the University of South Carolina Provost's Humanities Grant.

Kelly Wolf, you have survived with me through my dissertation, seven surgeries, a car accident, my hearing loss, countless pleas for puppies and kittens, and now this book. I admire you for your strength, your bravery, and your patience. It's been clear from the beginning who the strong one is in this relationship—in every possible way. I love you more than I could ever love anything, even Fiona. Thank you for driving me all over Ireland and New Zealand and remembering to ask the questions that I forgot. This book would not exist without your labor. I am grateful to Rosenberg and Garbo for getting me through the early stages of this manuscript and to River and Scully for keeping me company while I finished it.

The anonymous referees provided me with invaluable feedback. Their constructive advice helped me to deliver a much stronger version of this book than I had imagined possible. I want to extend my heartfelt gratitude to all of the fans who answered my questions and helped me to better understand which concerns to prioritize in the writing of each chapter. I also required the assistance of the Thai Film Archive, and they graciously assisted me with some translation work on Chinese-Thai names. The stunties and industry experts whom I interviewed for this project gave me insight into areas few academics are privileged to know. I thank the following exceptional individuals for their time, their kindness, and their insight: Eimear O'Grady, Dayna Grant, Lucy Lawless, Zoë Bell, and Peter A. Marshall. I also want to thank Dane Grant and Michele "Mishi" Fairbank for facilitating my interviews and visit to the *Ash vs Evil Dead* set in Auckland and to the *Ash* stunt team for letting me hang with them and for sharing their stories. I also want to thank Giedrius "Gee" Nagys and the Stunt School Ireland for letting me participate in their training day and for setting me on fire, literally.

This book could not have been written without the support of the Steimer and Wolf families. I thank Patricia Steimer, James Steimer, Pamela Wolf, and Joe Wolf for their endless support and the pet care they provided during my research trips. I also want to thank my sisters and brother, who have been my support network through this process: Susan Francis, Christine Steimer, Annie Wolf, and Pat Wolf.

My coworkers (and their pets) have been like a second family to me here at the University of South Carolina. Mark Cooper read an early version of my manuscript and provided me with key lines of thought for its revision. He and Heidi Rae Cooley also supported me through countless trips to the hospital and helped to keep my aging pets alive. Laura Kissel has been an absolute mensch throughout this long process. I could not have done this without her help. I thank her and Julie Hubbert for the time they spent with me in the hospital and Julie for just generally being my partner in crime. Teaching with her helped me to be a better writer. Sue Felleman brought me food and told me when I was taking on too much. I want to be like Sue when I grow up. She taught me how to be a mentor. Mark Minett and Heather Heckman have been a refuge for me as I wrote this book. I thank them for their friendship, their advice, and the unfettered access they give me to their cat, Monster. My production colleagues have taught me how to be a more responsible film and media scholar and how to properly account for media production labor and laborers. I thank Simon Tarr, Jen Tarr, Evan Meaney, Northrop Davis, and Carleen Maur for teaching me to be more responsive and responsible.

My dissertation group was there for me when this project was in its infancy and helped me to stay sane in those early days of its writing. Thank you, Ragan Rhyne, Leshu Torchin, Rahul Hamid, Doug Dibbern, and Sky Sitney. I am grateful to Miranda Banks, Toby Miller, Chris Straayer, and Anna McCarthy for the time and effort they put into helping me with this project. I am forever in the debt of Zhang Zhen for looking at countless revisions and examining my manuscript with intense attention to detail. The first chapter ever written for this book was edited by Bliss Cua Lim. It was Bliss who helped me to realize the potential of this research. Joel David supported me in every way imaginable. I aspire to someday know one-tenth as much as he does about Asian cinemas. Liza Greenfield has been my sage and my muse for over twenty years. She's always my stuntwoman. Lucas Hilderbrand taught me what was worth caring about and how to write with my own priorities and drown out negative chatter. Though this book lacks the eloquence of Elena Gorfinkel's writing, it is imbued with her revolutionary spirit. Alisa Lebow doesn't like it when I thank her for teaching me to be a better thinker, so I'll just have to thank her for her enthusiastic support of my creative writing. Her engagement with that writing made me more confident that I could write this book and that it might find a willing audience.

I want to thank all of my students at the University of South Carolina; the University of California, Irvine; and New York University. You inspire me to be a better teacher, researcher, and writer every day. I would also like to thank Jennie Jackson, in particular, for reminding me to stay hydrated.

I had the good fortune to meet both Chris Holmlund and Meaghan Morris at conferences, and those meetings changed my life forever. I had admired their work for so long, and getting to know each of them in person has been transformative for me and my work. Meaghan and Chris are the inspirations behind this project, and I am forever in their debt.

If I have forgotten anyone, please remember that I told you that my attempt at acknowledgments would be a failed venture from the start and know that you have my gratitude. This book is dedicated to the sixth floor of 721 Broadway because it was born there—born in conversations had, lessons learned, friendships made, and a life transformed by that space shared by the cinema studies and performance studies departments.

EXPERTS IN ACTION

Most Westerners, in their initial encounter with Asian masters of in-body disciplines are so overwhelmed by the sheer virtuosity of technique, the fluidity of practice, and the powerful presence of the performer that both "what" that virtuosity is and "how" the performer achieves that state is left unexplored.

——PHILLIP B. ZARRILLI, "WHAT DOES IT MEAN TO 'BECOME THE CHARACTER'"

I fear not the man who has practiced 10,000 kicks once, but I fear the man who had practiced one kick 10,000 times.

——BRUCE LEE, *TAO OF JEET KUNE DO*

In the summer of 2015, I visited the *Bruce Lee: Kung Fu, Art, Life* exhibit at the Hong Kong Heritage Museum and stood transfixed in front of a few old pieces of paper on the wall as other museum visitors swiftly moved past me to get to presumably more enticing items like Lee's yellow *Game of Death* jumpsuit and video clips from his films.[1] I must have looked highly suspicious to the guards because I stood there staring at the pieces of paper for at least fifteen minutes, and I kept looking over my shoulder to check that I was not obstructing anyone's view. To my shock, as I stood there rooted to the floor in awe with butterflies in my stomach, losing any sense of composure, I obstructed no one's vision. The two people who accompanied me had already finished much of the exhibit and came back for me, inquiring as to why I looked so flushed. In front of us was a handwritten description of Lee's training regimen, and I needed to write it all down. Shortly afterward, I repeated this process when I found Lee's choreographic notes for the *Way of the Dragon* Coliseum fight in another room.[2] I was not overwhelmed to be in the presence of an object that Lee had written/touched, though I do understand that inclination and expect that may have been why there were small crowds around the nunchaku and the jumpsuit. I am a scholar of action technique and performance with an investment in production cultures, and access to this type of work product is exceedingly rare. I was starstruck by the data, by access to the "how" (practice/training) and "what" (choreography) of Lee's virtuosic technique.[3]

For decades, the field of film and media studies has tackled the how and why of stardom with tenacity, but we have always had difficulty speaking to the specifics of performance in relation to Hong Kong–style action stardom. We tend to narrativize the action, identify thematic conflicts, or rely on adjectives rarely drawn from lexicons of bodily practice to differentiate between the styles of distinct performers. To paraphrase Bruce Lee, we have been concentrating on the finger and missing all the heavenly glory.[4] There is a more direct and specific way to speak to the creation and reception of virtuosic action spectacles. This project originated as a means to answer two seemingly simple questions: how can the field of film and media studies more clearly describe action genre performance, and what is meant by "transnational" action media? This deceptively simple point of origin spawned an intricate network of related queries concerning the production of action film and television spectacles and the degree of training required for their creation, the transnational ascendancy of Hong Kong–style action aesthetics in contemporary media, the relationship of fandom and reception to the performing body of the stunting star, and the relevance of research on expert performance to the mediated body of the martial arts adept.

Throughout this book I use the term *stunting star* and not *stunt star* or *stuntie* (a trade term for any stunt person). I use this term both to reinforce the progressive nature of stunt work and training (as acts in progress) and to distinguish the stunt *double*, who consistently performs the same role and is sometimes credited but relatively unknown to most audiences, from the performer who is marketed to audiences in a manner actively referencing their history as a stunt performer. The stunting star is a key component of Hong Kong–style action, if only because stunt performance distinguishes certain Hong Kong action stars from most other stars in the action genre. Stunting stars are not common in contemporary Hollywood action films and television programs, which dominate foreign screens. Because the division of labor for large-budget films and television programs actively disperses risk to stunt workers, outside of Hong Kong–style productions stunt performers are experts in action, and action stars are (possibly) experts in acting. The stunting star is possible only in production contexts lacking union and regulatory oversight: a figure precariously positioned in a perfect nexus of calculated risk, flexible labor, and corporeal spectacle. As this book addresses the production and reception of the expert performance of Hong Kong–style action spectacles in film and television, it regularly returns to the work of stunting stars and expert stunt coordinators and in doing so prescribes a means of discussion and analysis of their labor.

Hong Kong–Style Action

Esther Ching-mei Yau notes that Hong Kong movies made an indelible mark on cosmopolitan style cultures by the turn of the millennium. She links the stylistic contributions of Hong Kong cinema to transnational transactional economies of distribution and consumption, which pushed Hong Kong stars, films, and aesthetic repertoires far beyond the confines of the territory. Yau refers to the distinctive "imprints" of Hong Kong stars as "unusual" in this globalized landscape overpopulated by Hollywood films and Americanized products.[5] As Poshek Fu and David Desser note in their own anthology on the subject, "Hong Kong cinema had arrived" by the early 1990s through transnational distribution, strong video markets, positive critical response, and active fan reception practices.[6] In so many ways, *Experts in Action* revisits the subject of Yau's anthology—Hong Kong cinematic style and its unusual types of stardom—after the fall of Hong Kong cinema. After the decline in film production in Hong Kong in the mid- to late 1990s, films and television programs approximating Hong Kong aesthetics and structures of stardom proliferated in the places where Hong Kong had previously "arrived." This project does not approach Hong Kong cinema's stylistic contributions to visual culture as broadly as Yau's collection or Fu and Desser's. *Experts in Action*, as the title suggests, follows more in the footsteps of Meaghan Morris, Siu Leung Li, and Stephen Chan Ching-kiu's *Hong Kong Connections: Transnational Imagination in Action Cinema*. Morris, Li, and Chan expound in much greater detail on Yau's contention that Hong Kong cinematic style permeated the visual culture of "world cities" in the 1990s in such a way that the style transgressed national boundaries. The editors of this anthology frame Hong Kong action cinema as a "convergence point" or "contact zone" for scholarly discussion of the many elsewheres operating in and through Hong Kong cinematic traditions.[7] Borrowing Morris's astute observation in her introduction to that volume, *Experts in Action* is also "not a book *about* Hong Kong action cinema."[8] There is a great deal of scholarly writing about Hong Kong action cinema and about Hong Kong films and stars of the 1970s through the 1990s. This book is more interested in the aftereffects of the success and global circulation and reception of those films and stars. As Yau argued, Hong Kong cinema left an imprint on the world, and this project is keen to unpack that imprint's material effects on aesthetics, legal restrictions, craft practices, and audience expectations in the world beyond Hong Kong.

This book regularly uses the phrase *Hong Kong–style action* to indicate an assemblage of elements most commonly associated with action design work from Hong Kong cinema of the 1980s and 1990s: stunting stars, Asian martial arts, complex fight sequences with multiple points of physical contact between cuts, and dynamic and fluid wirework. Some of these elements are also common to earlier periods of Hong Kong cinema history and to cinematic traditions beyond Hong Kong. For example, a small number of stars did their own stunt work in Hong Kong, Hollywood, and Thailand (as well as many other localities) during even the earliest period of film history, but the specific attributes associated with the stunting star (as a marketable commodity who in actuality does most of their own stunts) are exceedingly rare and genealogically linked to the rise and transnational circulation of Jackie Chan as a star. Many stars have claimed to do their own stunts, but very few actually do, and none has demonstrated Chan's longevity. Additionally, martial arts combat as action spectacle (in the form of boxing, kung fu, fencing, etc.) has been a standard element of a number of action subgenres in Hong Kong, the United States, the United Kingdom, and many other national media contexts the world over since "early cinema," but the manner in which staged screen combat is organized, blocked, movement-serialized, filmed, and edited (a process increasingly referred to as *action design*) differs by period and locale. The preference for martial arts fight scenes choreographed so that one protagonist can take on multiple combatants simultaneously or in very quick succession, and shot in longer takes with a high number of points of physical contact in each shot, is linked to the rise and transnational circulation of 1980s and 1990s Hong Kong action films. The wirework design for Hong Kong action films of this period was also much more elaborate than Hollywood wire rig designs of the same period, was constructed via a trial-and-error process on set, and was created with fewer resources and minimal labor restrictions compared to the Hollywood context.

These action design and wirework techniques from Hong Kong were shared and emulated within transnational stunt *communities of practice*. Following Jean Lave and Etienne Wenger, I consider communities of practice as collective learning environments in which the knowledge and resources of a group of participants in an individual domain or intersecting domains are shared.[9] Stunt communities of practice are transnational and local, as many expert stunt workers participate in a flexible labor economy, and the production of action spectacles is an increasingly translocal enterprise. In the United States, from the height of the studio era to the 1990s, it was most common to shoot shorter fight beat (choreographed movements and points of contact) sequences with only one to three points of contact because stars were tied under contract and had to be paired with expert stunt performers to execute the choreographed movements without injury. Hollywood stars rarely have expert status in either on-screen fight choreography or other stunts. Shorter beat sequences did not strain their learning capacities and limited the likelihood of an accident that might delay the production. Over time, members of stunt communities of practice operating (most commonly) in the United States became well versed in this system of action design via shifts in training habits within their networks of practice, which they also spread to other localities when members or teams worked abroad. However, the influx of Hong Kong action films into the United States from the 1980s and 1990s changed the reservoir of technique for stunt laborers working on US-produced film and television (which were sometimes shot offshore), and the influx of talent from Hong Kong like Yuen Woo-ping (袁和平) contributed to a major stylistic shift in action design. Action design has always required expert stunt performers, and as action aesthetics from Hong Kong infiltrate various production contexts, those localities draw on expert local stunt workers, stunt teams, and stunting stars, whose trained bodies become action spectacle.

Hong Kong–style action by definition is both rooted in the globalized circulation of Hong Kong films, stars, choreographers, and stunt workers and also rootless, in that it is *of* Hong Kong without necessarily being made *by* or *in* Hong Kong. Hong Kong–style action was born of the transnational transactional economies of distribution and consumption identified by Yau and realized via the points of convergence explored by Morris, Li, and Chan. The moniker *Hong Kong–style* is inherently transnational because it is a relational category that calls out cultures of influence. Each chapter in this manuscript situates the production of Hong Kong–style action within those cultures of influence (e.g., production cultures, reception contexts, aesthetic repertoires). Simultaneously, each chapter addresses the specific localized manifestations of Hong Kong–style action in the Thai, US, and New Zealand film and television industries. Hong Kong–style action develops differently in each context in relation to legal restrictions, local production structures and hierarchies, funding and available resources, training contexts, and glocally networked stunt communities of practice. Hong Kong–style action, like the stunt labor forces that subtend its production, is inherently flexible. It is always expanding its archive of technique, always on the move, and inherently adaptable to local conditions of production and consumption. Individual expressions of this style of action in films, television programs, and live performance are culturally specific to the site of production, while the concept more broadly considered is in a near-constant state of metamorphosis. Hong Kong–style action can be found in Hollywood, South Korea, Japan, Australia, New Zealand, the Republic of Ireland, mainland China, and an increasing variety of national media industries and global production hubs. This book is based on research that I conducted in California, New Zealand, and the Republic of Ireland. Hong Kong–style action is an adapted and adaptive form in that it changes in accordance with local resources. Each chapter offers the reader a new avenue for transnational analysis of Hong Kong–style action based on defining attributes of this style: differential risk economies, modes of stardom linked to exhibition and distribution cultures, practices of communicative translation, and technical and educational exchange within transnational stunt craft networks. As a paradigm, Hong Kong–style action points both to the past and to the future of globalized action design and in the same movement points both to and away from Hong Kong. This paradigm is indebted to the aesthetic traditions as well as the production structures, rituals, and techniques common to Hong Kong action films of the 1980s and 1990s and simultaneously operates in transit and through translation beyond the confines of Hong Kong.

Film and media studies regularly approaches performance as a text decipherable through detailed discursive analyses of technique, genre constraints, and star texts. Film and media performance analysis is indebted to work in star studies that examines the meaning-making functions of stardom as an apparatus as well as more specific discursive formations that adhere to individual stars. This project has an affinity with contemporary film and media performance studies and theories of stardom in that it enables the reader to attend to action performance with greater specificity and with attention to both genre constraints and the reception and performance histories of individual stars and expert stunt workers. However, this project departs from the current trend in cinema and media performance analysis in four ways: it prioritizes action performance over acting; it employs industrial analyses and production studies methodologies to more directly assess what transnational labor flows add to performance, and how they do so; it adapts the analytic criteria of the scientific field of expert studies to humanistic inquiry into media labor; and it looks to fans to aid in the evaluation of expert performance in action. In the past decade, as film and media studies has taken a performative turn, many scholars in star studies have focused in greater detail on acting as a newfound object of analysis. Scholarly work in this area might anatomize the training process; examine recurring patterns of gesture, cadence, and expression; or deconstruct the affective register of a particular performer. To a certain extent, *Experts in Action* participates in these same practices. However, this book is reticent to engage with acting, both because other scholars have addressed it in great detail and because acting has often been prioritized to the exclusion of other types of screen performance. This is not to say that action performance has little to do with the craft of acting; I simply want to draw attention to a system of performance for which most scholars do not currently have a detailed operating vocabulary. This project contends that a *traceur*'s parkour-style *kong vault* (a headfirst dive in which the hands are used for propulsion against a stationary object) in a James Bond film or a stuntwoman's tae kwon do *yeop chagi* (옆 차기; side kick) in an episode of *Xena: Warrior Princess* is most productively addressed in the context of (1) the material and mediatized histories of the action's production (transnational training histories and production/exhibition contexts) and (2) the degree to which such actions command the attention of spectators.[10]

The application of production studies methodologies—in particular, on-set observation and interviews with expert action performers—provides the reader with a new operational vocabulary for discussing transnational action aesthetics and histories. The expert studies approach allows us to examine the entire performance process, from training, to production, to on-screen event. The combined use of industry studies and production studies approaches and the adoption of the metrics for performance analysis identified by expert studies accomplish something that has heretofore exceeded the grasp of film and media studies work on performance and action: this project makes action design, stunt work, and fight choreography legible to analysis. For too long, film and television analyses have avoided detailed discussion of action design, effectively rendering it ineffable. Deconstruction of action star images often provides illuminating and highly descriptive discussions of the star's body, but assessments of movement are rarely as illustrative. This book carves a new path for studies of action stars and performance, making plain an expressive register for future discussions of the work of action. It introduces a new emphasis on the labor involved in the production of action spectacles, as well as the specialized language necessary to bring this work into view. Additionally, the book considers the transnational movement of style and technique and in doing so comes to terms with the effects of cultural policies, production structures, and financing arrangements on the creation of action spectacles and the laboring bodies of producers. All of the stars and stunt workers discussed in this book demonstrate modes of expert performance in the domain of Hong Kong–style action media and, as such, share the mediating mechanisms most commonly associated with experts: decade-long training and early childhood exposure to deliberate practice, retraining, and adaptation.

Expert Performance

Scientists have been trying to map the unique mechanisms for the production of expert performance for over a century and have since identified a style of training (deliberate practice) and a duration of training (ten years) as necessary factors in the creation of exceptional and reproducible performance. While researchers have studied expert performance in fields as varied as typing, chess, combat aviation, and dance, certain defining attributes held true regardless of the domain: an *expert* commonly has on average ten years, or ten thousand hours, of training in their *domain* of expertise. As early as 1899, William Lowe Bryan and Noble Harter established the "ten-year rule" for expert performance in their study on telegraphers, and this rule has remarkably held fast in the face of countless studies on experts of all varieties.[11] The domain is a field of knowledge that may be narrowly or broadly conceived depending on the study. Experts most often begin their training in early childhood with a daily regimen supervised by an esteemed instructor and then supplement or refine their skill set later in life by further training and/or on-the-job practice. The style of training in any discipline takes the form of *deliberate practice*. As defined by K. Anders Ericsson, a premier scholar in expert studies, deliberate practice is a form of knowledge acquisition in which the tasks needed to achieve mastery of a domain are broken down into smaller segments (identified by George Miller in 1956 as "chunks") and repeated with supervision and correction by an instructor.[12] As each chunk is perfected, another is added, and the level of difficulty increases as the memorized chunks conglomerate into the whole performance sequence. The student learns the skills necessary for expert performance in the domain through a graduated cycle of instruction, practice, failure, and achievement. William Chase and Herbert Simon isolated the mediating mechanisms of memory that distinguished expert performance from novice performance, theorizing that experts use the chunks from training stored in long-term memory to make decisions during a performance, a process called *chunking*.[13] The chunking processes of expert performers are analogous to Richard Schechner's "restored behavior," or twice-behaved behavior.[14] Much of the research in expert studies demonstrates that expert performances are not the result of natural talent but of a history of deliberate practice evoked by restored behavior. Experts are not born; they are cultivated.

In the sciences, scholars define expertise as a collection of skills that contribute to *measurably superior* and *reproducible* performance. Studies on expert performance emphasize *measurability* and *reproducibility* on demand as defining attributes of the phenomenon, as laboratory study under controlled conditions has been the ideal method for identifying expertise in the cognitive sciences because it allows for observation of approximated conditional effects on cognitive and perceptual-motor skills. Researchers observe experts completing tasks common to their domain and systematically evaluate and identify the mediating mechanisms that affect the measurable quality of their performance. For example, a study of expert typists, in which the subjects' actions were recorded on video and played back in extreme slow motion, identified visual access to upcoming words (the "look-ahead strategy") as a mediating mechanism for measurably superior typing rates.[15] Not all expert performance is reproducible under laboratory conditions. Some researchers employ ethnographic observational methods similar to those used in performance studies, while others look to retrospective interviews, concept maps that illuminate the ontological structures of expert knowledge, or biographies for data that scholars cannot acquire in the lab. Historiometric approaches to expert performance trace career trajectories to determine maximum and minimum degrees of output and critical reception. This method can turn qualitative evaluations (conducted by other experts) of an expert's performances into more compliant quantitative data.

Though film and media studies and expert studies approach performance through distinct methods, utilize seemingly antithetical qualitative and quantitative evaluative criteria, and assess performance for unique purposes, there is still great value in a dialogic approach to expert performance that incorporates the concerns of both disciplines. This project harmonizes these disparate approaches to performance. Each discipline is uniquely suited to supplement the shortcomings of the other. While stardom and performance analyses in film and media studies struggle with the ineffability of action design and stunt work, expert studies lacks the tools to grapple with the intangibility of screen performance as an inherently complex object. The material body of the expert performer becomes intangible to expert studies because it is not easily mappable, measurable, or quantifiable during the act of mediated performance. Though the body of any expert in screen performance is material at some stage of the production process, the mediated performance itself is always somehow intangible—a collection of processes congealed into a representation. Unlike the labor of experts whom researchers can study under laboratory conditions, the work of screen performance cannot simply be measured in terms of speed, dexterity, or the reproducibility of learned practices and behaviors. Fortunately, film and media studies has spent decades developing a fairly standardized linguistic toolbox designed to identify the contributions of cinematography, editing, and mise-en-scène to screened performance. Additionally, this same discipline situates any performance in relation to genre standards within a national media context. Last, it also provides a more detailed cultural context for the study of mediated expert performance through the examination of cultural policies, industrial practices, and production cultures. In short, this book demonstrates that any approach to expert screen performance must simultaneously contend with the ineffability of the practiced body in motion and the intangibility of mediated corporality by using a convergent methodology drawn from both disciplines.

Expertise

In expert studies, the two primary criteria for expertise, performance that is both measurably superior and reproducible, are problematic markers for expertise in screen performance because editors most commonly select that type of performance for reproduction precisely because it is measurably superior to other recorded footage. It is necessary to reduce the expert studies model of expertise to its two core attributes when applying it to screen performance—recognition and reproducibility. Recognition and reproducibility are key markers of expertise in screen performance via both analytic reception and production practices. Film and television scholars and fans *recognize* expertise when some part of an individual's performance exceeds viewers' horizon of expectations based on that performer's past work and the work of the performer's contemporaries. Fans and scholars of genre and star performance can identify this type of expertise because of their extensive frames of reference. This skill is honed through years of attentive viewing and research practices. Additionally, these same scholars and fans are drawn to individual sequences, scenes, or brief instances of screen performance not because these examples are reproducible, as all screen performances are, but because of their *reproducibility*. The recognition of expertise results in a desire to rewind and replay the event and to relive the experience of viewership. These individual sequences, scenes, and instances, more than the whole films or programs from which they originate, drive the engaged spectator toward repeated viewings. Expertise becomes identifiable via acts of communication between expert performers and expert observers. It requires not simply a skilled performer but also a perceiving subject knowledgeable in the intersecting domains of that performer. In regard to the subject matter of this book, those domains are the production of action spectacle and the reception of action spectacle, both requiring extensive training. To trained eyes, expertise in screen action performance is instantly distinguishable and inherently rewatchable.

Much as the disciplinary preoccupations of film and media studies require us to adjust the parameters for expert studies approaches to screen performance, expert studies methodologies call for a shift in focus in film and media studies discourse from action stars to action performance. Work on action cinema is commonly preoccupied with both individual stars and the distinctive markers of action stardom. Even as film and media studies have recently taken a performative turn, discussions of action performance often fall prey to the very industry discourses on action stardom they are trying to unpack. Studio publicity machines manufacture action stars, and scholars analyze the various ways in which action performance originates from and is sutured to the action star's body without ever addressing the fact that most on-screen and prescreen action labor is not performed by stars. The expert studies criteria used to identify experts make it possible to differentiate between individuals who exhibit different levels of training in a given field based on the degree of reproducibility and superiority as correlated with the type and duration of training in that field. Film and media studies has a great deal to gain from adapting expert studies approaches as they provide us with guidelines for analyzing expert, intermediate, and novice performance. These methods help us to see more of the mythmaking functions of behind-the-scenes featurettes and interviews on the weeks to months of training some action stars undergo for a role, whereas expertise requires a regime of daily practice for around a decade. Adopting expert studies criteria has the potential to change not simply how we talk about action performance but also whose labor we analyze in the most detail. This approach facilitates a necessary shift in perspective on both above- and below-the-line action labor.

Though this shift in perspective allows for a more detailed understanding of the division of labor between acting stars and stunt performers, the goal of this project is not to create a new hierarchy. It should be possible to identify what distinguishes experts from novices without investing in the previous drives toward coverage of "great masters." In that respect, *Experts in Action* shares Julietta Singh's contention in her book *Unthinking Mastery: Dehumanism and Decolonial Entanglements* that "pitting mastery against mastery" only serves to reinscribe power into structures of domination.[16] This project does not proclaim action performers or choreographers as the "new action auteurs" but does call into question our very investment in the auteur concept, which for too long has clouded our vision and blinded us to the conditions of action labor production. As Singh argues, "By continuing to abide by the formulation of 'mastering mastery,' we remain bound to relations founded on and through domination. In so doing, we concede to the inescapability of mastery as a way of life."[17] At first glance, the skilling processes of performers working in Hong Kong–style action have seemingly little in common with the drives toward and functions of mastery in the twentieth-century decolonization movements that Singh investigates, but both use mastery as a form of protection and a means of legitimation. For both groups, Foucauldian practices of self-mastery abound and, arguably, produce distinctions between masterful selves and less masterful others. The drive toward mastery produces difference and inscribes value. Like Singh, I have no interest in reproducing these valuation structures, but I see great value in her project of "staying with the trouble" of "where, how, between whom, and to what futures mastery is engaged."[18] In that regard, this project is not designed to help us identify expert performance so that we can valorize it above all other forms of performance but to understand why, where, and by what means expert performers in action become necessary. In this manner, this book, much like *Unthinking Mastery*, strives to "reorient" the field with a "new vitality," encouraging action scholars to turn toward labor.[19]

Expert Performance in Action

This project requires a mode of performance analysis specific to the skills of expert performers working in Hong Kong–style action. Traditional star studies is useful but inadequate to the task of expert analysis. The method employed in this book integrates analysis of the defining attributes of expert performance with the concerns more typically addressed by star studies, to name the labor of stunting stars and expert stunt workers. This method examines histories of training on- and off-screen as well as the circulation of information about training and craft. This formulation takes the laboring body of the expert action performer as a site for analysis. This book examines action performance in a manner that captures the determining influence exerted on the expert action performer by the moments in which the performer becomes a *body spectacle*, a unique form of visual display common to a set of film and television genres (e.g., the musical, the martial arts film, the pornographic film, slapstick comedy) that is generated by and consists of the laboring body of a virtuoso performer expertly skilled in deftly choreographed corporeal manipulation. The representative tasks/body spectacles associated with Hong Kong–style action as a domain linked to training in Asian in-body disciplines include, but are not limited to, martial arts techniques, gymnastics and acrobatic maneuvers, wire-bound harness work, and device-aided jumps and flips. The method employed in this book draws lexicons of practice from the craft traditions linked to the training histories and workaday lives of the stars/subjects (e.g., stunting, martial arts, Peking opera, gymnastics) to bring into view the work of expert performance through acts of naming.

Pierre Bourdieu's idea of the *laborer's labored-over body* as physical capital is particularly germane to this work.[20] Both Bourdieu and Chris Shilling call attention to the ways in which individuals commute physical capital into economic and cultural capital.[21] In harnessing the physical capital of the expert action performer as an embodied form of spectacle, Hong Kong filmmakers (and those working in Hong Kong–style action) have attempted, with great success, to convert physical capital into economic and cultural capital in the form of film profits and a generic signature (the body of the martial arts virtuoso) unique to these films.

The Virtuoso Reception Context

Experts in Action adapts the identificatory criteria for expert performance to a method of star analysis focused on the laboring performer's body and discourses on the virtuoso in performance studies. The virtuoso is not an individual performer but rather a relationship between the performer and the spectator generated by the body spectacle and the dissemination of training discourse. The expert stunt performer or stunting star is not synonymous with the virtuoso because the virtuoso is not a performing body in itself but a reception context. Two texts inform this particular formulation of the virtuoso: Paul Metzner's book *Crescendo of the Virtuoso: Spectacle, Skill, and Self-Promotion in Paris during the Age of Revolution* and Judith Hamera's essay "The Romance of Monsters: Theorizing the Virtuoso Body." Metzner's redefinition of the virtuoso, with its focus on spectacle, reception, and the circulation of information about the technician/performer, is invaluable to my formulation of the status of the virtuoso as formed both in moments of cinematic spectacle and in the dissemination of information on the performer's training regimes. Metzner's virtuosi are not cinema stars; their performances and devices predate even the earliest modes of cinematic production. Those magicians, musicians, automaton builders, and chefs of seventeenth- and eighteenth-century France emerged as great artists because of Napoleonic policies aimed at modernization, the practices of revolutionaries that opened public space to the populace, the technological euphoria that accompanied the Industrial Revolution, and of course the circulation of text and images concerning the performers, made possible by advancements in print technology.[22] The performers discussed in this book are seemingly quite disparate from those analyzed by Metzner in terms of time period, nation, and areas of specialization. What the Peking opera performers, martial artists, and stunt performers of this study share with Metzner's virtuosi is a tendency toward the spectacular effected by deliberate practice, a corporeal formation explored in detail in each of this book's case studies.

Judith Hamera echoes Metzner's interest in the spectacular body. Hamera's piece alters the commonly held definition of the virtuoso and ponders the manner in which virtuoso performance effects the clarity and precision of body writing. The act of performance and the process of spectatorship define Hamera's virtuoso. For Hamera, the virtuoso is simultaneously a performing body and a mode of reception; she "explore[s] a model of extraordinary physicality as a tactic for inventing a particular kind of relationship between the dancer and the critic—an interspecies relation, if you like, and a spectacular one in the etymological sense of *specere*, to look or behold."[23] I use Hamera's model of the virtuoso as a performer-spectator relationship, extending the reception context beyond the critic to media consumers with prior knowledge of the expert action performer's spectacular dispositions (fans). Taking this reception context as a starting point, I am interested in exploring the project that Hamera discards, that of "developing specifics of a new technique for writing about the virtuoso body."[24] Hamera argues that virtuoso performances defy contemporary forms of body writing because of the precision with which virtuosi execute movements, the innovative manner in which they combine forms, and the modes of overly engaged spectator response that such performers provoke.[25] This book borrows from Hamera's reconceptualization of the virtuoso as created in the act of informed spectatorship and responds to her move to address the adept performer-in-motion as a process confounding language. The methodological contribution that this study makes to Hamera's theory of the virtuoso is the identification and analysis of the specific bodily dispositions that contribute to the shifting performance styles of individual virtuosi.

To explore resonances between this project and Bourdieu's account of the body, I borrow the term *bodily disposition* to characterize the disciplined and technologized body of the stunting star. For Bourdieu, disposition is key to an understanding of the habitus (a system of dispositions that is the generative principle of a person's practices, products, and judgments).[26] Disposition is a complex notion in Bourdieu's thought, a "semantic cluster" that ranges from aesthetic cultivation to bodily attitudes. Bourdieu defines disposition as "a way of being, a habitual state (especially of the body) and, in particular, a predisposition, tendency, propensity, or inclination."[27] Bourdieu's emphasis is on how class is embodied, as he argues that "the body is the most indisputable materialization of class taste."[28] This volume deploys the idea of bodily disposition not so much to address the classed body of the stunting star but to trace the debts of this body to a historically and culturally specific web of bodily disciplines deliberately practiced in such a manner as to produce a body with a predisposition, proclivity, or propensity to, for example, fly through the air in a martial arts film. The idea of a culturally and historically situated bodily disposition sheds light on the conspicuous differences between the bodies of many Hollywood stars and those of Hong Kong action stars.[29] The body spectacle is formed in the simultaneous visual articulation of the actual performing body, the cinematographic manipulation of that body, and the virtuoso relationship between performer and knowing spectator.

This book's approach to experts problematizes the essentialism underpinning structures of power common to academic writing in film and media studies and linked disciplines. We often make the mistake of assuming that *expert* and *academic* are synonymous. There are fans and industry professionals who have long histories of training that run parallel to and intersect with our domains. This book looks to them as expert interlocutors. Fans have been treated as subjects worthy of rigorous academic study for years; however, this book's contribution to fan studies is unconventional. Convention organizers, documentary filmmakers, and media producers have positioned fans as experts before. Fan knowledge has been utilized as a valuable industrial resource and as an object of scholarly investigation, but what is new in this volume is the incorporation of the knowledge of expert fans of Hong Kong–style action to guide analysis. When I call on fans as experts, I am not explicitly referencing the knowledge base of acafans (academic fans with a scholarly interest), nor am I excluding it. I wish to make very clear that this book does not hierarchize expert scholarly knowledge over expert fan knowledge. I turn to fans as colleagues, as experts in an adjacent and at times intersecting domain. Fans may approach Hong Kong–style action differently from Hong Kong action scholars, and we can benefit greatly from exploring the points of intersection of our adjacent domains. To that end, I do not psychoanalyze the responses I have collected from fans, just as I would reject the impulse to do that to the scholarly work of colleagues in the field of film and media studies. Fans are interlocutors in this project, not objects of analysis.

Transnational Media Studies:
Polymorphic Analysis of an Object in Flux

This book traces distinct, embodied histories of transnational exchange by isolating and defining unique forms of expert performance common to contemporary globalized action film and television genres. While Hong Kong may be an obvious starting point for a book on action media, the selection of Hong Kong poses problems for trans*national* analysis. Hong Kong cinema is commonly referred to as a national cinema or at the very least as a body or work comparable to other national cinemas (e.g., those of Korea, India, the United States), when in point of fact Hong Kong is a "special administrative region" (SAR) and not a sovereign nation and has been slowly transitioning from British to Chinese rule, a program called "one country, two systems" that will be complete in 2046. Other authors have addressed the particular predicament of speaking of Hong Kong cinematic productions as a "national" media context. Strictly speaking, Hong Kong cinema does not fit the auteur-defined models of national cinemas, oppositional to Hollywood in both aesthetics and ideology. Bliss Lim refers to Hong Kong cinema as a "national cinema effect," articulating the paradox of Hong Kong cinema, a cinema that is not national but that scholars have historically addressed as if it were. Lim proffers an analytic category that is simultaneously indebted to the manner in which the scholarship on Hong Kong cinema has historically tended toward national models and also highly cognizant of the cinematographic, economic, and thematic affinity between Hong Kong films and those produced elsewhere.[30] This book posits an account of Hong Kong cinema as, in Lim's terms, a "national cinema effect" and also considers the operation of Hong Kong action cinema aesthetics, production structures, and techniques abroad as manifestations of Hong Kong–style action operating in transnational cultural economies that are not singular or linear.[31] The polymorphous manifestations of Hong Kong–style action beyond the SAR require not one singular approach to transnationality but diverse approaches to the shifting logics of transnational media production and consumption at a key point of convergence: action design requires the labor of expert stunt performers.

The expert performers discussed in this book are transnational not simply because of the global marketing, distribution, and reception of their films and television programs but because the act of production adapts techniques and corporeal practices common to Hong Kong action films to localized media contexts (e.g., the United States, New Zealand, Thailand). These technical histories of corporeal practices congeal in the body of the expert action performer. In addition, the transformation of training regimes and bodily maintenance into the visibly laboring body of the expert action performer is augmented by distinctly filmic elements (e.g., cinematographic decisions, structures of editing) that amplify the effect on the spectator of the specialized labor (e.g., dance, martial arts, stunts) performed in individual sequences. The body spectacles of the prominent performers selected for this study are distinct in that the remarkable physical accomplishments captured by the camera and transformed by cinematography and editing illuminate a transnational history of embodied practices ranging from martial arts training to film production and marketing.

Many books already address pre-1997 and post-1997 Hong Kong cinema, and while no scholar would likely deny the emergence of a "crisis cinema" in Hong Kong around this key date, *Experts in Action* speaks to a different moment of departure and convergence in the history of transnational Hong Kong cinema, 1994. In 1994 the Hong Kong government instituted the Organized Crime and Triad Ordinance, and the triad funding for local film production started to dry up, with production going from 234 films in 1993 to 153 films in 1995, with numbers declining sharply each year thereafter.[32] Additionally, the Thai film tax was lowered in 1993, and within the year US and Hong Kong films began to flood the market. The following year, Hong Kong studios increased their investment in the exhibition market in Thailand.[33] Also in 1994, New Zealand revised its film and television tax incentive plan, and production increased dramatically. *Xena: Warrior Princess* began production in New Zealand the following year. Finally, in 1994 China agreed to the importation of ten first-run Hollywood films in order to increase profits through revenue sharing, which would lead to an increase in the production (and coproduction) of Hollywood films designed to appeal to Chinese audiences.[34] This mid-1990s tipping point in cultural policy design may not have simply prompted the shift to Hong Kong–style action design abroad, but it more than facilitated transitions in transnational physical and aesthetic stunt craft traditions.

This book traces a variegated trajectory by which the Hong Kong film industry's reliance on experts in Peking opera and martial arts contributed to action aesthetics (created in an accelerated production environment and lacking corporate or governmental oversight) that would be circulated outside of the Hong Kong SAR and re-created by experts working in stunt communities of practice in the United States, Thailand, and New Zealand. This book approaches the transnational circulation of aesthetics and technique in the action genre in relation to the industrial need for and creation of experts. All of the primary experts in action discussed in this book have followed somewhat similar career paths from stuntie to action choreographer or stunt coordinator, though most stunt performers will never ascend to a managerial position as a choreographer or coordinator. In an era when computer-assisted action spectacles predominate, an extremely limited number of stunting stars and expert stunt performers will rise from obscurity. Though stunting stars are generally expert stunt performers, the inverse is not always true. Some expert stunt performers have effected the transition to Hong Kong–style action abroad and risen from obscurity to revered status within their peer group but lack public attention. This book seeks to make their labor more apparent, and, as such, the book transitions from a discussion of stunting stars like Jackie Chan, Tony Jaa (จา พนม), Jeeja Yanin (ญาฉิน "จีจ้า" วิสมิตะนันทน์), and Zoë Bell to an analysis of expert stunt coordinators Chad Stahelski and Dayna Grant. The adoption of Hong Kong–style action spectacles in transnational action media after 1994 aided in the ascent of these stunt experts, trained in somewhat different bodily disciplines and working in polylocal and translocal media production industries. In their simplest form, the chapters of this book examine the means by which the circulation of Hong Kong action films outside the borders of the SAR both effected a new breed of stunting star and also relied on as well as transformed the domains of expert stunt performers in Hong Kong, Thailand, the United States, New Zealand, and beyond.

Elsewheres and Imprints:
Transnational Hong Kong–Style Action in Context

This book is organized such that the chapters following this introduction enact a double movement by addressing production contexts increasingly less spatially proximate to Hong Kong and also shifting the focus from analyses of stunting stars to other expert stunt performers. The specific articulation of Hong Kong–style action in any given context (e.g., film, television program, sequence, or scene) is heavily determined by four characteristics: mechanisms for the mediation of risk, Hong Kong cinematic exhibition and reception cultures, local translation tactics, and the flow of craft practices. Each of these elements makes expertise a requirement and results in distinctive forms of expert performance. The relationship between the financial risk of the production and the physical risk of the performers informs Hong Kong–style action design in all contexts, just as all Hong Kong–style action requires the previous circulation of Hong Kong films to establish a horizon of expectations among audiences and standard criteria for producers. The transnational expressions of Hong Kong–style action always necessitate translation practices owing to differences in production environments, labor structures, and regulatory contexts. Additionally, innovative stunt work in Hong Kong action (and other) traditions requires the training opportunities provided by transnational craft networks. In an effort to track down the elsewheres and imprints of Hong Kong action cinema, to find the many places where Hong Kong action cinema left discernible marks on production cultures and aesthetic traditions, each of the chapters that follows focuses on one of these four attributes of Hong Kong–style action design.

While risk aversion may be common to all Hong Kong–style action production contexts, the first chapter highlights the most glaring example of differential relationships to risk in the Hong Kong and Hollywood media industries. Prompted by fans' astute observations that Jackie Chan's Hollywood films and his Hong Kong films feature remarkably distinct action aesthetics though they showcase the same expert performer, this chapter explores the use value of the same expert in action in two different contexts. This chapter examines the mutually informing economies of corporeal and financial risk that distinguish Hong Kong–style action in US production contexts from the body spectacles produced in Hong Kong. In Hollywood the expertise of stunt performers (as recognizable based on performance histories and as reproducible on command) ensures safety on the set. In Hollywood, not only is safety ensured on set, but it is also key to the authorization of insurance on set. Owing to labor and insurance regulations in Hollywood, action stars are not recognized as experts in action performance and are restricted in their corporeal contributions to fights, falls, and other stunts. This chapter identifies the legal, industrial, and financial mediating mechanisms that alter Chan's expert performance in Hollywood productions in comparison to his earlier work in Hong Kong.

There is a consistent relationship between financial risk and the imperiled body of the stunting star in many East Asian and Southeast Asian media contexts. The star who not only is *known* for doing their own stunts but actually *does* most of their own stunts is a rare commodity that is much more common in Asian production contexts. This is likely due to more flexible labor structures than those in Hollywood, as demonstrated by Sylvia J. Martin's ethnographic research on stunt work in the United States and Hong Kong, along with less formal and rigid relationships between financing and insurance.[35]

The second chapter discusses the divergent effects of the Asian financial crisis of 1997 on the Hong Kong and Thai film industries. Thailand bounced back more quickly than did Hong Kong, whose film industry had already experienced a huge drop in production. Hong Kong action films had long dominated the Thai box office. The decrease in the number of Hong Kong action films on-screen created a gap filled by Thai stunting star Tony Jaa. Jaa's films and stunts, and the star text of the stuntman-turned-star, mimicked so closely those of Jackie Chan, with the great exceptions that Jaa's body spectacles were drawn from native Thai martial arts traditions and that he demonstrated his expertise on command by reproducing the stunts in live performances without the assistance of wirework rigs. This chapter explores the imprint left on Thai action cinema by the history of Hong Kong action cinema exhibition in Thailand. In particular, this imprint caused Hong Kong action production structures, techniques, and star formations to operate as a mode in new Thai action cinema. While action scholars have defined the parameters of action as a mode (e.g., spectacular bodies, speed of movement, and sound effects and music as accentuating pulses), Hong Kong–style action operates as a mode in the Thai context via production contexts that mimic those of 1980s and 1990s Hong Kong action design and simultaneously surpass those spectacular designs in both dexterity and danger. The domestic and transnational financial success of this mode resulted in a new model for Thai action stars.

The distribution of Hong Kong films abroad left lasting imprints on the action design aesthetics and the training requirements for expert stunt performers far beyond Asia. The transnational flow of Hong Kong movies to video rental stores in the United States introduced new forms of action design to cult audiences. Some of the fans drawn to the distinctive character of Hong Kong action techniques and aesthetics were also US film and television producers. Chapter 3 explores the repurposing of Hong Kong action aesthetics by the US fanboy media producers of the New Zealand–produced, globally syndicated television series *Xena: Warrior Princess*. As there was little crossover between the New Zealand and Hong Kong stunt communities in the early 1990s, Kiwi stunt workers had to improvise in terms of both technology and technique. This chapter considers their attempts to reproduce the overall effects of Hong Kong action set pieces as a form of communicative translation. This translation required an expert with training in both gymnastics and martial arts—stuntwoman Zoë Bell. She worked as a stunt double for Lucy Lawless on *Xena: Warrior Princess* as Bell had a bodily disposition that was ideal for the uncommon action design techniques used for the show. Bell's on-set work for the program further contributed to her domain-specific training in Hong Kong–style action techniques, transforming her into not simply an expert stunt performer but, more specifically, an expert in Hong Kong–style action. These forms of training made her the ideal candidate to double for Uma Thurman in the *Kill Bill* series and led to her star turn in Quentin Tarantino's *Death Proof*.[36] This process led to Bell's transformation from an expert stunt performer to a stunting star with a virtuoso reception context.

In the fourth chapter, we move from the local translation practices addressed in the previous chapter to the transnational flow of technique in the years following the release of *The Matrix*.[37] We return to Hollywood and New Zealand to trace the imprints of Hong Kong action techniques and labor structures in stunting communities of practice. This chapter investigates the importance of expert stunt performers operating in transnationally linked craft communities of practice. The chapter considers the transnational flow and adaptation of stunt craftwork from Hong Kong in relation to the training regimes and work product of expert stunt workers. This chapter reorients the analysis of Hong Kong–style action in two key ways: it shifts perspective from stunting stars to expert stunt performers, and it redirects our attention from the individual stars of the previous chapters to the team dynamic of stunt craft practice as overseen by action designers and coordinators. This chapter looks at the work of New Zealand stuntwoman and stunt coordinator Dayna Grant on *Ash vs Evil Dead* as well as that of Hollywood stuntman and coordinator Chad Stahelski (as well as his partner David Leitch) and the 87eleven Action Design team.[38] These experts facilitate the flow of technique as they add to their domains of expertise through the skills they learn in transit in the new international division of cultural labor.

The conclusion of this book is a call to action that provokes the engaged reader to consider how expert labor enables the production of spectacle far beyond the action genre as well as in and beyond film and media. The conclusion argues that while the formula for the analysis of expert performance laid out by this book may be easy to apply to well-known performers, actors, or stars, it is just as viable for analyzing the on- and off-screen craft practices of experts as a whole. The method employed in this book has much broader applicability and is best used as a political weapon to make visible the labor of lesser-known experts working behind the screen and in the shadows.

Experts in Action does not propose an overarching grand theory of transnational media analysis but rather suggests that we start from the shared and intersecting skill sets of certain laborers working in media production in different localities. From those points of convergence, we can consider the effects of policy, industry, and production strategy on these workers and the work they do. There is no one way to approach transnational media because the effects and histories of transnational media are always also local and never singular. This book sheds light on the laboring bodies of experts that leave us transfixed by the action, and it names their work.

ONE

RISKY BUSINESS / Financial and Physical Risk in the Action Stardom of Jackie Chan

This chapter situates Jackie Chan's training in Peking opera within this discipline's larger historical relationship to stunt communities of practice in Hong Kong cinema. The chapter addresses Chan's bodily disposition as predicated on his ten years of deliberate practice in Peking opera techniques at the China Drama Academy, one of the five primary opera schools supplying stunt performers, actors, and choreographers to the Hong Kong film industry. Chan has consistently drawn from this training as an archive for restored behavior, as is evident in the body spectacles on display in his Hong Kong films. These striking corporeal displays shock or move the spectator into a state of awe. Scholarly and popular writing on Chan's Hollywood films often mentions the legal restrictions that affected his performance style, but few have considered this worthy of prolonged examination. This chapter contributes to film and media studies discourses on Chan by situating Chan's expert performance historically in relation to the conditions of production in the Hong Kong film industry and industrial practices related to financing and insurance in Hollywood. Fans have commented on the marked difference in body-spectacle production in Chan's Hong Kong films versus his Hollywood films. This chapter identifies Chan's use value to Hollywood studios, beginning in the mid- to late 1990s and continuing into the early 2000s, in relation to the distribution of economic risk. A history of physical risk characterized Chan's expert performance, which made him a major box-office draw and later facilitated financing agreements, which limited economic risk for Hollywood studios because Chan's films could be presold to exhibitors in certain markets. A history of physical risk precluded the mediation of economic risk. What follows is an attempt to answer three simple questions:

1   What types of deliberate practice/restored behavior inform Jackie Chan's expert performance?
2   What are the specificities of Chan's body spectacle?
3   Prompted by concerns brought up in his virtuoso reception context, why are his body spectacles different in his Hollywood films?

To better contend with these questions, this chapter explores the relationship between the Peking opera and Hong Kong cinema history as well as legal controls that produce differences in Chan's US film productions. This description is animated by Chan's bodily disposition as effected by his training in Peking opera, augmented by his control of production at Golden Harvest, and transformed by the legal requirements of Hollywood film production. Though much has been written on Chan in film and media studies, no one has yet addressed in much detail the legal structures that force distinctions between Chan's work in Hollywood and his Hong Kong productions. In particular, this chapter considers the effects of Hollywood insurance regulations on the production of Chan's body spectacles. This analysis understands Chan's body, as well as the dynamic spectacles to which it is linked, as subject to history while his stardom also makes him an agent of power.

The Historical Economy of Expert Performance in Hong Kong Action Cinema

Hong Kong–style action cinema requires the skilled bodies of experts in different Asian in-body practices behind and in front of the camera. Many performers working in Hong Kong action genres have bodily dispositions formed by years of training in Peking opera, martial art forms, acrobatics, and dance (e.g., Yuen Biao [元彪], Angela Mao Ying [茅復靜], Josephine Siao Fong-fong [蕭芳芳], Mars [火星], Michelle Yeoh) and produce filmed kinesthetic corporeal spectacles that have contributed to their reception as stars. A host of the Peking opera–trained second-unit performers, extras, stuntmen, and action coordinators working in Hong Kong martial arts cinema in the 1960s and 1970s have since become stars well known for the body spectacles they help to craft as directors and choreographers (e.g., Sammo Hung Kam-bo [洪金寶], Corey Yuen [元奎], Yuen Woo-ping, Yuen Cheung-yan

[袁祥仁]). While many Peking opera–trained performers have found success as actors or directors in the Hong Kong film industry or as action coordinators in Hollywood, no performer has surpassed the earning power of Jackie Chan, the Hong Kong star most recognized for the demonstrable dexterity and precarious posturing of his body spectacles. The first few pages of this chapter address the historical connections between communities of Peking opera practice and Hong Kong action film production, and then I outline the deliberate-practice activities that characterized Chan's training in the discipline.

The selection of expert Peking opera performers as participants in and designers of Hong Kong action sequences has had lasting effects on both the aesthetics and the production practices of action films and television. Peking opera and Hong Kong cinema are historically interdependent and have had a shared labor force since the earliest Cantonese-language productions. Additionally, the "operatic mode" in Hong Kong cinema, as identified by Chris Berry and Mary Farquhar, "includes all the genres and subgenres of the Chinese cinema spun out of opera conventions, including opera film itself, as well as martial arts, costume film spectaculars and the long tradition of opera within film."[1] Zhang Zhen discusses how the presentational style of early Chinese cinema hewed close to that of the theater, specifically in the symmetrical organization of perspectival relations (frontal, in medium long shot) and the privileging of spectacle over narrative. Zhang identifies this form of early filmmaking as *xiren dianying* (戲人電影; the cinema of theater people) and compares its spectacular tendencies to those of Tom Gunning's "cinema of attractions."[2] Both opera and cinema made the transition to theatrical venues with more formal seating arrangements in the early 1910s, but neither fully eclipsed the spectacular mode of address. Opera performances utilized ornate flowing costumes (some costume design included *shui xiu* [水袖], or "water sleeves," which helped to accentuate the kinesis of the performers), loud singing, and acrobatic fight choreography to hail the crowds. Hong Kong action cinema has retained the opera's tendencies toward an embodied hyperbolic visual display because of the shared history of the two forms and the crossover of opera performers to film. As Yung Sai-shing has argued, "The cinematic techniques are there to help foreground the actions of an actor. They are employed in order to encourage the audience to concentrate on the actions displayed in the mise-en-scène. Like its counterpart on the Chinese opera stage, the body of an actor has become the spectacle."[3] The draw of Hong Kong–style action is most often the tendency of the star to become body spectacle. This process is made possible via the skilling practices of Peking opera training. Some of the earliest examples of Chinese cinema were opera films featuring prominent stage performers. Cinema helped opera troupes to reach a larger audience, but with the growth of the Hong Kong studio system and its coterie of stars after the Japanese occupation, most opera performers were relegated to background action. Though opera films were popular in the 1950s, the influx of a new cultural labor force from the mainland would force a shift in genre to swordplay films.

After the occupation of Hong Kong by the Japanese, the Cantonese film industry experienced a surge in production. As Yung has noted, Peking opera academies came to prominence after World War II and, via "severe and demanding training, . . . played a decisive role in nurturing new blood for the Hong Kong action cinema."[4] During this period, martial arts academies and Peking opera schools funded many Cantonese-language Hong Kong action films. The teachers and students from these academies of Chinese in-body practice performed all of the dangerous stunts, choreographed the fights, and trained the stars to look credible in their roles as martial arts masters. As Bryan Chang comments, "Opera personnel began to gain footholds in the staging of combat, [and] martial artists from various disciplines gravitated towards the industry."[5] Historically, production companies did not commission this assistance for the stars; the lead actors paid Peking opera masters like Lau Kar-leung (劉家良) to work with them directly.[6] Four generations of action choreographers were known as Dragon-Tiger Masters (*longhu wushi*; 龍虎武師), commonly drawn from the five major training academies in Hong Kong: the China Drama Academy (中國戲劇學校), Spring and Autumn Drama School (春秋戲劇學校), Eastern Drama Academy (東方戲曲學校), Chung Wah Drama Academy (中華戲曲學校), and the training squad of Yuen Sui-tien (袁小田).[7] These schools produced Hong Kong's most prominent action stars and choreographers, including Yuen Woo-ping, Lam Ching-ying (林正英), Mars, Alan Chui Chung-san (徐忠信), Sammo Hung Kam-bo, Yuen Biao, and Jackie Chan.

Opera waned in popularity in the 1960s.[8] This was an effect of the push toward modernization, the growth of the film industry in the 1960s, and the availability of opera performances on the newly established television network TVB (Television Broadcasts Limited), owned by Shaw Brothers Studio and launched in 1967. Television led to increased accessibility of opera in the home but reduced the number of touring troupes: spectators could watch from the comfort of home, and fewer people attended live performances.[9] Peking opera performers trained for seven to ten years in *wu gong* (武功; martial-acrobatic arts) but had difficulty finding work in the opera. Many of these performers (and their children) were subsequently employed by a variety of studios in the Hong Kong film industry as actors, directors, choreographers, and stuntmen. The Peking opera provided leading cast members for the Huang Fei-hong (黃飛鴻) film series: ninety-nine films in this Cantonese series starred Peking opera performer Kwan Tak-hing (關德興) as the legendary folk hero Huang Fei-hong. Hector Rodriguez contends that Cantonese immigrants' desire to "reaffirm their own identity" played a role in the transnational success of films like these. Rodriguez likens the Huang Fei-hong films to other culturally specific gatherings — opera performances, guilds, temples. He explains that the Huang Fei-hong series operated as an archive of cultural practices. By this he means that the martial arts styles specific to certain southern regions of China, practices that had a cultural relevance to Cantonese audiences living outside of the mainland, were preserved on film and experienced in a group sharing the same cultural heritage.[10] Rodriguez does the valuable work of sketching the intimate relation between production and exhibition. He stresses the degree to which the "authenticity" of action sequences was privileged by directors, as the series served an archival cultural function (to "faithfully preserve and disseminate a range of putatively authentic martial arts postures and movement").[11] However, with the shift in power from small Cantonese studios to the vertically integrated Mandarin-language giants (Shaw Brothers and Cathay) in the late 1950s and early 1960s, referred to by I. C. Jarvie as the "Mandarinization of Hong Kong cinema," many Cantonese-speaking, opera-trained performers were forced into second-unit work and background action in the assembly-line system of production employed by Shaw Brothers Studio.[12] Not until the rise of Golden Harvest after 1970, the transition to Cantonese-language cinema in 1973, and the generic shift to the *gong fu* (功夫; skilled effort), or "kung fu," film did many Peking opera–trained experts become major action stars in their own right, including Jackie Chan. The star-making function of some 1970s kung fu films is clearly identifiable in the casting of lead performers with visually arresting body spectacles (Jackie Chan, Bruce Lee, etc.), an action amplified by the mythmaking functions of shooting body spectacles in long shot and long take. Some films also featured the antics of trained opera performers working as a team to create elaborately choreographed numbers.

The opera continued to decline in the early 1970s as more Hong Kong households turned to television for entertainment, and many young opera-trained artists looked for work in the film industry. These actors, who had trained in the martial-acrobatic arts, displayed a skill set that drastically altered the tenor of the martial arts film formula, which had been dominated by *wuxia pian* (武俠片; martial hero films) in the 1960s, moving the emphasis from swordplay to hand-to-hand combat. The swordplay film was one of the Shaw Brothers Studio's most successful genres in the 1960s, but very few of their contract players had the skill set to pull off dynamic body spectacles. For this reason, the studio hired Peking opera performers to choreograph the on-screen action, work as body doubles, and provide background action. The distinction between the Mandarin-language productions of the wuxia pian in the 1960s and the opera is not simply that one required the professionalized cultivation of a certain body technology (after all, many stars spend hours perfecting their star image) but rather that the particular technologized star bodies that were required for the martial arts genre were skilled in body maintenance in a cultural register that was distinctly Chinese and familiar to fans of the Cantonese martial arts cinema that was eclipsed in the years of Shaw dominance. In contrast, the 1960s swordplay formula showcased actors harnessed to wires and Peking opera–trained stuntmen bouncing into the air via self-crafted small trampolines. These "minitramps," as they are referred to in transnational stunt industries, are small aerobic rebounders (trampolines) used to provide actors and stunties with extra lift for flipping and simulated flying. These small trampolines are used because they are more easily approached from a running start and can be hidden from view of the camera, making it appear as though Peking opera–trained stunt workers could fly without effort. In contradistinction, the kung fu films of the 1970s featured heroes whose only technological resources were harvested from their own bodies. Both genres made use of expert opera-trained performers, but the martial arts films that came to prominence in the 1970s did not simply use opera experts as choreographers or stunt performers but also made some of them stars in their own right and therefore established a distinctive formula for media production that relied on expert action performance.

Jackie Chan's Training in Peking Opera: Bodily Disposition and Deliberate Practice

Jackie Chan's bodily disposition is indebted to a large extent to his ten years of training in the Peking opera, but the same could be said for his schoolmates, Sammo Hung and Yuen Biao. As K. Anders Ericsson and various scholars have repeatedly demonstrated, expertise is the effect of the cultural conditions of productions and not a matter of natural talent.[13] So, instead of beginning with the all-too-familiar positioning of the star as exceptional, seemingly ordinary but also extraordinary, as is often done in star studies, let us begin from the premise that the routine and systematic application of the training techniques of Master Yu Jim-yuen (于占元) across a ten-year period produced a collection of expert performers at precisely the moment when the local film industry needed actors with such bodily dispositions. Yu's tutelage is key to the production of this collection of expert performers, as Stefan Degner and Hans Gruber have demonstrated that "the acquisition of high levels of expert performance in a specific domain is based on the availability of guidance from an expert who is able to design the most relevant and effective practice routines depending on the learner's preexisting skills, personal traits, and prior knowledge."[14] In a related study, these scholars and their colleagues insist that figures like Yu must be acknowledged and rescued from the "shadows" because his influence fostered the necessary conditions for expert performance and he provided the guidance necessary to aid his students in careers in the Hong Kong film industry.[15] Yu not only monitored the training of all students at the school but also selected individual students for more specific deliberate-practice routines based on their skills and weaknesses.

The structure and content of Chan's daily training routine at the China Drama Academy have been touted in Chan's autobiography, confirmed in interviews with Sammo Hung, and reinforced by the available historical and ethnographic research on standard pedagogical practices at Peking opera academies. The training Chan discusses in his autobiography, which is consistent with pedagogical structures identified by other Peking opera performers trained in this period, conforms to the deliberate-practice model needed to produce expertise, in particular the eighteen-hour workday with repeated stretching, acrobatic, and weapons exercises corrected by an expert teacher. As discussed in the introduction to this book, deliberate practice was identified by K. Anders Ericsson, Ralf T. Krampe, and Clemens Tesch-Römer as a cardinal component in the creation of expertise in a wide variety of domains and consists of repetitive tasks that are corrected by a mentor and performed and improved on daily.[16] Deliberate practice requires professional oversight to ensure that pupils do not revert to automaticity. Coaches and trainers optimize the potential for improvement by correcting mistakes and establishing ever-increasing performance goals.[17] Daily exposure to this structured routine over the course of ten years, or ten thousand hours, produces demonstrated adaptations in cognitive, physiological, neural, and motor capacities.[18] The end result is performance that is both superior and reproducible.

The deliberate-practice activities inherent to opera, in the words of Richard Schechner, "call into existence new means of training, which means new ways and means of transmitting performance knowledge—new to the West but not new to Asia or Africa."[19] Embodied knowledge is passed from expert teacher to novice student via repeated and corrected actions, a process remarkably less similar to Western drama-teaching processes than to training for sport. These deliberate-practice activities act as an incubator for restored behavior, a process that "raises physical skills to the level of performance art."[20] Schechner identifies restored behavior as "the main characteristic of performance." This defining element is drawn from "source" material that "may be unknown or concealed" and is "worked on" and rearranged in the process of rehearsal.[21] In the case of Jackie Chan (and, I would argue, all experts), the source of this restored behavior is years of deliberate practice, and the cognitive, physiological, neural, and motor capacities generated and altered by this training are equivalent to Chan's bodily disposition. The telltale markers of deliberate practice in Peking opera that are evident in Chan's bodily disposition are flexibility, coordinated implementation of objects, group work, and tolerance of pain.

Children are commonly enrolled around the age of seven in Peking opera training, and Chan is no exception to this rule, as he was enrolled at that age in *sifu* (師父; master) Yu Jim-yuen's China Drama Academy, where Chan lived and trained in acting, singing, martial arts, and acrobatics for a decade.[22] The students at the China Drama Academy were schooled in a variety of forms of corporeal manipulation, including *tanzi gong* (毯子功; mat or rug work), *yaotui gong* (腰腿功; waist and leg work), and *bazi gong* (把子功; weapon work and fighting). Training at the academy was structured around an extended workday organized into discrete sessions for stretching and acrobatics (tanzi gong), martial arts and weapon work (bazi gong), singing (*chang*; 唱), and dance-acting (*zuo*; 做). Tanzi gong is a movement program similar to the floor exercise programs of most gymnasts as well as the barre routines of trained dancers. Yaotui gong are a series of crouching positions, leg raises, and flying kicks. The students were often forced to hold the stretched postures of yaotui gong and the handstands common to tanzi gong for up to one hour. This training reinforces the student's conscious perception of their center of gravity and therefore prepares them to make microcorrections during acrobatic maneuvers so as to maintain control over movement and landing. The yaotui gong stances and tanzi gong maneuvers aid in the development of four elements: flexibility, muscle strength, balance, and control.[23] Forcing students to hold stances like the *chao tian deng*

(朝天凳; standing split) for at least an hour, endlessly walk in a crouched position for hours, and propel themselves through the air in moves like the *ce kong fan* (側空翻; aerial cartwheel without hands) helped the opera students to acquire the requisite flexibility, strength, balance, and control to perform in front of a live audience and, later, to repeatedly perform stunts on-screen.

These procedures generated a repeated and prolonged exposure to pain designed to push the performer's lactate threshold, a very painful learning process. *Lactate threshold* is a modern term used by physical trainers to indicate the moment at which athletes can no longer use their muscles because the level of lactate in the blood has been elevated by overactivity. Most athletes colloquially refer to the pain one experiences when reaching the threshold as "hitting a wall." The lactate threshold is specific to each athlete and can be manipulated by endurance training; that is, it can be "pushed." Vivian Sobchack has explained that pain causes subjects to gain a reified relationship to their own bodies, creating "an increased awareness of *what it means to be a material object.*" That is to say, the subject-in-pain, which Sobchack refers to as the body-subject, comes to conceive of their body as a thing.[24] Pain is how we come to know our bodies and how we establish our physical limits. Students at the drama academy became accustomed to pain as necessary to their improvement. It was of primary importance to the skilling process, as explained by Joshua Goldstein:

> The physical hardships of actor training had many layers of emotional and social significance. There were no books, diagrams, or student improvisation; training was a physical process, communicating skills from one body to another. Young actors needed to have their bodies reshaped; they were immersed in a set of vocal and physical practices that were tremendously difficult until they became second nature (parallels to ballet, foot-binding, tattooing, and Olympic gymnastics come to mind). Physical pain was an unavoidable part of this training, as was the requirement that students begin quite young. Only after being remolded into properly supple and receptive material, physically and mentally, were students deemed ready to receive instruction by expert actors in their specialty plays.[25]

The students of the China Drama Academy were chosen so young because their muscles were still quite pliable, and their small stature made it easier for them to propel themselves through the air. Though the painful stretching and repeated flips helped students to master their individual skills so that they could become opera stars, the training process also emphasized the troupe dynamic, which would become very important to Chan's body spectacles in his work with Golden Harvest. I would also suggest that, though not described in most academic accounts of deliberate practice, the corporal punishment endured by Chan and his contemporaries played a role in his drive to perfect his performance; as Mackerras explains, "Corporal punishment was common, with savage thrashings even for minor offenses. It would be accurate, although incomplete, to say that the art of the Peking opera was literally beaten into these boys."[26] The skilling of Chan's body was inseparable from the ritualized relationship to pain that is continually rearticulated in the on-screen display of Chan's performative failures in the "no-goods" that run during the closing credits of his films. During the no-goods, we are made privy to the mishaps that happened on set while the filmmakers were trying to complete the film's stunts, as is discussed in greater detail later in this chapter.

The students were trained for at least one hour each day in bazi gong, usually consisting of gong fu and coordinated play with long- and short-form weapons: broad swords, spears, shafts, knives, and so on. While students had to learn to synchronize their acrobatic movements, weapons training required precision timing and positioning so as not to do great physical harm to other performers. The children memorized the movements of all actors onstage and developed timed cues to avoid injury. Opera students are more than proficient in the coordinated interplay of bodies necessary to group performance, and this skill set would prove useful to Chan in the future. The dynamic symmetry of fluid movement and the terpsichorean staging of multiple-character fight choreography would become marked characteristics of Chan's body spectacles, and his classmates at the academy would aid in the process of making Chan a star. Practice, as it turns out, does not make perfect. Practice makes the expert so prepared for failure that the performer can quickly borrow from an expansive and diverse archive of restored behavior to lessen the degree of failure or completely circumvent it. The unique character of Chan's performance style can be identified in Chan's distinctive admixture of choreography and editing, the theater of pain visible in his outtakes, the integration of objects from the mise-en-scène in fight choreography, the coordinated troupe dynamic of staged combat sequences, and the risky nature of his stunt work.

Star Studies and Chan's Expert Performance

The extant star studies on Chan tend to examine the transnational quality of his star text, or, more specifically, his divergent star texts in Asia and the United States. Within the discipline of film studies, Chan is the most heavily textualized transnational Hong Kong star, which is fitting given that he is the star with the widest audience base in all of Asia. However, only a small percentage of the work on Chan focuses on his star text in the East Asian market, whereas in recent years there has been a proliferation of writing on the problems posed by the North American distribution of Chan's films. Most of the writing on Chan's Hong Kong films and his reception in East Asian markets tends toward both biography and a detailed description of the production context for individual films and stunts. The writings of Mary Farquhar and Craig D. Reid are notable exceptions. Both Farquhar and Reid examine Chan's choreography in greater detail. Farquhar argues that Chan's body spectacle is effected by both generic conceits and his bodily disposition from the opera: "Chan's brand of kung fu comedy therefore appropriates, integrates, and transforms a range of theatrical forms and performance styles. By emphasizing operatic movement, comic plots, and bodily farce in martial arts films, kung fu comedy added laughter as a counterpoint to the chivalry, blood, revenge, and tears that previously saturated the on-screen martial arts world."[27] Farquhar approaches Chan's bodily disposition with a greater attention to detail than other writers. She examines the contribution of Chan's opera training to the "rhythmic punctuation" of his body spectacles and argues that Chan's opera training can be observed in his choreography.[28]

Like Farquhar, stunt coordinator and academic Craig D. Reid addresses Chan's tendencies to both use and transform standard choreographic arrangements as key elements that produce Chan's body spectacles. Reid makes use of occupational vocabulary in his analysis, identifying the three standard sequence structures for fights: MAM ("Many Against Many") sequences in which multiple participants on opposing forces engage in combat; OHM ("One Hits Many") sequences in which (traditionally) a solitary hero takes on two or more assailants; and Triple O ("One On One") sequences, in which single individuals from opposing forces engage in lengthy fight scenes. He explains that Chan's fights often conform to either the MAM or OHM formula, formulas that "truly test the choreographer's and actor's capabilities."[29] Reid argues that Chan's body spectacles require greater dexterity and precision than most other action sequences because they avoid the style of cinematography and editing most common to Hollywood action films: the MSSQUE ("Many Shot, one Strike, QUick Edit") and the BEE ("Beginning-End Edit"): "The MSSQUE sections are shot by first filming one or a series of several techniques from three or four different cameras simultaneously. These shots are edited together to give the illusion of speed.... For a BEE, close-ups of the same strikes are then shot. The middle frames of the close-up shots are edited out while the beginning and the end of the strike's movement are spliced together. Hence the name 'Beginning-End Edit.'"[30]

The MSSQUE and the BEE help to punctuate performance, but they also make it possible for the performer to seem more skilled, as the editing obscures physical technique. Reid explains that Chan designed his own style of cinematography and editing to capture the fluid movements of the accomplished members of his stunt team. Reid refers to this method as the PMT ("Perpetual Motion Technique"):

The PMT (Perpetual Motion Technique) method was invented by Jackie Chan, and only he can use it to maximum effect. Directors, producers, and artists worldwide consider Chan to be the best fight choreographer in the film industry. The premise of his PMT method is the maintenance of continuous body motion throughout the entire fight sequence to give the impression of nonstop action. Chan's fights already contain continuous action, but his constant body motion enhances the emotional desperation of the conflict.[31]

The PMT is a combination of fast editing and continuous body movement such that the performer's body never appears static during cuts. This can be accomplished more easily when every take of an action sequence begins with the performer charging into the shot in some manner. One of the benefits of the PMT is that it often uses a wider (long shot/extreme long shot) and deeper field of vision (deep focus), which accentuates the capabilities of the performers in MAM and OHM sequences. One additional technique used in the construction of all of Chan's fight sequences is the YEBET method ("YEll Before Each Technique"), which helps performers to sync their movements to the timed cues of the verbal outburst "based on the—successful—logic that the faster the actors yell, the quicker their movements will be. The Chinese further perfected this method so that the yell and the technique delivery occurred simultaneously."[32] The YEBET technique is quite commonly associated with the work of 1970s martial arts performers, in particular Bruce Lee's primal howl. The Jackie Chan Stunt Team not only uses this method but has refined it such that different vocal cues (yells) inform the stunt performers on how to respond and where to position themselves. Reid's educated dissection of Chan's fight choreography is indispensable to any analysis of Chan's body spectacles and provides valuable insight into the distinctions between Chan's Hong Kong and Hollywood work, as discussed later in this chapter.

Jackie Chan's Virtuoso Reception Context: Fans and Expert Performance

The final group of expert interlocutors to aid in my examination of Chan's unique corporeal contributions to his Hong Kong and US productions are the fans who serve as a sample of Chan's virtuoso reception context. Expert performance requires observation and the recognition of individuals well versed in the performance techniques of the individual or in intersecting performance domains like martial art forms or action genre performance more generally. The reception and identification of expert performance is possible only through the virtuoso reception context. I chose to approach members of the Jackie Chan fan community for their expertise in this area. I conducted three fan surveys on Chan's virtuoso reception context: the first two in 2009 and the third in 2015. The first two surveys solicited respondents via message-board postings, and the last was facilitated by Chan's US Fan Club and the "Jackie Chan Is the Best" Facebook group. The three surveys together received ninety responses; the respondents predominantly identified as male (63 percent), and their ages ranged from seventeen to seventy. The self-identified Chan fans originated from the United States, Hong Kong, Canada, Germany, Switzerland, Hungary, Spain, the United Kingdom, Italy, India, and Japan. English was the most common first language, followed by German and Japanese. Fans were asked how they would prefer to be identified if they were quoted in this book and given three options (for example, anonymously, Jane D., Jane Doe), and their wishes have been respected because I desire to recognize these fans not as research subjects but as expert interlocutors on Chan's action design. Respondents were asked a total of nine questions about Chan:

1 How many Jackie Chan films have you seen?
2 When did you first start watching Jackie Chan, and in which film/TV show, etc.?
3 What is Jackie Chan's most memorable action sequence or ability, and why?

4 What is Jackie Chan's least memorable action sequence or ability, and why?

5 On which format do you commonly watch Jackie Chan's work?

6 Do you ever watch individual Jackie Chan action sequences multiple times, and why?

7 What makes Jackie Chan distinct from other action stars?

8 How often do you watch Hong Kong–style action films/TV shows, and for how many years have you been watching them?

9 Is there any other topic that you would like to address that was not mentioned above?

The largest percentage (35.5 percent) of the respondents began watching Chan's films in the 1980s, followed by a smaller group (23 percent) who began to follow his work after *Rumble in the Bronx* was released in 1995, and a third set (15.5 percent) who first encountered Chan in the installments of the *Rush Hour* series in the late 1990s though the early 2000s.[33] The smallest percentage of respondents first encountered Chan's work in the late 1970s. The members of the virtuoso reception context identified in this series of surveys have watched from fifteen to more than seventy Jackie Chan films, with the greatest number of respondents identifying at least forty Jackie Chan films they had screened thus far. While ninety self-identified Jackie Chan fans are not by any means representative of Chan's entire virtuoso reception context, many of the fans who participated have had greater exposure to Chan's performances than average action film spectators, and their observations on Chan's most and least memorable performances are invaluable to any study of action performance. The two trends that are most apparent from this research are the beliefs that Chan's most dynamic performances were during his heyday with Golden Harvest and that his work on US productions in the past twenty years has been comparatively disappointing.

The Virtuoso Reception Context:
Chan's Expert Performance in Hong Kong Films

In the early 1980s, kung fu films were waning in popularity, and Chan needed to produce more elaborate body spectacles to create a box office draw. Chan forced a transition in the action genre in the 1980s with the creation of the *wu da pian* (武打片; fight film), the key characteristics of which were "athleticism, martial arts, and dangerous stunts."[34] Most of the survey respondents

(88 percent) identified Chan's body spectacles in his wu da pian Golden Harvest films as the most dynamic of his career. The organization of Chan's films for Golden Harvest allowed him greater control over the production process but forced him to take increasingly dangerous risks to ensure funding for future productions. Chan's work in this genre in the 1980s and 1990s showcased five types of body spectacle that were remarked on by the members of his virtuoso reception context. These techniques are indebted to his deliberate-practice training in opera: feats of flexibility and dexterity, complex staging of OHM fights, integration of objects from the mise-en-scène, death-defying stunts, and the no-goods as a theater of pain. Though these modes are distinct, Chan integrates them in many of his body spectacles for his films with Golden Harvest.

The hours of stretching exercises and muscle conditioning in Chan's Peking opera training helped to produce body spectacles that demonstrate flexibility and dexterity: wall jumps, stylized poses, and grappling techniques. Chan commonly includes these techniques in his films as brief visual flourishes. In *Police Story* (警察故事), Chan completes one of his customary wall jumps instead of simply opening a gate.[35] These stylized movements are featured in long shot so that all of Chan's body is visible as he propels himself over the obstacle in two short moves. He grabs the top of the gate and positions his feet on the adjacent wall for leverage, then swings his legs over the gate and completes the jump (figure 1.1). Chan explains in the documentary *Jackie Chan: My Stunts* (成龍:我的特技) that he prefers to scale objects rather than simply open doors.[36] He "likes to jump" because it is more captivating for audience members; he explains that while it could be done with camera trickery, he has the "ability" to complete these difficult maneuvers. Chan's skill and dexterity when scaling a wall in two swift movements set him apart from other action stars of the 1980s and 1990s. Some fans do take note of these flourishes. One of Chan's fans, Jake M., a thirty-four-year-old male from Scotland, explained that he "love[d] to watch Chan move on screen, he makes simple gestures more interesting with his talent."[37] Chan demonstrates his dexterity with a "simple gesture" in *Drunken Master II* (醉拳二): Chan leans backward so that his back is nearly perpendicular to the ground while leaning on a combatant.[38] As the man positioned under Chan pulls away, Chan retains his position, a backbend, one of the common stretches taught to young opera students (see figure 1.2). Chan's body spectacles, even the briefest, are designed to startle the spectator, to force a recognition of Chan's great ability.

1.1 Jackie Chan leaps swiftly over a gate in *Police Story*.

1.2 In *Drunken Master II*, Jackie Chan demonstrates dexterity by performing a backbend.

This process is most effective when Chan integrates these feats of dexterity into his stunt sequences. Chan demonstrates his incredible flexibility and phenomenal grappling strength in the bus chase sequence from *Police Story*. Chan's character, the policeman Chan Kakui, must stop a drug kingpin from escaping on a double-decker bus. Chan runs after the bus with only an umbrella in hand and hooks the back of the bus with the umbrella handle. Chan is dragged behind the bus before pulling himself onto the bumper. Chan's full body is in view as the scene cuts to a shot of Chan struggling to keep his feet off of the road (see figure 1.3). Chan eventually hooks the top window of the bus, and perpetual motion forces him into the air at every turn (see

1.3 Jackie Chan is dragged behind a bus in *Police Story*, struggling to keep his feet off the ground.

1.4 In *Police Story*, the bus's movement causes Jackie Chan to swing out from the bus.

figure 1.4). Chan grasps the umbrella, supporting his full body weight, as the oncoming traffic forces him to lift his legs over the cars in his path. He then kicks the antagonist inside the bus. Chan performed that without a harness or safety wire, though the umbrella handle was made of steel, making it more durable. Chan falls from the bus but concludes the scene with one final flourish, jumping feetfirst over a barrier. This stunt, as well as the high jump in a mall that closes the film, demonstrates the distinct nature of Chan's body spectacles because, as twenty-nine-year-old US respondent Aaron Nicewonger argues, such performances "show his willingness to put himself in harm's way to get the perfect stunt."[39]

Though Chan is best known for the singularity of his accomplishments, the troupe dynamic that was fostered by his years at the academy and supported by his contract with Golden Harvest lent itself to the construction of multiple-combatant body spectacles that feature the complex staging of OHM fights. One example occurs in *Drunken Master II* and features Chan's PMT. In *Drunken Master II*, Chan plays the young Huang Fei-hong. Fei-hong's mother, portrayed by Anita Mui, is besieged by ruffians trying to steal her jewelry.[40] She instructs Fei-hong to recover the necklace and to demonstrate his *zui quan* (醉拳; drunken boxing) as a means of promoting the family's training academy, Po Chi Lam (寶芝林). Drunken boxing imitates the uncoordinated movements of someone who is inebriated, but performing the style accurately requires great coordination and balance, as Chan demonstrates in this OHM sequence. The antagonists are members of Chan's stunt team, and each yells as he approaches Chan, using the YEBET technique. Chan explains the coded system of yells used by his stunt team in *Jackie Chan: My Stunts*: the phrasing for the outburst informs Chan of the positioning and the mode of attack (high punch from behind, low kick from the front, etc.), and the speed of the utterance helps Chan to adjust his reaction time. The YEBET system facilitates Chan's PMT as three assailants attack him at once. The staging is made more dynamic by the use of a low-budget special effect common to Hong Kong martial arts films: baby powder. Chan and his team place baby powder in all impact zones to accentuate each strike and to generate the appearance of motion lines so that the bodies never seem still in the frame (see figure 1.5). Chan leaps over opponents or uses their bodies for leverage to grab prop bottles of alcohol and quickly imbibe from awkward positions. Chan was able to simulate the symptoms of drunkenness (red face, bloodshot eyes, etc.) by performing prolonged headstands before each take. The integration of objects from the mise-en-scène in fight sequences is common to Chan's OHM body spectacles and amplifies the dynamism of the coordinated bodies in motion.

Chan plans the action sequences in his films around the use of particular objects that seem naturalized in the mise-en-scène, as referenced by US respondent Keith Wayne Crumpler Jr., who describes Chan's unique "ability to move and seemingly react without thinking [and] to see everyday objects and find clever new uses for them."[41] Yung Sai-shing has deftly unpacked Chan's use of opera-honed object-integration skills, including the use of *yizigong* (椅子功; chair skill) and *zhuozigong* (桌子功; table skill) in *Drunken Master*.[42] Yung links the practice to Chan's training, explaining that "these basic props on the opera stage become the most convenient objects for the opera actors to show off their acrobatic and stunning actions."[43] Yung connects Chan's masterful handling of objects from the mise-en-scène to the familiar furniture found on sparse opera stages. This restored behavior from

1.5 In *Drunken Master II*, baby powder was used to accentuate the impact of each strike.

Chan's years of deliberate practice on- and offstage animates his workshop activity, the second stage of Chan's "whole performance sequence" as defined by Richard Schechner.[44]

In *Jackie Chan: My Stunts*, Chan explains that he organizes his fight choreography in relation to objects he experiments with in his stunt lab. Action numbers are created first, and the narrative impetus for their occurrence is decided at a later point. Two OHM fight sequences that demonstrate Chan's dexterity with objects in the mise-en-scène are the refrigerator number from *Rumble in the Bronx* and the ladder fight from *Police Story 4: First Strike* (警察故事4:之簡單任務).[45] In *Rumble in the Bronx*, Chan plays a Hong Kong police officer on vacation, defending his uncle's grocery store from a street gang in the Bronx. The film was shot in Vancouver, and Golden Way (Chan's satellite company) was required to hire Canadian talent, many of whom are cast as gang members. However, few were used in the scene because the choreography required familiarity with Chan's style. This film was one of many attempts to help Chan break into the US market. The producers cast many white actors as gang members to make the film appear less Chinese, but Chan has only an average of one or two Caucasian stuntmen on his team. Most attack sequences feature Asian members of the gang or Chinese stuntmen in long (often blonde) wigs to make them appear white. The gang's hideout is filled with seemingly innocuous objects that Chan uses as weapons; he uses refrigerator doors to hit his opponents and traps them inside in the refrigerators. Chan also uses a shopping cart to increase the impact of a

1.6 In *Police Story 4*, Jackie Chan assumes a stylized pose, a technique used in Peking opera at the end of a scene.

kick, and he employs a snow ski in the manner of a *gun* (棍). A gun is a Chinese long staff weapon used by practitioners of *wushu* (武術; "martial art") and *taichi quan* (太極拳; "flowing energy fist"). Chan uses this object to defend himself against six attackers. Chan performs a similar maneuver using a variety of objects in an OHM fight sequence from *Police Story 4: First Strike*. Chan protects himself using the head of a Chinese lion dance costume, two brooms, a wushu gun swiftly stolen from one of his attackers, and, finally, a large metal folding ladder. Chan flips the ladder over his back and thrusts it at his assailants, played by members of his stunt team. He jumps through the ladder, swings it over his head for use as a shield, and trips and traps his foes with it. Chan propels himself through the rungs of the ladder before twirling it around his body to end the scene with a stylized pose (see figure 1.6), two techniques common to opera performance: the skillful manipulation of a weapon before the close of a scene and the *liangxiang* (亮相; stylized pose).[46]

Though Chan is well known for his "prop dances," the body spectacles that helped to solidify his relationship with Golden Harvest and created the greatest box office draw were the increasingly dangerous stunts commonly performed as the climax to each of his wu da pian films. Chan was generally allotted higher budgets for each succeeding film, and to attract both financiers and audiences, Golden Harvest needed Chan to risk greater harm with life-threatening maneuvers. Near the conclusion of *Project A* (A 計劃), Chan, a fan of silent comedies, attempts to re-create a sequence similar to Harold Lloyd's clock-tower stunt in *Safety Last*.[47] This was identified as the most memorable action scene by 12 percent of survey respondents. In the scene Chan is clutching the hands of a clock and falls from the tower

1.7 In *Project A*, Jackie Chan dangles from a clock, holding onto the clock hands, before falling to the street below.

through an awning to the street below, landing on his neck (see figure 1.7). Heiko Gottschalk, a thirty-two-year-old German respondent, explains that the sequence is highly effective even upon repeated viewing: "I really hold my breath whenever I see the 'Clock Tower Fall.'"[48] The stunt emphasizes the unique qualities of Chan's performance, and, as such, this sequence is shown multiple times from slightly different angles, as is customary in Chan's films. At the close of *Police Story*, Chan leaps from the top floor of a shopping mall and slides down an illuminated pole, causing lights to explode as he passes (see figure 1.8). Chan received second-degree burns on his hands from the lights, which were turned up to full voltage, and dislocated his hip upon landing, but he still managed to finish the scene by getting to his feet to continue the chase. For *Armour of God* (龍兄虎弟), Chan's character, Asian Hawk, is supposed to jump from a cliff onto the top of a hot air balloon.[49] Chan accomplished the stunt by free-falling from a small plane, and the result is astonishing. In *Police Story 3: Supercop* (警察故事3: 超級警察), Chan jumped from the top of a building to a ladder attached to a moving helicopter.[50] Chan then clung to the ladder as the helicopter flew over Kuala Lumpur. In Chan's final film for Golden Harvest, *Who Am I* (我是誰), he delivers what was billed as his most dangerous stunt to date, a twenty-one-story slide down the side of a building in Rotterdam (see figure 1.9).[51] The stunts that Chan performed in these films may have attracted audiences, but many fans have suggested that the no-goods are more spectacular than anything that happens before the credits roll.

As previously mentioned, a series of mistakes known as "no-goods" is showcased for the audience at the close of every Chan wu da pian. Many

1.8 In *Police Story*, Jackie Chan slides down a pole as the lights explode.

1.9 Jackie Chan slides twenty stories down a building façade in *Who Am I*.

fans who participated in two surveys that I conducted, in point of fact an astounding 40 percent, reported that the most memorable part of any Chan film made by Golden Harvest was the no-goods.[52] In the no-goods for *Police Story 3: Supercop*, we see Chan hanging from the helicopter ladder as he kicks his shoes off; they fly hundreds of feet to the ground. In this same credit sequence, we observe Michelle Yeoh jump a motorcycle onto the top of a moving train on her third try. Over the credits for *Armour of God*, we witness Chan fall from a tree branch and punch a hole in his skull. He bleeds profusely, and the stunt team rush him to the hospital. The no-goods at the close of *Rumble in the Bronx* reveal that Chan completed some of the fight sequences with a broken foot in a cast that was disguised to resemble a sneaker (see figure 1.10). In one of my surveys, Scott N., a twenty-six-year-old from New York, explained that the no-goods "confirm the lengths to which Chan is willing to go for our entertainment. They make everything

1.10 Jackie Chan places a fake shoe over the cast on his foot in the no-goods for *Rumble in the Bronx.*

more believable. They show us why he is a star."[53] Many fans reported that they reviewed the fight sequences and stunts after seeing the bloopers and that knowing the hazards of the production process made them feel a greater proximity to Chan. Gwendolyn W., a twenty-eight-year-old from California, described the process as a newfound "empathy, a physical connection to Chan's body."[54]

Chan's virtuoso status, his reception as a uniquely talented individual, is contingent on his body spectacles and the confirmation of the dangerous labor necessary to produce them. Spectators like Gwendolyn feel a physical proximity to Chan, a process that Aaron Anderson has identified as "muscular sympathy." Anderson, quoting dance scholar John Martin, explains:

> These ideas of "felt blows, palpable echoes of gestures, and reflexively repeated movements" conform to what dance theorist John Martin calls "metakinesis" (communication through movement) and "muscular sympathy" (the phenomenological "feeling" associated with this communication). Central to the idea of muscular sympathy is the innate knowledge that a body cannot conceivably be made to do anything that the body cannot do. Yet while this is necessarily true of live performance, film may manipulate human movement in ways that affect our kinesthetic understanding of that movement. Since editing techniques and special effects can create the illusion of bodies doing things and moving in ways they conceivably should not be able to, any bodily understanding of movement may take on new dimensions in relation to certain filmed images or movements.[55]

Expert action viewers are physically moved, jolted in place, and sympathetically engaged by Chan's unique abilities, abilities that defy the limits of the possible. The no-goods reaffirm to expert viewers that what they watched was more than just a mirage created by constructive editing. Chan offers a unique type of corporeal cinematic pleasure.

While it is often difficult to isolate and translate the unique quality of a particular virtuoso performer, it is somewhat easier to identify what makes stars like Jackie Chan, Michelle Yeoh, and Sammo Hung more captivating than the other actors with whom they share the mise-en-scène. An anonymous twenty-four-year-old respondent from India remarked, "When I [watched] all these stunt[s] and movements, I realized this is the first time I am seeing a human doing all these nonhuman physical things, later on I found that [it was] only Jackie Chan in the world who did all that."[56] The stunting star has a unique effect on knowing spectators. The knowledge of the prefilmic and profilmic dangerous labor that contributes to the on-screen body spectacle combined with camera placement (long shot, extreme long shot) and editing (PMT) creates a special relation to the on-screen virtuoso body. Chan's virtuoso status, the reception of his body as phenomenal, was made possible in his work with Golden Harvest because of the structure of his contract: his lack of budgetary constraints, the artistic freedom that comes with satellite deals, and the ability to choose his own stunt team. Chan would not be so fortunate in his work in the United States. The legal requirements of production in the Hollywood system would limit and transform his body spectacle and thus his reception as a star.

Economies of Risk in Hollywood: Above and Below the Line

It is irresponsible to address Chan and other stunting stars without drawing attention to the apparent labor power (and production structures) necessary to the creation of certain body spectacles. Film is a collaborative enterprise, and far too often cinema and media studies treats the object of study as a simple text, akin to the manner in which English departments historically approached the novel. Taxonomizing the form and function of film narratives is a valuable service to the field, but surface readings tend to obscure the substantial labor force that is necessary to media productions and ignore the historical circumstances and working conditions that contribute to the finished product. In his work on film adaptation, Robert Stam has identified the tendency to position film as a lesser art form that is "suspectly easy to make and suspectly pleasurable to watch." He refers to this under-informed presumption as the "myth of facility."[57] By examining the differential aesthetic outcomes of the US production model for the creation of Hong Kong–style action spectacle in relation to the model common to Hong Kong productions, we can identify multiple conditions that contribute to this difference, in particular that in the US context (1) the action star is not an expert action performer; (2) regimented safety mechanisms have been put in place to regulate the star's behavior on set; and (3) financing and insurance arrangements are predicated on a well-run set that is observably compliant with contractual agreements.

1. The Star Is Not an Expert Stunt Performer

As Steve Fore has asserted, Chan is an anomaly in the Hollywood action marketplace. Chan's status as both star and performer has been the primary dilemma for producers.[58] Actors in the United States do not generally do their own stunt work, though they often make claims to the contrary. In the years preceding the studio era, actors often performed their own stunts if they were physically able to.[59] Once actors became stars, known commodities tied under contract to individual studios, they were no longer allowed to perform their own stunts. At the height of the studio era, studios could insure some of their stars, but all of the major players working on a project were not required to sign individual insurance contracts. If an actor was injured on set, production could be halted until the performer could recover (or the actor could be replaced by another contract player). The demise of the classical studio model of star management (which, when necessary, allowed for substitution) and the fall in theatrical attendance in the US market have led to a valuative model in which financing arrangements are predicated on particular stars with a history of solid theatrical performance in specific markets. It is therefore counterproductive to place stars in precarious situations, and for that reason the US film and television industries rely on expert stunt performers.

The creation of dynamic and groundbreaking body spectacles for action film and television productions the world over requires expert stunt performers. The restored behaviors that these performers draw from were developed through years of deliberate practice in a variety of disciplines that constitute their domain. The domains of Hong Kong stunt performers and US stunt performers intersect but are not identical. There are historical, industrial, economic, and governmental reasons for these distinctions.

Stunt communities of practice evolved (and continue to evolve) differently in Hong Kong than in Hollywood. The Hollywood model for financial and physical risk is historically different, with a separation of the expert star and the expert stunt worker. The process of governing through risk in Hong Kong media productions shares certain strategies with Hollywood, in particular the reliance on expert stunt coordinators, choreographers, and performers from dynastic communities of practice, as Sylvia J. Martin has addressed:

> Stunt coordinators and action directors who rehire the same team members remark that working with the same team—particularly family members—is a common tactic for reducing physical risks, since members of the network are familiar with the individual's limitations as well as their strengths, and directions are thus more easily conveyed. As with many industries, family hiring practices are maintained not only to pool economic resources but also to instill a sense of trust. While family hiring practices involve complex dynamics and are exclusionary, the kinship ties in the Hollywood and Hong Kong film industries should be understood as a strategy for avoiding physical risk.[60]

In the Hollywood context, the risk relationship is mediated by insurance contracts and on-set oversight. The familiarity fostered by nepotistic hiring practices and a team dynamic controlled by the stunt coordinator, as well as the use of stunt personnel in place of actors, minimizes the likelihood of a production delay. These techniques reduce the risk of injury to both stunt workers and stars. The greater risk created by stunt work is mediated financially through the personal insurance stunt workers carry in addition to that provided by the union representing the stunt workers and stars, the Screen Actors Guild - American Federation of Television and Radio Artists (SAG-AFTRA). Hollywood insurance executive Peter A. Marshall explains that "[stunt workers in Hollywood] have to provide their own insurance for their own workers comp[ensation] and disability because it is such a high-risk profession, and it really stands outside of the Screen Actors Guild usually. And so, the production doesn't get indemnified [the] extra expense of delay of their injury, and the performer is not indemnified by the production directly for their own injury."[61] In the Hong Kong context for Golden Harvest films, the satellite-deal model used profit sharing to limit the creation of moral hazard, as did the filial structure of the Jackie Chan Stunt Team, in which Chan is expected to finance medical care for accidents.

When studio production was at its peak in Hollywood and stars were tied to each studio, mishaps and production delays did not pose the serious threat they do today. The Hollywood film industry has experienced a steady decline each year in production and returns, fewer large-budget films are made, and many films fail to recoup their costs domestically. The incredible sums of money involved in producing a contemporary Hollywood motion picture require insurance policies to increase the likelihood of a return on investment. Chan can reportedly no longer perform dangerous stunts because they affect a studio's ability to secure a lower-cost production insurance package. Peter A. Marshall explains the process by which insurance companies evaluate stunt work on Hollywood productions as such:

> So, for instance, on *The Matrix* or some of the movies that do a lot of practical stunts, meaning they're not computer generated and they're not green screened with very controlled elements, you will have somebody who is like an adjuster, except they come before the accident. They come out there and they look at the plan. They talk with the coordinator and they suggest ways to make it safer, if they have those, and they advise the company about what kind of restrictions to put on for insurance.[62]

Marshall added that when stars are involved in a "gag" (or stunt), even in a limited capacity, that can affect premiums and, more commonly, deductibles. He explains that "there could be elevated deductible and additional premium, pending on what the loss control person [on set/working with the production] hears, sees, and then advises the carrier."[63] In his work with Hollywood studios, Chan has had to adjust his body spectacles to meet the requirements of insurance companies as well as the restrictions of the US Occupational Safety and Health Administration.

2. Regimented Safety Mechanisms Have Been Put in Place to Regulate the Star's Behavior on Set

The Occupational Safety and Health Administration (OSHA) was established by the Nixon administration's Occupational Safety and Health Act of 1970, was operational by 1971, and has since regulated workplace safety and established a coded system to be enforced by OSHA personnel.[64] Businesses that did not conform to the code were issued hefty fines, which cut into profits. As such, these businesses were pushed into compliance with the law. The successful passage of the act was aided by the strong support of union representatives because the act was expected to respond to safety concerns that were left unresolved by the collective bargaining process.[65] In most businesses OSHA cannot enforce regulations because of "the small number of inspections it conducts relative to the total number of establishments covered by the act and the low level of fines received by inspected firms."[66] Given the number of companies OSHA is responsible for, it cannot respond to small-scale complaints, and OSHA often relies on grievances filed by union representatives before conducting an on-site inspection. Hollywood productions have a substantial union presence; as such, in recent years, the industry has been careful to abide by OSHA regulations. Productions generally have a safety officer assigned to ensure compliance with all rules and to therefore limit union complaints. Hollywood's self-regulation has had profound effects on Jackie Chan's performance techniques.

The two rules most commonly applied to Chan's work on set relate to personal protective equipment and fall protection.[67] The rule about protective equipment requires an employer to pay for and issue devices that help to eliminate the risk of injury or death. The regulation for fall protection requires the installation of safety bars and restrictive devices for falls over six feet, like those in Chan's Hong Kong films *Police Story* and *Project A*. Chan has been forced to wear wired harnesses for many of his Hollywood films. These devices protect Chan from harm but greatly limit movement, which affects the terpsichorean character of Chan's body spectacles. As many of the sequences from Chan's Hong Kong films involve falls from a great height or precarious positioning on rooftops, Chan has had to greatly alter his action aesthetic to conform to OSHA policy. Chan must change his comportment, and adjustments must be made cinematographically so that the protective devices are less apparent.

3. Financing and Insurance Arrangements Are Predicated on a Well-Run Set That Is Observably Compliant with Contractual Agreements

Financial and physical risk have historically been distributed differently in Hollywood than in Hong Kong, but much like contemporary Hollywood studios, Golden Harvest historically financed production via large-scale loans from international banks and distributed the films it produced to theaters that it owned (or rented). The vertical integration of the studio limited risk, as did restricting production to star vehicles and genre films. Hong Kong does not have a history of state intervention on set, and the lack of formal insurance arrangements may be an effect of the filial nature of Chinese capital (as Chan reportedly pays for the medical needs of his injured crew members) and of illegal enterprises' historical control over productions. The triads, who were legally expelled from the industry in 1994, did not require the assistance of big banks to fund their films. Golden Harvest structured its production system on the satellite-deal model, in which the studio handled funding, while Chan's production company, Golden Way, was in charge of day-to-day operations and creative decisions. The production of a star whose body was decidedly endangered by the process of filmmaking was aided by creative freedom, a lack of studio oversight, and the absence of safety regulations. In Hong Kong, under Golden Harvest, Chan became a profitable star precisely because of the risks he took on set. The Hong Kong film industry's lack of formal safety regulations made Chan's striking displays of dexterity possible. In turn, the marketing of the increased risk associated with each new film helped to make Chan's films successful.

Hollywood studios commonly finance films via a combination of government subsidies, presales, gap financing, and large-scale bank loans.[68] Domestic and international theatrical presales as well as television presales help to defray part of the cost of production, but investors require the security created by a star with a solid track record. In the late 1990s, major studios were increasingly looking to team with smaller production units that had already arranged some financing, organized international distribution through global partnerships, and retained a bankable international star under contract. Such arrangements were classified as low-risk investments. In 1998 producers Roger Birnbaum and Gary Barber, reveling in the success of *Rush Hour*, formed Spyglass Entertainment and signed an exclusive five-year deal with Disney to produce internationally marketable low-risk films in this model, including *Shanghai Noon* and *Shanghai Knights*.[69] International banks covered the bulk of the financing for these films, but because film was an increasingly risky investment, these banks required insurance policies. Insurance can cover the producer's financial obligations should something happen to one of the film's stars; the actor can no longer simply be replaced in an era when financing is tied to the star's performance history in foreign markets. Quite ironically, companies reportedly refuse to provide insurance for Chan because of the body spectacles that have given him international box office appeal, as the threat of physical harm poses too much financial risk.

One primary distinction in governance of risk in Hong Kong is that production insurance does not structure the relationship to personal physical risk on set. Though Hong Kong has been a hub for the insurance industry since 1841 and the industry was booming in the 1970s, Hong Kong film and television industries have avoided investment in injury insurance for action performers.[70] Owing to the lower budgets, profound speed of production, and less formally regimented/unionized production culture in Hong Kong, the action choreographer takes responsibility for the safety of performers on set. Risk is governed by the paternalistic reverence for the Dragon-Tiger Master and belief in their expertise. Members of the Jackie Chan Stunt Team are not covered by insurance policies in Hong Kong productions. Chan employs his team under multipicture contracts and covers any medical costs incurred from mishaps on set. While accidents occur in Chan's Hong Kong–based productions, they are rare and are mostly incurred by the star performer himself.

The Other Jackie Chan: Stunts or Stardom in Hollywood

The fan-participants whom I surveyed as part of Chan's virtuoso reception context voluntarily added sentiments akin to "anything he does in America is his worst," noting that "only Chan's Hong Kong films should be considered when weighing the quality of his work."[71] These responses are no surprise, as I have heard similar declarations from my students over the years, but these complaints do beg the question: what are the differences between Chan's Hollywood and Hong Kong action sequences? The answers are legion because the mediating mechanisms that adjust Chan's expert performances in Hong Kong and Hollywood films are many: age, lighting budget, second-unit directors, and so on. However, in an attempt to highlight heretofore-neglected elements of Chan's performance, the three characteristics that mediate difference in the performance of body spectacle in Chan's Hollywood and Hong Kong films are the pressure to alleviate financial risk for both studios and banks, legal and financial distinctions between stunt performers and stars in Hollywood, and regulatory compliance with US workplace safety standards.

Chan's first major box office success in the US market came in the form of the 1995 *Rumble in the Bronx*, and Hollywood studios took note. When the theatrical presales market began to dry up, studios became desperate for stars bankable in multiple international markets. Securing Chan enabled studios to continue to distribute financial risk to exhibitors. Hollywood tried to capitalize on funding schemes linked to Chan's success after 1995 because of his bankability in foreign markets based on his stunting stardom and career of physical risk taking, which made it easier to secure theatrical presales abroad.

The body spectacles of Chan's Hollywood films show a number of marked distinctions from his Hong Kong work that can be identified via a discussion of the following: the stunt performers, fight beats (choreographed movements and points of contact) per shot, use of props as a form of compensation, special effects, cinematography, and editing. For most Hollywood productions Chan does not use his full stunt team for on-screen labor. He works with his team to choreograph the stunts, but most of the men visible in the finished product are often union stuntmen with long Hollywood careers. Working with a team that has no Peking opera training can alter the nature of Chan's OHM body spectacles. In a sequence from *Shanghai Knights*, the reaction time of the stunt crew is incredibly slow (in terms of the number of fight beats per shot) compared to Chan's team, and Chan's OHM body spectacles lose the effect of perpetual motion. In an OHM fight sequence in which Chan's character, Chon Wang, is attempting to rescue a young Charlie Chaplin from some criminals, Chan is confronted with the limitations of the stunt team.[72] Instead of a coordinated sequence of blows, the team hits him simultaneously or in Triple O scenarios. The timed hits are much slower than in Chan's Golden Harvest films, and he compensates for these differences with the increased use of props as weapons. The use of props natural to the mise-en-scène as weapons is common in Chan's Hong Kong work, but what is distinct in his Hollywood films is the overuse of this technique. The members of the stunt crew for *Shanghai Knights* were fungible laborers; if they were injured during the course of production, they would be replaced by new stunt workers with minimal delay. Chan could use these stuntmen as slow-moving targets (see figure 1.11). In the chase sequence from *Shanghai Knights*, Chan flips over tables, attacks his assailants with umbrellas, and causes the stuntmen to spin through the air. Chan's movement is limited, and for this reason he adds a choreographed dance routine to the close of the action sequence. Chan's body spectacles have been transformed by the different training regimes of the stunt labor force in the United States as well as by policy restrictions designed to protect the star's body.

As previously stated, most Hollywood actors, no matter what they might say to the press, do not perform their own stunts because of insurance restrictions, and most stunt performers are covered under personal insurance policies. As stunt performers are considered independent contractors, they are not employees under OSHA regulations.[73] Producers do not need to en-

1.11 In *Shanghai Knights*, Jackie Chan uses Hollywood stuntmen as props.

sure the safety of stunt workers to the same extent that they must cover actors involved in the film. Even though Chan has traditionally fulfilled dual roles as star and stuntman, his activity on set must be adjusted to meet OSHA regulations because he is an actor and thus classified as an employee. However, Chan's stunt team would be considered independent contractors. Chan does not insure his stunt performers, as it is not required by OSHA policy and it is not customary to do so in Hong Kong, where the team trains. Again, even in the US context, Chan will cover the medical costs of team members should they be injured on the job.[74] One of the primary effects of this distinction between actors and stunt workers is that stuntmen and stuntwomen are allowed to produce more dynamic body spectacles than Chan in his US films. In US productions, stars and stunt performers are commonly segregated into first-unit and second-unit work. The few moments of crossover occur when stars are needed for master shots that will be edited together with vignettes of stunties reacting to the star's performance. In these moments of convergence, US stunt performers are expected to ensure the star's safety and to make the star look credible. Though Chan's stunt team also performs these functions in his Hong Kong films, his Hong Kong–produced OHM action sequences are distinct from his Hollywood productions. In the Hong Kong context, though Chan's risk taking might still suffer the mediating mechanisms of age or possibly fear, the process is not mediated by legislative restrictions. The OHM action sequences in Chan's Hollywood films bear a resemblance to his Hong Kong work because Chan requests that the director of photography shoot the action sequence in continuity instead of relying on master shots. This shift in production techniques also requires a change in technique by the stunt workers, who must keep Chan safe for extended periods and interact with the star at length instead of simply responding to a punch thrown in the master shot. The most glaring differences between Chan's Hong Kong and Hollywood films are evident in the number of choreographed fight beats per shot. The reduction in fight beats per shot, as a single articulated movement or point of contact, is an effect of both the need to protect Chan from possible mishaps and the lack of time the mostly American stunt team has to learn complex multibeat sequences requiring the coordination of human movement and camera placement. The Hong Kong fight-design process is often done on set, whereas contemporary Hollywood fight choreography is planned in advance of production by the stunt crew and coordinator. Stunt performers are always learning on the job, but because of the high number of beats between cuts in a typical Jackie Chan fight sequence, Hollywood stunt workers on his films face a very fast learning curve.

Chan's Hollywood films offer body spectacles distinct from those in his Hong Kong productions because of restrictions designed to ensure his safety and continued survival as well as to protect the investment of the financiers. The substantial expenditure necessary to produce a film in the United States contributes to the policing and protection of star bodies. In contrast, in Hong Kong the structure of production at Golden Harvest enabled the creation of a star whose body was decidedly and purposefully endangered by the process of filmmaking. Other nations have increasingly been introducing safety regulations that affect the laborers working in their film industries.[75] The loss of Chan to Hollywood (and later to mainland China), the economic uncertainty that came with the handover of Hong Kong to China in 1997, and an overreliance on foreign investment briefly forced Golden Harvest out of film production, though they still operate a successful cinema chain and have now entered the Asian film marketplace as a financier. With Chan's increasing age and the increasing restrictions on his activity in his Hollywood productions, his striking corporeal kinetic displays of skill and dexterity are being replaced by the capabilities of computer graphics in the United States and the talents of stars like Tony Jaa from national film industries with underregulated labor contexts. In an era in which Hong Kong is producing fewer films than ever, and Chan is aging and being regulated out of stunt work, Hong Kong–style action aesthetics have reached a palpable moment of transition.

TWO

HONG KONG ACTION CINEMA AS A MODE IN THAI ACTION STARDOM / Tony Jaa and the New Stunting Star Model

In 2003 Thai action cinema, which had been a mainstay of rural Thai exhibition circuits, expanded its reach not only to Bangkok multiplexes but far beyond the boundaries of the domestic market. The canny marketing strategies of one of Thailand's largest studios, Sahamongkol Film International (บริษัท สหมงคลฟิล์ม จำกัด), and the uncanny body spectacles of stunting star Tony Jaa, otherwise known as "Jaa Phanom," made this possible. Jaa's body spectacles are uncanny in many senses in that his propensity for flight is preternatural and the perilous stunts that Jaa performs in his early films evoke in the expert action spectator a feeling of "the familiar in the strange." Jaa's early work evokes that of Jackie Chan, but the alien qualities of Jaa's bodily disposition are the effect of deliberate practice of Asian in-body performance practices that are distinctly Thai. After the success of *Crouching Tiger, Hidden Dragon* (卧虎藏龙) in 2000, why would the next transnational action star to rise to the attention of audiences originate from Thailand and not from a country steeped in the traditions of Chinese-language cinemas?[1] The answer is at once simple, in that Jaa's body spectacles act as a seemingly contrapuntal antithesis to those of the wuxia (martial hero) cycle, including those on display in *Crouching Tiger, Hidden Dragon* and in following films, and complex, in that, as Saskia Sassen has suggested, "globalization consists of an enormous variety of micro-processes that begin to denationalize what had been constructed as national."[2] Jaa's rise to action stardom in the early to mid-2000s is an effect of the flow of Chinese immigrants as flexible citizens and, relationally, of Hong Kong films into Thai cinemas; a history of shifting regulation of imports; the decrease in production in the Hong Kong film industry following antitriad legislation in 1994; the economic conditions brought on by the Asian financial crisis of 1997; and the marketing of Jaa as a well-trained martial arts expert and stunt performer. An examination of the early work of Jaa (and to a lesser extent "Jeeja" Yanin Vismitananda) demonstrates that Thai action producers very astutely adopted the Hong Kong action model: expert stunting stars and a consistent selection of members from stunt choreographer Panna Rittikrai's stunt community of practice, flexible specialization in the form of satellite-model production, eschewal of financial-risk-distribution practices common in Hollywood, and documentation of the conditions of production as a form of marketing.[3] Thai action cinema offered virtuoso performances distinct from those of the wire-heavy wuxia epics being produced in Chinese-language cinema. However, between 2010 and 2020 we have also witnessed a decline in the transnational profile of Thai action cinema owing to globalized shifts in exhibition trends and the contractual rigidity distinct to the Thai market. This chapter concerns two national film industries deeply affected by the Asian financial crisis of 1997: Hong Kong and Thailand. In particular, this chapter examines the body spectacles of stunting stars working in post-1997 Thai production contexts: Tony Jaa and Jeeja Yanin. Following this, the chapter explores the relationship of Thai cinema exhibition history and the Asian financial crisis to Jaa's body spectacles and global reception context. This chapter examines the relationship of the laboring body of the expert stunting star to other special effects, as informed by production models, industrial histories, exhibition contexts, and cultural policies.

Tony Jaa has commonly portrayed rural villagers fighting the ills of foreign invaders and modernizing forces. A standard analysis of Jaa's star text would most typically (1) discuss the martial arts icon as a national hero, (2) read the characters he plays as symbolizing the national condition, and (3) analyze his performance as an articulation of the conflict between modernity and tradition. I am interested in Jaa for the ways he is linked to the nation—but not because of the characters that he has played, the symbolic conflicts between modernity and tradition that such characters face, or the traditional martial art forms, *muay thai* (มวยไทย) and *muay boran* (มวยโบราณ), that he practices. (While muay thai is a form of Thai kickboxing that makes ample use of the knees and elbows to attack enemy combatants, muay boran is an ancient form of Thai combat that is lethal and requires more flexibility.) Instead, I argue that Jaa is iconic of the nation and in particular of the national film industry of Thailand because of the manner in which his body spectacles and virtuoso reception context have been determined by national economic predicaments and globalized exhibition cultures. It would be simple to address Jaa as a nationalist icon with embodied connections to a state-sanctioned martial art form through aesthetic analysis, but to do so without examining Jaa's body spectacles, as well as the "special effects" of the Asian financial crisis on the common production model in Thailand, would serve to reinforce the naturalized absence of discussions of labor arrangements, production hierarchies, funding structures, and exhibition cultures in cinema and media studies. As such, this project is less interested in offering an argument about muay thai expert Tony Jaa and the national heroes he has played on-screen. This chapter is more concerned with articulating the manner in which exhibition cultures, distribution cycles, and cultural policies have led to the revaluation of the martial arts body spectacle, and of Jaa in particular, as well as to a rise in reception cultures of disbelief, a newfound "aesthetic of astonishment."

This piece addresses the rise of Thai action film star Tony Jaa as an expert stunting star and the formation of a new model for Thai action stardom based on a horizon of expectations established by Jaa's dynamic body spectacles. Both the unique characteristics of Jaa's stunt work and the systems that have informed his international stardom are addressed in detail in an attempt to lay bare the mechanics of transnational action stardom in the Hong Kong model. The function of this chapter is not to analyze the appearance of similar choreographic techniques and cinematographic styles across national borders in the name of global action cinema scholarship but to link the generation of body spectacles by action stars and performers to the material circumstances of the *transnational* flow of media and cinema as an economic enterprise. For this purpose, I solicited participants for online English-language surveys. I posted links to the surveys on the listservs run by fan websites connected to each of the stars and also contacted fansite administrators and asked them to circulate information on the surveys to their members. Participants were asked to indicate their name, sex, and country of residence as well as to answer four short questions on the star's work:

1 What is the star's most memorable action sequence or ability?
2 When did you first notice the star?
3 On what media format do you commonly watch the star's work?
4 What makes this star distinct?

The surveys were kept concise to encourage more participants, but most respondents replied with extensive comments on the star. I received replies from fifty-six Tony Jaa fans and thirty-two Jeeja Yanin fans located in the United States, England, Australia, and France. I conducted these surveys on Jaa's and Yanin's virtuoso reception contexts in an attempt to make formal analysis of their body spectacles relevant to the concerns of audiences. Fan research in film and media studies has historically been concerned with early film spectators, stardom, or the cult text. but more work must be conducted on action film fandom in our discipline.

This case study proceeds by recounting the history of foreign involvement in exhibition, distribution, and cultural policy in the Thai motion picture industry because the transnational aesthetic dispositions of "new Thai action cinema" do not emerge and continue to evolve without historical precedent; as Sassen proclaims, "The new is messier, more conditioned, and with older lineages than the grand new global institutions and globalizing capabilities suggest."[4] While many scholars define national film industries by their production histories, the following pages attempt to demonstrate the importance of exhibition, distribution, and policy changes to production strategies, genre elements, and labor conditions. The chapter explores the relationship of this history and the Asian financial crisis to Jaa's body spectacles and global reception context. Hong Kong action cinema operates as a *mode* in contemporary Thai martial arts films, and Jaa is of primary importance to the rise of Thai cinema in Hong Kong's moment of decline. This chapter attempts to identify both Jaa's spectacular corporeal disposition and the much broader conditions necessary for the production of Jaa's stardom, including the historical dominance of Hong Kong action film distributors, the effects of the 1997 Asian financial crisis on Hong Kong film production, and the concomitant rise of new Thai action cinema in the wake of Hong Kong cinema's decline in production.

The Asian financial crisis of 1997 has most commonly been attributed to Thailand's decision to peg the baht to the US dollar after the real estate crisis of the mid-1990s. During the 1980s and early 1990s, the baht was performing well, as Thailand was one of the "Asian tigers" involved in the East Asian "economic miracle." However, owing to an inflated sense of security, many domestic Thai banks began borrowing large sums in US dollars. The real estate crisis was prompted by the risky lending practices of underregulated banks, which led to investment in greatly inflated stocks owing to a "false impression of soundness."[5] The Asian financial crisis was, in so many ways, the prequel to the global financial crisis of 2008 and 2009. However, the International Monetary Fund, which provided a bailout plan for the struggling Asian nations, instituted neoliberal policies to cut government spending and increase taxes, in stark contrast to the Obama administration's Keynesian response to the 2007–2009 US economic crisis. Salaheen Khan, Faridul Islam, and Syed Ahmed have suggested that the Asian financial crisis of 1997 created a sustained and widespread effect in countries located close to Thailand owing to the significance of interregional trade between these nations beginning in the 1970s.[6] They describe the effect of this interdependence as a "contagion" spreading along trade routes connecting South Korea, Singapore, Malaysia, Indonesia, the Philippines, Hong Kong, and Thailand.[7]

I contend that the crisis's contrasting outcomes for the film industries of Hong Kong and Thailand are due to two primary factors: (1) the changes in the Hong Kong film industry preceding and following the 1997 handover of Hong Kong and (2) the history of US and Hong Kong domination of film distribution and exhibition arrangements in Thailand. Hong Kong cinema was struggling before the Asian financial crisis, but many of those preexisting problems were further exacerbated by the funding crisis that the Hong Kong film industry experienced after 1997, including the loss of key members of the labor force, a substantial decrease in investment following the criminalization of triad business practices in 1994, competition with Hollywood products heavy on special effects, and the need for ensemble films with young "bankable" casts to secure financing through distribution arrangements and DVD presales. The financing predicament faced by the industry forced a shift in genre prescriptions toward more Hollywood-style, effects-driven martial arts films. This shift to computer-generated effects-heavy action films adjusted the requirements and expected skills necessary for generating on-screen body spectacles, which is to say, the films were inundated with wirework and light on stunts. Hong Kong also suffered losses owing to decreased revenue from distribution in the markets affected by the Asian financial crisis, including Thailand, with which the United States had recently negotiated lower film import tariffs in exchange for a similar concession for Thai agricultural exports.

The Thai film market has historically been dominated by a foreign presence, but in the years immediately preceding the Asian financial crisis, the most prominent imports were from the United States and Hong Kong. The US manipulation of the film import tariffs allowed Hong Kong and Hollywood films to flood the market. This effected a decrease in local Thai production from 113 films in 1990 to 32 in 1996.[8] The decrease in production in Thailand along with the growth of the television market has led to more calculated efforts to ensure success for the few films that studios release. To compete with Hollywood special effects and Hong Kong martial arts, as well as to appeal to the teen market at mall cinemas and the traditional action film market at the open-air cinemas in the provinces, Thai studios and stunt houses have developed a martial arts star formula that necessitates perilous body spectacles on the part of the stunting star. This formula is not new to this national cinema; during the golden years of Thai cinema, successful action stars under long-term contracts were expected to shoot as many as five films at once. As fewer films were being financed in the years after the Asian financial crisis, maintaining long-term control over marketable stars became a priority for studios looking for financing. Studios returned to the contract-driven arrangements of the 1970s but adopted Golden Harvest's satellite production model. The particular confluence of Thai studio-era business practices (placing stars under restrictive contracts), Hong Kong cinema production structures (like the satellite deal) designed for martial arts stars like Bruce Lee and Jackie Chan, and Thai action cinema's historical preference for "real" stunts led to the emergence of a new Thai action star formula. This formula necessitated marketing the expertise of the stunting star. The formula was modeled after the success of Thailand's most famous martial arts star, Tony Jaa, and required constant and adaptive deliberate-practice training to ensure product differentiation for each succeeding film in an action star's oeuvre. Jaa, and the star formula based on him, has provoked a distinct virtuoso reception context marked by astonishment and disbelief.

Thai Cinema History: Decline and Resurgence

Far too often genre histories are examined, and star texts revealed, without any consideration of a national cinema's exhibition circuits, distribution cycles, and cultural policies. What follows is an attempt to address the long-standing effects on Thailand's film industry of the early Japanese design of exhibition cultures, Chinese manipulation of film distribution cycles, and US intervention into cultural policies. The following pages examine the history of Thai exhibition cultures in relation to cinema ownership, distribution practices, genre prescriptions, and cultural policies. Like many national markets, the exhibition cultures of Thai cinema are dominated by Hollywood productions, but Thai film history has a lengthy and varied relationship to cultural imperialism. While Thailand proudly proclaims its status as the only noncolonized nation in Southeast Asia, Thai cinema has always been dominated by a foreign presence. The etymology of the Thai term for the cinema reveals the complex cultural genealogy of cinema as a foreign media form. At the beginning of the twentieth century, when Japanese businesses dominated the exhibition market, film was referred to as *nang yipon* (หนัง ญี่ปุ่น; Japanese shadow puppet theater). As cinemas filled with European and American productions before and during World War I, the common term for film became *nang farang* (หนัง ฝรั่ง; Caucasian or foreign shadow puppet theater). In recent years, as Thai outfits increased local production, the phrase for cinema has been shortened to simply *nang* (หนัง). The term *nang* is inherited from Thai shadow theater, or *nang talung* (หนังตะลุง), a type of performance native to the southern provinces that uses leather puppets, illuminated from behind to project the outline of the puppet onto a screen. As Zhang Zhen has noted, early Chinese cinema shares a connection to traditional forms of shadow puppet theater, albeit native Chinese varieties.[9] Any thoroughly rigorous analysis of the Thai film industry cannot simplify the national cinema context to a history of local production. Foreign influences on distribution and exhibition practices have had long-standing effects on the genealogy of Thai film production, in particular, the structure of the star system, the formation of genre conventions, and the style of performance.

Foreign control over theater ownership and the management of film distribution has persisted in various forms in Thailand from the earliest *cinématographe* screenings to present exhibition contexts. In the 1910s the Japanese ran the exhibition industry in Thailand, but they were quickly replaced by Sino-Thai businesses like the Siam Cinema Company. One of the earliest vertically integrated film distributors in the nation, the Thai-Chinese-owned Siam Cinema Company, originated in the exhibition business and quickly eliminated competitors by acquiring the distribution rights to French, American, and Hong Kong productions and expanding the cinema network to rural areas beyond Bangkok. Siaw Songuan Sibunruang (เซียวซอ งอ้วน สีบุญเรือง), who, Scot Barmé argues, was "arguably the most important figure in the early history of the Thai cinema," ran the company.[10] Before managing the film company, Siaw worked for many years as an accountant at Siam Electric, and he later used his investment in the electric rail, and the development of the transportation network to rural areas, to further the expansion of Siam Cinema's holdings, organizing traveling film shows to provinces located close to the southern railway line. Siaw was one of the first exhibitors to attempt outdoor screenings. Siaw positioned the local screenings at stops along the rail line. Owing to Siaw's early efforts, the growth of cinema in the provinces was linked to the expansion of the public transportation network.[11] The development of the outdoor provincial theater system, the circulation of Hong Kong and US films to rural areas, and the vertically integrated distribution-exhibition network were remarkable accomplishments. Each of these infrastructural advancements fostered the development of an audience base for Chinese films in Thailand and would greatly alter the formula for Thai action films in the decades to come. After Siaw's empire collapsed, the continued distribution of Hong Kong films in Thailand was facilitated by the American manipulation of Thai import tariffs.[12]

In a strange turn of events, the lobbying efforts of the United States greatly benefited the Hong Kong film industry. Like Hollywood producers, Hong Kong studios also took advantage of the lowered import taxes in Thailand. During the years in which the Thai government bowed to US wishes, mainland Chinese films were not imported, but Thailand had a substantial Chinese immigrant community. Golden Harvest and Shaw Brothers were happy to serve the needs of this community and anyone else interested in Hong Kong action films. In the mid-1970s, the import tariff system was adjusted, and as the Americans fled the market, Hong Kong film distributors and Hong Kong–owned exhibitors shared the newly available screen space with Thai productions.

In 1976 Professor Thanin Kraivichian (ธานินทร์ กรัยวิเชียร) became Thailand's new prime minister and almost instantly made changes that would have a profound impact on the Thai film industry. The Thai Motion Picture Producers Association, Thailand's first film trade union, which was established in 1967, lobbied the Kraivichian administration to limit the number of foreign imports and to decrease the film admission tax. The first obstacle to the success of the Thai film industry, the admission tax, was set at 50 percent of the ticket price and was charged directly to patrons. The motion picture association argued that the tax dissuaded people from attending the cinema. The Kraivichian regime quickly lowered this tax to 10 percent. Following this, the administration attempted to reduce the foreign saturation of the market by changing the import tariff, increasing it from US$0.11 to US$1.20 per meter of imported film stock. The Motion Picture Export Association of America responded by boycotting the Thai market from January 1977 to May 1981. The US government and the association lobbied Thai celebrities and the press to pressure the Kraivichian government, to no avail. Eventually, the United States gave up on the boycott and reentered the Thai market in 1981, but by that time the domestic film industry had rebounded and was producing new films at an all-time high.

The growth of Thailand as a tiger economy and the Hollywood boycott of the late 1970s to early 1980s were two key factors that prompted the surge in production during this period. It was easier to secure funding from banks for films made in the 1970s and 1980s. There were also more free screens, with less Hollywood product flooding the market. During the 1970s many filmmakers attempted to capture middle-class audiences in the urban center with "artful" social problem films.[13] By the 1970s most Thai filmmakers had made the transition to thirty-five-millimeter stock, with the exception of some working in the action genre, for whom production budget and ease of use were of primary importance in the drive to supply films to the outdoor theaters in the provinces as quickly as possible. In the 1970s and 1980s, many Hong Kong films from Shaw Brothers and Golden Harvest were flooding the market and had gained a foothold in many of the theaters that had previously held Hollywood product. However, Hong Kong action films, much like the low-budget Thai actioners, captured most of their profits from the upcountry outdoor circuits. The outdoor circuits included *nang lorm pha* (หนัง ล้อม ผ้า; cloth-surround films) and *nang klang plaeng* (หนังกลางแปลง; open-air films). Both of these configurations require a screen, a projector, and a transportation system (car, boat, or oxcart) to move between villages. At nang lorm pha screenings, a cloth fence is set up so that admission can be charged. Nang klang plaeng were free public films sponsored by a member of the community or the government and often included news programs.[14] Hong Kong films (and to a lesser extent Taiwanese films) performed incredibly well in Thailand. Golden Harvest and Shaw Brothers even extended their exhibition empires to urban centers in Thailand. Shaw Brothers International (SBI) united with the local Union Odeon Company to buy available cinemas in heavily populated areas of Thailand and ran over one hundred theaters in the country by the 1970s.[15] However, Hong Kong action films performed best at open-air theaters in rural areas. To gain distribution to these locations, the major Hong Kong studios, such as Golden Harvest, developed long-term business relationships with certain Thai distributors, most notably the Sino-Thai-owned Sahamongkol Film, the studio that would later produce all of Tony Jaa's films.[16]

The Thai box office success experienced by Thai and Hong Kong filmmakers in the 1970s and 1980s would be cut short in the mid-1990s owing to the pre-1997 collapse of the Hong Kong industry, the adjustment of the film import tax, and the growth of the multiplex. As discussed earlier in this chapter, the Hong Kong film industry was quite negatively affected by the loss of creative personnel and by difficulty securing loans, among many other issues. Hong Kong was not delivering as many releases to Thailand as it had in the boom era. When the United States pushed for a significantly lower film import tariff in 1992, the Thai government conceded in exchange for a reduced import tax for Thai agricultural products being shipped to the United States.[17] Hollywood instantly benefited from this arrangement, as the import tax was dropped to 30 percent of the level it had been set at in 1976. The tariff went from US$1.20 per meter of imported film stock to a shocking US$0.40 per meter. The United States had been working around the tariff for years by sending prints to be processed in Thailand, as the tax did not distinguish between positive and negative footage, but once the tax was adjusted, Hollywood studios were the first to benefit, more than doubling their number of imports. Many of these Hollywood films were screened at the new multiplexes, which began to spring up in 1994.

As the Asian financial crisis worsened, fewer films were made in Thailand, with fewer than ten being produced per year by the end of the decade. As Anchalee Chaiworaporn and Adam Knee point out, particular genres were quickly eliminated, including most action films and lower-budget productions:

> B-grade productions were the first to be affected by the flood of Hollywood films: with an abundance of available titles, regional Thai distributors (those concentrating on provinces *outside* Bangkok) opted for Hollywood action films with better production values than those of the local product. Hong Kong movies likewise should have gained an advantage from the reduced import tax, but that industry was experiencing a dramatic decline in the early 1990s and hence was in no position to reap potential benefits.[18]

Ubonrat Siriyuvasak has echoed this sentiment, explaining that the first effect of the decline in domestic production was a marked lack of diversity in genre production, and the second was the disappearance of independent production companies.[19] The few companies that survived the crash adjusted their product to the mall and multiplex audiences, and many films made during this time were designed to appeal to the teen market.

In the late 1990s, while the Hong Kong film industry was faltering, the Thai industry witnessed a spike in production, as noted by Chaiworaporn and Knee: "Although Thai film making had a substantial lull in the mid-1990s, it has actually experienced a relative boom since 1997 (the year of the Asian Financial Crisis), with production picking up markedly over the course of a few years (from little more than two dozen features in 1997 to an estimated sixty in 2003) and Thai films generating significant interest at international film festivals."[20] The two authors make it clear that this recent boom is in no way equivalent to the Thai film industry's success in the 1970s and 1980s, owing to the return of US studios to the market.[21] Hollywood films have retained a large market share of ticket sales in Thailand since the end of World War I, but these films have always been met with stark competition from Hong Kong films, other films from Asia, and local productions.[22] As I have demonstrated, Thai cinema was dominated by the presence of US and Hong Kong productions for decades. There is an extensive history of foreign control over film exhibition and of US meddling in Thai cultural policy decisions. Thai films have historically tried to compete with and emulate both Hollywood and Hong Kong action films in attempts at success in the domestic context. However, owing to the budgetary restrictions of the industry, Thai action film aesthetics have tended more toward Hong Kong body spectacles than Hollywood special effects. Knee has addressed the need to consider structures of influence more broadly when approaching the relationships between national cinemas, as many analyses of globalized cinema tend to focus too exclusively on Hollywood when analyses of the relationships between regional cinemas such as Thailand and Hong Kong can be just as telling:

> In the effort to more fully understand Hong Kong cinema's global context—and to avoid an over-reliance on sometimes problematic East/West oppositions in doing so—it is particularly productive to examine that cinema's connection to Thailand. Thailand's relationship is especially strong in that the country that has long been a significant market for Hong Kong film, in that numerous Hong Kong–Thailand coproductions have been mounted over the years, in that Hong Kong has wielded a strong stylistic influence over Thailand.[23]

Knee explains that two key developments in Thai action cinema in the late 1970s and early 1980s were the "influence" of Hong Kong–style martial arts films and the use of stuntmen. Thai film scholar Alongkorn Klysorikhew credits both of these developments to the import duty protection, which helped to reduce the number of US imports during this period.[24] Before this time, action film actors normally did their own stunts, as actor Sombat Metanee (สมบัติ เมทะนี) explains: "At my time, we did what we could. We were not afraid of pain, nor death, taking all risks, falling from hills, using real bullets, jumping through closed windows, or doing somersault jumps."[25] Thai filmmakers, desperate to compete, altered the standard action formula to include more hand-to-hand combat and acrobatics. These techniques would also help to distinguish Thai action cinema from foreign competitors in the years following the Asian financial crisis.

The Thai studios that facilitated the distribution of Hong Kong films in Thailand quickly adapted to the effects of the Asian financial crisis. Thai distributors, like Sahamongkol, had become major film producers in the years following the US boycott. The Thai studio system experienced increased growth following the Asian financial crisis, when smaller competitors and independent filmmakers were eliminated. In an attempt to capture the teen market of the mall multiplexes, studios became interested in young directors, many of whom had worked in the music video industry and developed innovative visual techniques. Thai films were influenced greatly by the Hong Kong films that had historically circulated in the Thai market. Given the negative effects of the Asian financial crisis on Hong Kong production, Thai filmmakers tried to fill the empty screens with lower-budget alternatives that would appeal to younger viewers and provide pleasures missing from Hong Kong and Hollywood martial arts films. The new formula promises greater thrills, though substantially fewer visual effects. These films avoided wirework and safety equipment, eschewed computer-generated imagery, and forced some stars to perform all of their own stunts. The formula, facilitated by the skills and daring of actor Tony Jaa, was so successful that Thai cinema was, for a time, considered the great successor of Hong Kong action cinema, and new Thai action stars were molded to fit the Jaa model.

Jaa's exploitative long-term contract, adapted to the satellite-deal paradigm, and the use of Jaa as a model for new Thai action stars are indicative of the concerns of the Thai film industry in the aftermath of the Asian financial crisis. In the Thai market, Jaa's body spectacles, for a time, seemed to command greater exchange value than the special effects sequences of Hollywood or the flying wuxia heroes of Hong Kong films. However, Jaa has found success in foreign markets as well, a very rare event for a Thai film star. The marketability of Jaa and the Jaa model beyond the confines of the domestic market enabled greater financing for Thai productions. Sahamongkol successfully secured more funding for Jaa's films through DVD presales for European and American markets. Jaa's films have also been screened outside of Thailand: in Hong Kong, parts of Europe, and major American cities. Though some Thai films have made it to international film festivals in the years following the Asian financial crisis, none of these films have been distributed as widely as Jaa's work. In the years following the financial crisis, the dangerous body spectacles of stunting stars like Jaa and Jeeja Yanin have ensured the security of the Thai film industry in an era of economic uncertainty.

Tony Jaa and the New Thai Action Cinema

Based on biographical information distributed to the press, Tony Jaa is a Cambodian-Thai martial artist who grew up in a small village in northern Thailand and spent much of his free time as a boy playing with his family's pachyderms and watching Hong Kong and Thai action films projected on a large white sheet set up by the local traveling film program.[26] According to studio publicity material designed to authenticate Jaa's lifelong deliberate-practice training and link him to Hong Kong stars, Jaa would reenact the flips and kung fu moves of Bruce Lee, Jackie Chan, and Jet Li at home, and when he had trouble matching the height of wire-bound actors, he would use his pet elephants to gain better leverage.[27] Jaa briefly trained in muay thai under his father and graduated from high school at fifteen so that he could work with his idol, Thai stunt legend Panna Rittikrai (พันนา ฤทธิ์ไกร). Rittikrai was one of the first real stuntmen in Thailand. In the 1950s and 1960s, most actors did their own stunt work, but with the influx of martial arts films from Hong Kong in the 1970s, the audience expectations for the action genre were greatly altered. Spectators, particularly in the provinces, where the genre was most popular, expected Thai action films to contain more spectacular action sequences. Rittikrai wrote, directed, choreographed, and starred in many of his own films, including the film that had phenomenal success in the provinces and inspired Jaa to become a stuntman, *Born to Fight* (เกิดมาลุย), directed by Rittikrai in 1979.[28] While Jaa was being trained as a stuntman, he worked as a production assistant for Rittikrai's Muay Thai Stunt Team until Rittikrai felt Jaa was prepared for on-screen work. Rittikrai quickly realized that Jaa had a unique ability to jump to impressive heights and remain airbound for an astonishing amount of time. He explained that this skill made Jaa uniquely marketable: "He could jump higher and stay up in the air longer than others. He had immense determination. He would die for movies. He did not want to do it just for the fame, but to prove that he could do it. He was a genius in the martial arts—he could learn any discipline. If Jackie Chan could spin two rounds, Tony Jaa would train until he could do three."[29]

Rittikrai suggested that Jaa attend Maha Sarakham College of Physical Education to diversify his martial arts knowledge. In many ways, Rittikrai acted as a "person in the shadows" during Jaa's early career. According to Hans Gruber and colleagues,

> the other persons often remain in the shadow, mainly serving as facilitators of expert careers. . . . Their role is underestimated. Although they are not distinguished by bright performance, they set the standards of deliberate practice for the bright experts, they decide the next steps to be trained and improved during the acquisition of practice, they often take part in experts' superior performance (e.g. in sports, music, or science) and they thus contribute to excellence. The presence (or absence) of the appropriate persons in the shadow might well influence whether or not an individual engages in 10-year long deliberate practice within a domain.[30]

At Rittikrai's suggestion, Jaa is reported to have trained at Maha Sarakham and other locations for a total of eight years in various martial art forms, in particular muay thai, to prepare for his starring role in *Ong Bak: Muay Thai Warrior* (องค์บาก) in 2003.[31] Jaa benefited greatly from Rittikrai's experience in the Thai film industry, though Jaa's work is better known than that of his mentor, who had been working in the industry since the late 1970s. Rittikrai continued to work with Jaa after he returned from Maha Sarakham, training him as a stuntman, grooming him as a stunting star, and even choreographing the action design for his early films.

Hong Kong Action Cinema as a Mode

Film and television scholars address action as both a genre and a mode operating across genres like the action-adventure film, the spy film, and even detective dramas. Instead of conceptualizing these types of films as subgenres of action, scholars like Lisa Purse and Yvonne Tasker have drawn attention to the presentational style of these genres, their use of the spectacular body, and the heightened sense of urgency in their audience address. For action film scholars like Purse, Tasker, and Chris Holmlund, the action mode is defined by these attributes and conveys more than speed and spectacle, as it is a formula for storytelling.[32] Purse argues that action as a mode is a "style of presentation," the function of which is to "repeatedly foreground the body's active physicality."[33] Purse sees emphasis on the body in motion as key to the operation of the action mode. The overall effect of the moving and spectacular body is then amplified by fast-paced editing choices, perfectly timed sound cues and score selection, and framing via a (commonly) mobile camera. Tasker argues that action utilizes this presentational style not simply to advance the narrative components of a film, as she contends that these techniques are also employed as forms of storytelling in and of themselves:

> As a mode action has as much to [do] with a way of telling a story—or perhaps more exactly visualizing that story—as the *kind* of stories that are told. Both action sequences and action films emphasize the dynamism of the moving image, whether that is expressed via movement within the frame or an accelerated pace of editing. Music and sound play an important—and relatively underexplored—part in the action sequence/film, anticipating and complementing the sense of urgency expressed through character and vehicle movement. Such an emphasis on speed, conflict and movement is routinely juxtaposed with an aesthetic that celebrates scale, one that invites viewers to contemplate—even immerse themselves in—the effects, sets and spectacular scenes.[34]

Though Purse and Tasker emphasize spectacular address as the organizing principle of action as a mode, the formulation of Hong Kong–style action as a mode expands on their configurations via additional frameworks. Each of the frameworks for Hong Kong style as a mode arises from the historical specificities of the national/regional (Thai, New Zealand, mainland Chinese, etc.) production culture's exposure to Hong Kong action cinema (e.g., reception context, import history, labor flows). Action as a mode is the rationale for foregrounding Jaa's body as spectacle. It motivates the speed of the editing, the use of slow-motion effects, and the loud rhythmic soundtrack during action sequences. The conditions that effect a framework for Hong Kong–style action as a mode beyond and in addition to these elements are (1) the long presence of Hong Kong action films in Thai film exhibition contexts, (2) the precipitous decline in Hong Kong film production in the late 1990s, and (3) the degree to which Hong Kong and Thai action films compete in the greater Asian film marketplace. While performance-enhancing special effects, materializing Foley work, high-concept music, editing for impact or emphasis, and a mobile camera can highlight or amplify the spectatorial effects of any action star's body spectacle, the unique repertoire of a specific stunting star or expert stunt worker is the defining attribute delineating Hong Kong–style action as a mode. In the Thai context and in Jaa's work (and that of Jeeja Yanin), that means Hong Kong–style action is expressed as a mode in relation to production tactics that emulate those of Hong Kong stunting star Jackie Chan and also in relation to the degree to which the body spectacles of Thai stunting stars exceed the horizon of expectations generated by Hong Kong action films and deliver something new.

Hong Kong cinema works as a mode in Jaa's Thai action films but is nativized by the presence of generic elements related to the Thai "heritage" film. Hong Kong action cinema operates as a mode in Thai production contexts owing to the historical circulation of Hong Kong films in Thailand, at mall cinemas, and, most successfully, at outdoor screenings in the provinces. Hong Kong action films were often distributed to the small, open-air village cinemas that had also always been a profitable market for Thai action films. With the decline in production in Hong Kong during the Asian financial crisis, Thai action films have recently attempted to fill the void at provincial screening venues. However, Thai action cinema has generally been considered a low genre unworthy of wide release to mall multiplexes in urban centers. Thai film producers have attempted to adjust the action formula borrowed from Hong Kong action cinema texts in order to appeal to a more diverse audience base. These filmmakers have combined the characteristics commonly associated with the generic variants of the Hong Kong martial arts film (e.g., flying bodies, complex stunt work, no-goods) with those connected to the genre labeled the "heritage" film, such as "an emphasis on marketing, high production values, the presentation of Thainess as a visual attraction, the pastiche of historical personages and traumatic episodes in the biography of the Thai nation, and most significantly the wishful claim to quality as films of a *sakon* or 'international/Western' caliber."[35] Not only does the use of such tactics help producers to reach wider audiences, but the combination of Hong Kong action aesthetics and the concerns of the heritage film helps to make Thai action films distinct.

Jaa's films are designed to compete with Hollywood and Hong Kong productions via two primary means of distinction evident in Jaa's body spectacles: "the presentation of Thainess as a visual attraction" and the promise of the new. These concepts are deeply intertwined in Jaa's work as his body spectacles tend to incorporate elements of Thai culture (muay thai, muay boran, traditional dance, Thai elephants, etc.) and death-defying techniques never before attempted in other action cinemas. Jaa's work is similar to that of Jackie Chan and Jet Li in that he attempts seemingly impossible stunts and catapults himself through the air, but in an effort to demonstrate that such actions are new and distinct, he does so without much protection and with minimal assistance. The distinguishing characteristics of Jaa's body spectacles that set his work apart from the pleasures offered by Hong Kong and Hollywood action films are the manner in which he seems to fly through the air, the lack of traditional assistive devices and protective equipment, his constant adaptation to new martial art forms as a means of product differentiation, and his work with trained Thai elephants.

One particular element associated with Jaa's body spectacles is of primary importance to his virtuoso reception context: his propensity for flight. Of the fifty-six people I surveyed regarding their consumption of Jaa's work, an astonishing 70 percent responded that Jaa's most impressive attribute was his ability to remain air-bound. At least half of these respondents replied with variations of the following statement: "Tony Jaa can fly!"[36] While action film audiences have become quite accustomed to seeing heroes launched through the air or suspended in midflight via the use of wires, harnesses, and computer-generated imagery, few have witnessed the shocking revelation of a performer who can manage this feat unassisted.

Most respondents referred to Jaa's ability as "superhuman," and, in particular, many of the survey participants spoke of a memorable moment from one film. A large number of the respondents suggested that Jaa's "most impressive attribute" could be best witnessed in "the scene from *The Protector* [*Tom-Yum-Goong*; ต้มยำกุ้ง] where he flies."[37] This moment from *The Protector*, a film about a young Thai villager trying to rescue his family's elephants from poachers in Australia, is quite fleeting but nevertheless memorable as Jaa is visible in long shot leaping from screen left and delivering a double variation of a muay thai *kao loi* (เข่าลอย; flying knee jump).[38] Jaa propels his body through the air and lands a double knee strike on the head of his opponent (figure 2.1). This scene may be remarkable in comparison to the skills of other martial arts performers or because Jaa accomplishes it without the aid of wires, but it is not exceptional in reference to Jaa's standard body spectacles.

Jaa's body spectacles are shocking not simply because his performance displays unique qualities but because they also defy expectations in reference to the horizon of possibilities established by previous action films. Jaa delivers a variety of flying kicks throughout his films to demonstrate his dexterity, agility, and ability to remain aloft without assistance. In *The Protector*, Jaa performs an assortment of astonishing leaps. Jaa propels himself feetfirst over a parked car, flips over a trench and lands a handstand on a ledge, kicks out a streetlamp bulb, runs up a wall and flips over his opponent, and kicks a man positioned in a flying helicopter (figures 2.2–2.6). In *Ong Bak: Muay Thai Warrior*, in which Jaa had his first starring role, he flips upside down sandwiched between two closely positioned pieces of glass, jumps feetfirst through a small wire hoop, and also delivers a kao loi with his pants lit on fire (figures 2.7–2.8). Though each of these stunts is jarring, the most mem-

2.1 Tony Jaa performs a flying knee strike in *The Protector*, a moment identified by survey participants as a key scene showing Jaa's abilities.

2.2 Tony Jaa jumps over a parked car in *The Protector*.

orable moment is Jaa's reenactment of Jet Li's shoulder-walking stunt from *Fong Sai-yuk* (方世玉) without the use of wires or a harness. Jaa runs swiftly down a narrow alleyway and jumps onto the shoulders of the men blocking his path.[39] To prove that Jaa provided a body spectacle free of special effects and distinct from that of Jet Li, Jaa performed the stunt live at screenings for audiences in Paris, New York, and Los Angeles.

Jaa's virtuoso status is linked to a reception context marked by disbelief, a new "aesthetic of astonishment," and is reinforced by the revelatory func-

2.3 Tony Jaa flips over a trench and lands a handstand on a ledge in *The Protector*.

2.4 Tony Jaa jumps up and kicks out the bulb in a street lamp in *The Protector*.

tion of his live performances. I do not wish in any way to suggest that modern martial arts film audiences are identical to the early film spectators discussed by Tom Gunning in his essay "An Aesthetic of Astonishment: Early Film and the (In)Credulous Spectator." However, Jaa's body spectacles do seem to exert a power over audiences that is somewhat similar to Gunning's cinema of attractions in that Jaa's films comprise a "series of visual shocks."[40] Gunning explains that early film audiences were not duped by camera tricks but, more likely, saw film as an art form that combined "realistic effects with a conscious awareness of artifice."[41] Modern action film spectators have been

2.5 Tony Jaa runs up a wall and flips over his opponent in *The Protector.*

2.6 Tony Jaa kicks a man positioned in a flying helicopter in *The Protector.*

so inundated with the artifice of martial arts spectacles that many find the "realism" of Jaa's performance physically jarring.

I am not the first scholar to argue this. One of the only other academics to write in great detail on Jaa's work, Leon Hunt, has commented that much of the writing by fans and journalists on *Ong Bak* tends toward declarations of astonishment. In particular, the fans recognize Jaa's body spectacles as distinct from Hollywood and Hong Kong models; Hunt quotes a fan who has posted a review of *Ong Bak* on the Internet Movie Database: "This has been the action/fighting movie I've wanted to see all my life. REAL fighting

2.7 Tony Jaa flips upside down while sandwiched between glass plates in *Ong Bak: Muay Thai Warrior*.

2.8 Tony Jaa jumps feetfirst through a wire hoop in *Ong Bak: Muay Thai Warrior*.

actions and sequences! No special effects, no wires, no disjointing cuts, no camera tricks, no CGI . . . full continuity from jump to hit to fall, and at what force!"[42]

Jaa's well-publicized eschewal of wires, harnesses, and safety equipment is authenticated by the live performances of action sequences from his films that often accompany each film's premiere. His deliberate-practice training as an expert stuntman and martial artist makes it possible for Jaa to reproduce on-screen body spectacles live, and the circulation of this footage qualifies his on-screen performance and distinguishes it from that of stars who claim to perform their own stunts but are commonly doubled by stunt workers and aided by computer-generated effects. Jaa performs astonishing kicks, walks on the shoulders of his stunt team, and demonstrates muay thai moves on various opponents. Many of Jaa's most shocking stunts are reenacted for the audience as proof of his talent.

Jaa's skills help to distinguish him from other martial arts performers like Jackie Chan in that Jaa undergoes a constant reskilling process to provide the audience with increasingly spectacular corporeal maneuvers in each succeeding film. Chan was able to secure more funding for each film he made with Golden Harvest by adding more difficult stunts to ensure a box office draw. While Chan's stunts were always phenomenal, as discussed in detail in the previous chapter, he generally drew from his reservoir of training in the Peking opera. Jaa is well known for spending months to years familiarizing himself with new techniques. He spent eight years studying muay thai and an additional year acquiring the techniques of muay boran to prepare for *Ong Bak*. For *The Protector*, Jaa developed a new style of muay thai that is an adaptive animal form based on the movement of elephants, elephant boxing. In the film Jaa demonstrates this style in a manner that suggests he is breaking the arms and legs of a room full of opponents. Jaa envisioned this sequence as a remake of the well-known one-hits-many (OHM) fight between Neo (Keanu Reeves) and the multiple variants of Agent Smith (Hugo Weaving) in *The Matrix Reloaded*.[43] The scene in *The Matrix Reloaded* required the use of computer graphics and stunt doubles (two of whom are discussed in chapter 4) to effect the large-scale OHM fight, but Jaa wanted to demonstrate that he could take on multiple opponents without using special effects while maintaining full contact with the "real" bodies of his combatants.

If the OHM scene that concludes *The Protector* provides audiences with proof that Jaa delivers a body spectacle that is distinct from Hollywood action films, the long-take OHM sequence in the same film distinguishes his performance from those of older Hong Kong martial arts stars. Jackie Chan commonly performed many beautifully choreographed OHM sequences in each of his films from the 1970s through the 1990s, but, as addressed in the previous chapter, even Chan relied on cinematography and editing to amplify the effect of such sequences with the perpetual motion technique.[44] The production of Jaa's body spectacle in what is designed to appear as a single-take sequence in *The Protector* makes great use of the revelatory power of cinematography while eschewing the heavy reliance on editing necessary to the perpetual motion technique in Hong Kong films. The long take follows Kham, the character played by Jaa, as he attempts to find his family's stolen elephant. In the course of the four-minute sequence, Jaa appears to climb four floors of a shopping plaza while taking on multiple combatants. Jaa avoids the stairs and climbs the wall in one jump to reach the second floor. The camera remains positioned on the first floor to record both Jaa's leap and the fall of the stuntman Jaa throws from the second-floor balcony. The camera then proceeds upstairs, following Jaa as he ascends to take on multiple attackers at once. As Jaa tosses a stuntman off of the third-floor balcony, the camera pans right and tilts down for an overhead shot of the stuntman falling onto a kiosk below. As Jaa enters a small room designed for illicit encounters, the camera follows him. The cameraman spins 180 degrees to reveal two men in the doorway looking for Kham. As these men leave, the cameraman tilts up to find Jaa, who has positioned himself in a split above the doorframe so as to remain hidden from view. All of this has occurred before two minutes have even expired on the take. At three minutes and twenty-two seconds into the take, as Jaa nears his target, having fought off over twenty combatants, the camera tilts down over the balcony to demonstrate the extent of Jaa's progress. The revelatory function of the narration enhances Jaa's body spectacle and provides a visual pleasure foreign to the work of Jackie Chan.

Jaa attempts to provide body spectacles distinct from those available in other national cinemas, and for this purpose, Jaa commonly includes Thai elephants in his productions. Thai elephants have historically been represented in art and mythology in Thailand as symbols of good fortune, and they served as the labor force for the logging industry until this was banned in 1989. Though some elephants are still used illegally in the logging industry, protectionist NGOs have sprung up in recent years, and there has been a surge in conservation efforts. Thai elephants are most commonly used in the tourism industry in Thailand and, as such, serve as symbols of the nation both nationally and internationally.[45] Jaa is particularly fond of working with elephants and spent months training and living with a stunt team of Thai elephants to prepare for a scene in *Ong Bak* 2 (องค์บาก 2) in which he runs with the herd and leaps between them (figure 2.9).[46] Jaa also performed a variety of flips and gymnastic maneuvers from the tusks of trained pachyderms in *The Protector* and *Ong Bak* 2 (figure 2.10). His work with animals has become so popular that he used the presence of elephant stunt work as a selling point for *Ong Bak* 3 (องค์บาก 3).[47] Jaa demonstrates a commitment to a constant cycle of reskilling to distinguish his work from that of other stars and from his previous performances.

2.9 Tony Jaa runs on the backs of an elephant herd in *Ong Bak 2*.

2.10 Tony Jaa flips off of an elephant's tusks to deliver a knee strike to the head of an opponent in *Ong Bak 2*.

Jaa has been so incredibly successful that the Muay Thai Stunt Team has devised a formula for the creation of new stars based on Jaa's model. This formula requires budding stars willing to sign long-term contracts, young actors committed to working without protective or assistive devices, rigorous training, and perpetual adaptation. Jaa often described his deal with Sahamongkol as a "slave contract" because the studio forced him to work for them; he could not, under any circumstances, work for a domestic or foreign film studio without their permission. Though many Hong Kong and US filmmakers asked to work with Jaa, Sahamongkol would not part with its most valuable commodity. When Jaa eventually started working on other projects, the company sued him and tied him up in court for two years, claiming his ten-year contract was automatically renewed even if he never signed it.[48] Jaa's Thai films had been made under the Golden Harvest–style satellite-deal model, with Sahamongkol funding production and Prachya Pinkaew's (ปรัชญา ปิ่นแก้ว) Baa-Ram-Ewe productions handling the daily operations on set. As discussed in detail in chapter 1, satellite deals are a form of decentralized production common to Golden Harvest productions in which the larger of the two studios controls financing, casting, scripting, and scheduling, while the smaller production company handles day-to-day operations. This process allows stars like Bruce Lee, Jackie Chan, or even Tony Jaa to have greater control over stunt design and permits the stars to hire their own stunt teams. In adopting this structure, Sahamongkol gave Jaa the freedom to work on projects that he found interesting and to choreograph or contribute to the action design, but they retained the rights to everything that he shot. Sahamongkol tried to duplicate its success with Jaa by manufacturing new young martial arts stars who would appeal to mall audiences. They quickly signed performers under contract and allowed them time to train with Panna Rittikrai. While more recently this formula has been applied to the child actors who starred in the film *Power Kids* (5 หัวใจ ฮีโร่; 5 Hawci Hiro), the first and most notable actor they chose for this experiment was Thai cinema studies student Jeeja Yanin, who had previously trained in tae kwon do and holds a fourth *dan* (단; degree, with the fourth being an instructor level) black belt in that sport.[49]

Gendered Difference: Jeeja Yanin and the Jaa Model

Jeeja Yanin was chosen for her talent and, in the words of Panna Rittikrai, because she "has cute looks and the position of foremost female action star is still vacant!"[50] The studio was attempting to manufacture a young female star they could market in the same way they sold Tony Jaa, similarly to how Golden Harvest and D and B films attempted to position Michelle Yeoh as comparable to Jackie Chan by casting her in policewoman films in the early 1980s. In Yanin's first film, *Chocolate* (ช็อคโกแลต), she demonstrated phenomenal dexterity, and her commitment to perpetual adaptation is unmistakable.[51] Though my project is not concerned with narrative, in this case the plot of this film greatly informed Yanin's training regimes. The film concerns a young autistic child by the name of Zen, played by Yanin, who has the unique ability to imitate any martial art style she sees demonstrated. Zen watches Bruce Lee films, she studies Tony Jaa in *Ong Bak*, she observes the muay thai students who train next to her apartment, and in the film's finale she faces off against another young martial artist, trained in the Brazilian martial art of capoeira, who has a neurological condition that produces repetitive gestures. The use of capoeira distinguishes the performance from those of Jaa and represents a break from the Thai and Chinese martial arts styles used up until that point in the film. Zen performs muay thai like Jaa and kung fu with the flair of Bruce Lee, and in the last fight scene, she quickly learns to mimic her opponent, defeating him with capoeira. The structure of this narrative required Yanin to not only train in kung fu, muay thai, and capoeira and perform dangerous stunts but also acquire the skills to perfectly mimic famous performers like Lee and Jaa.

In the capoeira fight sequence, Yanin demonstrates her talent for complex flips that would commonly be accomplished with the use of wires in Hong Kong productions. The sequence begins when her opponent flips himself upside down and spins his legs above his head (known as a *piao de mao*) to deliver a kick to Yanin's head. Many capoeira techniques require the *capoeiristas* to propel themselves into the air to increase the power of the impact. As Zen, Yanin's character, acquires her opponent's style, Yanin must attempt to mimic the performer's *ginga* (rocking motion). The ginga is designed to ward off attacks by making motion difficult to predict. Every capoeirista has a distinct ginga, making Yanin's re-creation particularly impressive. The close of the sequence contains Yanin's most arresting acrobatic flip routine as body spectacle. Yanin demonstrates a variant of the *mariposa* (butterfly twist), as she flips her body 180 degrees while flying through the air horizontally and delivers a kick to the performer positioned above her (figure 2.11). This sequence showcases remarkable dexterity and thrust and is distinct from Hong Kong–style wuxia films, which would require the use of wires for such a performance, and Hollywood films, which could not accomplish such a maneuver without the use of computer graphics.

Like for Tony Jaa's work, and that of Jackie Chan before him, a series of postcredit sequences, or no-goods, reinforces the authenticity of Yanin's performance, as discussed in the previous chapter. Though *no-goods* is Hong Kong production terminology for flubbed takes, stunt teams also use this phrase in Thai films starring Yanin and Jaa. The Thai postcredit scenes obviously emulate Chan's postcredit no-good reel of mishaps captured on film during dangerous stunts or fight sequences. Thai action film directors add these sequences not simply to demonstrate an affinity with Hong Kong action films and stars but to make evident the differences of the Thai context. The no-goods reveal that the full-contact capoeira maneuvers from *Chocolate* took a toll on Yanin. She was badly injured by a kick to the eye and was

2.11 *Chocolate*'s horizontal butterfly twist: Jeeja Yanin makes contact with her opponent.

allowed only one week to heal before resuming work on the film. She discussed the injury in an interview: "I played every scene myself. The worst blow I was dealt was after nights of shooting. I'm a girl, it was that time of the month and I was really tired. I didn't see a foot coming and wham! I couldn't open my left eye for a while and had to stop shooting for a week."[52] The no-goods showcase a series of her injuries and those of the stunt team but are careful to never reveal any footage of Yanin in a wired harness. It is clear that wirework was used for the final battle in the film, but the only cables visible are those for the stunt team members. The inclusion of no-goods in *Chocolate* is clearly a deliberate attempt to link Yanin's mode of performance not simply to Hong Kong–style action techniques but to Jaa's work as well.

Much as Jaa attempts to provide body spectacles that are new and distinct from those of Hong Kong performers, Yanin must continually differentiate the visual pleasures she supplies from those of Jaa. Yanin may have been modeled after Jaa, but her body spectacles are designed to appeal to a younger audience. Yanin trained for two years in a variety of martial art forms so *Chocolate* would offer audiences something more than simply a re-creation of *Ong Bak* with a female lead. After the success of *Chocolate*, Yanin was assigned to another Baa-Ram-Ewe and Sahamongkol coproduction called *Raging Phoenix* (คือ สวย คู่).[53] *Raging Phoenix* required Yanin to adapt to new styles though the film did not showcase her talent as much as *Chocolate*. As the film was geared toward the teen audiences of Thai mall multiplexes, the body spectacles were not designed to be accurate to martial art forms. Sahamongkol realized that Yanin's youthful appearance might appeal more to the teen audience than Jaa, who is considered less conventionally attractive in the Thai context. In her sophomore effort, Sahamongkol attempted to distinguish Yanin from Jaa, as a teen star, by having her participate in body spectacles that were a conglomeration of break dancing and drunken muay thai.

It would be unproductive to make a grand claim about the various manifestations of Yanin's distinction from Jaa (character design, stunt choreography, etc.) as holding broader implications for gender difference in Thai action cinema as Yanin's star text is currently informed by only three starring roles in total. Though she may be the most successful female action star in contemporary Thai cinema, as of yet she has no real competition for that title. There is no point in distinguishing Jaa's expert ten-year deliberate-practice training in stunt work and martial arts from Yanin's shorter training history, other than to note that the Thai stunt industry does not provide the same opportunities for long-term careers to stuntwomen as it does to stuntmen. However, Yanin's markers of gendered difference should not be ignored. In point of fact, she has fared better with the transnational youth market than has Jaa because of the successful marketing of the female star as a cute little girl. Yanin's gender may help to differentiate her from Jaa, but it has proven much less important than the two defining characteristics that have been key to both her marketing as a teen film star in Thailand and her reception abroad, youth and "cuteness." Though Yanin had a higher percentage of female fans than Jaa, based on my survey data from thirty-two respondents, none of her fans identified her gender as the element that distinguished her from Jaa; instead, most spoke of her size, age, and cuteness. While fans may or may not be able to identify the subconscious effects of gender on their preference for particular stars over others, instead of performing a presumptuous analysis of the degree to which sexual difference informs their reception, it might be beneficial to address the actual distinguishing characteristics these fans have noted. Yanin is cast to play infantilized female roles, as she is reportedly only 5'2" tall and is often choreographed in opposition to much larger on-screen fighters. The cuteness and youth of the star are most revealing in the marketing of Yanin across Asia. While there may be crossover between the pan-Asian teen market and the action marketplace, the marketing of Yanin has been distinct from that of Jaa in that she performs live choreographed stunts on talk shows and at shopping malls across Asia (Thailand, Hong Kong, Taiwan, Japan, etc.) to market her films, whereas Jaa demonstrates his skills at international festival screenings and sporting events. The two performers are clearly being sold as distinct products to unique audiences: the commonly shirtless and laconic Jaa is marketed as a masterful martial artist and showman to cineastes and sports fans, whereas Yanin, who is allowed to change into a fashionable outfit and have her hair and makeup refreshed between the stunt show and the interview, is presented to teens and other mall goers as a shockingly physically adept, charming, and polite young woman with a perpetual grin and keen fashion sense. It is impossible to deny that she is cute, and in the pan-Asian teen marketplace, cuteness has cross-cultural potency, as Thorsten Botz-Bornstein has noted:

> The aesthetics of cuteness (*kawairashisa*) has been developing in Japan since the 1980s, and in the late 1990s it turned into an explicit kitsch-culture. However, cute culture is not restricted to Japan, but has also been observed, for example, in Taiwan. Fluffy stuffed animals dangling from the cell phones of women in their thirties, men wearing Pokeman [*sic*] emblems on key chains, and the ubiquitous presence of Hello-Kitty and Doraemon figurines in households are indications of a culture that has been driven to such an extreme only in East Asia.[54]

The cuteness associated with Yanin's star image may provide her with the staying power that seems to be lacking in Jaa's career: both sequels to *Ong Bak* went far over budget and failed at the box office, whereas Yanin has had a successful run with the South Korean–Thai coproduction *The Kick* (더 킥).[55] Additionally, *Jukkalan* (จั๊กกะแหล่น), in which she had a small part, has been repackaged as *This Girl Is Bad Ass!!* with Yanin listed as the lead and the new English-language trailers proclaiming her "cute face with crushing fist" intercut with shots of her practicing bike-fu (choreographed bicycle fight sequences).[56] While there are a variety of nationalized forms of cuteness in the pan-Asian market, the distinctions between them seem to pose less of a marketing obstacle than the various, at times contradictory, nationally specific masculinities in this same transnational market, and, as such, Yanin may soon eclipse Jaa in popularity. There is room for variation within the Jaa model for stardom designed by Sahamongkol, and that variation is articulated in the production of continually evolving and transnationally marketable modes of body spectacle. Thailand was poised to reclaim the pan-Asian and international martial arts film marketplace from Hong Kong after decades of Hong Kong and American domination of the Thai domestic action film market.

While both Hong Kong and Thailand suffered from the Asian financial crisis, the crisis had divergent effects on stars working in each national context. The new model of film production in Hong Kong in the 1990s, characterized by ensemble casts and nonstunting stars, was a product of the financial crisis as well as antitriad legislation. The destabilized economic situation affected genres, contributed to shifts in the production process, and altered the aesthetic register of body spectacles in the Hong Kong martial arts film. Just as Hong Kong cinema had reached a moment of decline, Thai action cinema experienced a surge in production. The economic downturn provided Thai filmmakers with the screen space necessary to capture an urban audience, expanding their distribution beyond the traditional provincial market for the genre. The reduced circulation of Hong Kong films in Thailand was the impetus for generic transformation. Owing to the collapse of the Hong Kong film industry, the market saturation of the wire fu genre, and the devaluation of old forms of spectacle, a new martial arts film industry has risen in the East. The new Thai action cinema did not simply re-create Hong Kong–style body spectacles; instead, filmmakers simultaneously used Hong Kong action cinema as a mode of production and attempted to infuse films with a conception of Thainess. Tony Jaa and Jeeja Yanin were instrumental in this generic transformation, as their laboring bodies have helped to delineate the difference between Hong Kong and Thai action spectacles. The future of global action cinema is presently being written by the constantly evolving corporeal dispositions manifest in the graceful air-bound bodies of stunting stars crafted in the Hong Kong model but geographically far exceeding the confines of Hong Kong.

THREE

A HONG KONG RESERVOIR FOR *XENA* / Communicative Translation and the Bodily Disposition of Stunting Star Zoë Bell

This chapter addresses the manner in which genre affects labor, changing a nation's televisual and cinematic reservoir of technique. In particular, the chapter considers how the spectacles commonly associated with the action genre in general, and the wuxia genre more specifically, have been consumed and repurposed by fanboy media producers.[1] The term *fanboy* is commonly used to describe an obsessive consumer of media texts and collectible commodities who participates in a male-dominated subculture of appreciation for such artifacts as comic books, martial arts paraphernalia, fantasy films, and the works of auteur action film directors. In this chapter the term *fanboy* is not used with derision but rather is meant to identify individuals who actively participate in media consumption practices that are considered esoteric. This chapter examines the effects of Hong Kong action fandom on modes of action production in one of the many "elsewheres" in which Hong Kong style has proliferated. The chapter investigates a series of actions that caused the historical practices associated with one "national cinema effect" (that of Hong Kong) to become congealed in the body/person of performers trained in another national media context (New Zealand) in which Hong Kong action cinema operates as a mode. Generic translation across national frameworks has an effect on the laboring bodies of media producers and, in the case of action genres, has distinct and identifiable effects on stunt doubles. The adoption of Hong Kong wuxia aesthetics in contemporary action films has forced adjustments in shooting style, shoot duration, costuming, set design, editing, and rig construction: all of these alter the stunt performer's embodied experiences of work. For example, a *rig* is an apparatus designed to control the movement of stunt performers, actors, objects, or vehicles in front of the camera. While wire rigs might be controlled by an automated system in Hollywood productions for safety and planning purposes, the typical Hong Kong wuxia flying rig is a system of thin wires attached to a body harness on the performer and supported by a system of pulleys that allow teams of two to six "pullers" to lift the performer by pulling on ropes attached to the wire support structure. When these cinematic and televisual techniques and body spectacles associated with Hong Kong–style action are used by individual performers over time, this contributes to the star image of stunting stars. This is decidedly the case for Kiwi stuntwoman Zoë Bell. Bell's star image is clearly informed by a series of body spectacles made possible by her training in tae kwon do and gymnastics, the early spectacular embodiments evident in her Kiwi-style wire fu work on the set of *Xena: Warrior Princess*, the exposure of the conditions of her labor in the documentary *Double Dare*, her dynamic performances as a stunt double in Quentin Tarantino's *Kill Bill* series and as a stunting actor in *Death Proof*, and her award-winning high-fall work in *Catwoman*.[2]

In this chapter I examine the *communicative translation* of Hong Kong–style wuxia action sequences to the context of the Kiwi-produced television series *Xena: Warrior Princess* in an attempt to sketch the transnational reinscription of Hong Kong production practices in New Zealand and the requirements that such translations placed on the body of stuntwoman Zoë Bell. In the course of my research, I interviewed Bell and conducted a fan survey with forty-five participants. This chapter addresses Bell's everevolving repertoire of body spectacles, informed by bodily dispositions accumulated through her early training in gymnastics and tae kwon do as well as her work on the sets of various films and television programs. This is the first chapter in this book to discuss television, but the production strategies of the medium are as relevant to any consideration of expert performance as those of the films discussed in prior chapters, if not more so. The exhaustive production schedule of a syndicated weekly program like *Xena* with a dedicated second-unit crew fostered Bell's development as a stunting star. I argue that Bell has joined the ranks of the stunting stars of early cinema in that the knowledge of her laboring body in the production of spectacle has been revealed to audiences via the behind-the-scenes coverage of *Xena* in the documentary *Double Dare* and the casting of Bell as the self-inspired

"Zoë the Cat" in Tarantino's *Death Proof*. This chapter seeks to address a gap in the fields of both star studies and genre analysis: the material history of particular body spectacles.

From Hong Kong to *Xena*:
Communicative Translation and Spectatorial Effects

Little has been written in film and media studies on how many of the topics considered in this chapter intersect: stunt actors, genre, and labor. These elements converge in the transnational production context of *Xena: Warrior Princess*, a television show funded by US production companies, scripted by American screenwriters, acted in and directed by US and New Zealand talent, and distributed internationally as a first-run syndicated program.[3] The production context of *Xena* is worthy of further examination as a site of what Peter Newmark has termed "communicative translation," a model of translation theory concerned more with the symmetry between the reception contexts of translated texts than with semiotic mimicry. Newmark's translation theory distinguishes between semantic and communicative translation; he explains that "communicative translation attempts to produce on its readers an effect as close as possible to that obtained on the readers of the original," whereas semantic translation "attempts to render, as closely as the semantic and syntactic structure of the second language allow, the exact contextual meaning of the original."[4] For Newmark, semantic translation holds to the authorial intent of the source text while allowing for slight variability in cultural adaptation. In contrast, communicative translation is concerned with the needs of the reader; it focuses less on preserving the language of the source and more on relaying the source's context or effect on readers.[5] I contend that this theory of translation can be extended to film and television viewers as "readers," in that such spectators may also act as media producers, re-creating previously viewed material in an attempt to regenerate the effects of the original (awe, shock, "jerk reactions," etc.) for a new group of spectators.[6]

Xena provides an interesting case study for communicative translation in that the spectatorial effects elicited by the bodily spectacles of Hong Kong wuxia films were reconstituted three times in acts of communicative translation: in the use of Hong Kong action-sequence mixtapes as a template to sell the series, in the remediation of film to television and the shift in production context from Hong Kong to New Zealand, and in the congealment of corporeal practices and cinematic/televisual techniques in the body spectacle of stunting star Zoë Bell. In this chapter I analyze the communicative translation of Hong Kong wuxia body spectacles into analogous sequences in *Xena*, where superhuman bodies fly, flip, or move through the air in flames. As with Jackie Chan, Tony Jaa, and Jeeja Yanin, Bell's body spectacles are generated and constituted by her laboring body as a virtuoso performer skilled through years of deliberate practice. Bell's training in gymnastics and tae kwon do prepared her for the deftly choreographed corporeal manipulations required of a Xena stunt double. Such spectacles elicit powerful spectatorial effects in her fan base. The dexterous on-screen body of the expert stunt performer not only embodies spectacle but also mesmerizes the spectator with a stunning visual display of corporeal manipulation, choreography, cinematography, editing, and mise-en-scène complemented with jarring sound effects.

Though the previous chapter addressed the films of Tony Jaa as primary examples of Hong Kong action cinema as a mode, those films are not examples of communicative translation. The producers of Jaa's films were trying to re-create the success of Hong Kong action films and borrowed techniques common to the Hong Kong variants of the genre. However, the filmmakers actively "nativized" the style in an attempt to reach Thai audiences and to compete with Hong Kong films distributed in Thailand. The producers of *Xena* did not understand Hong Kong action films as competitors. The show's creators considered Hong Kong action genre films a "private reservoir," according to *Xena* director Doug Lefler, from which to borrow and actively attempted to re-create the effects of those films with the limited resources available in New Zealand.[7] As an homage to Hong Kong action cinema, *Xena* borrows genre elements of the wuxia film, but the program is delightfully polymorphic in its genre expression. More than just a hybrid, the show borrows at will from Greek mythology, Roman history, and various Eastern and Western religious traditions. Hong Kong–style action as a mode is a modular transnational paradigm, adaptable to the cultural, economic, and governmental conditions of its production. Unlike in the Thai context, there was no horizon of expectations to surpass. In many ways, the creative team behind *Xena* was starting from scratch in terms of the wirework training history of the Kiwi stunt labor force and the material resources on hand. Hong Kong–style action as a mode functions as a form of audience address facilitated through the communicative translation of Hong Kong–style body spectacles.

In *Xena* the communicative translation of wuxia body spectacles took the form of Kiwi-designed wirework, harness rigs, and minitramps. The translation of wuxia stunts into the distinct form of action spectacle that is Kiwi-style *wire fu* (a neologism coined by American fanboys in reference to new wuxia film action design) was inspired by the cinephilia of *Xena's* US producers, avid fans of Hong Kong films. The embodied translations of wuxia body spectacles in *Xena* were grounded in the material circumstances underpinning a Kiwi stunt crew's technically and stylistically innovative renditions of Hong Kong–style martial arts sequences. In what follows, I explore the history of the wuxia genre in Hong Kong; the relationship of the television series *Xena: Warrior Princess*, produced in the United States and New Zealand, to that genre as prompted by the practices of fanboy producers; and, finally, the body spectacle and bodily disposition of stunting star Zoë Bell as a repository for this transnational generic history.

Much of the critical work on *Xena* addresses its horizon of reception and the fan practices surrounding the television hit.[8] In contrast, there is little to no work on its transnational production context, particularly on how the action spectacles of a beloved US television series were generated overseas in New Zealand. While much scholarship has focused on the queer subtext of *Xena*, I am concerned, rather, to identify and elucidate the visual subtext of *Xena's* action sequences. These sequences exist as translations and embodiments of both the histories of training disciplines in China and Hong Kong for actors and stunt performers working in the wuxia genre and the generic predilections of the wuxia films specifically.[9]

Hong Kong action cinema operates as a mode in the national media context of a New Zealand–produced television program via the inclusion of elements common to the genre. Rick Altman has defined the thematic/structural elements of a genre as *syntactic*, and the constitutive elements as *semantic*. Altman explains:

> While there is anything but general agreement on the exact frontier separating semantic from syntactic views, we can as a whole distinguish between generic definitions which depend on a list of common traits, attitudes, characters, shots, locations, sets, and the like—thus stressing the semantic elements which make up the genre—and definitions which play up instead certain constitutive relationships between undesignated and variable placeholders—relationships which might be called the genre's fundamental syntax. The semantic approach thus stresses the genre's building blocks, while the syntactic view privileges the structures into which they are arranged.[10]

The wuxia film inherited from the Peking opera the semantic elements of elaborate costume design (flowing, brightly colored fabrics), acrobatic maneuvers, and a tendency toward flight. The translation/adaptation of Peking opera techniques to the wuxia genre dates to the earliest examples of the genre in Shanghai. The spectacular pageantry of corporeal display and costuming linked to early wuxia films was made more dynamic in the 1960s when Shaw Brothers released color films in the genre in an attempt to gain more of the market share. The wuxia's semantic elements (costumes, flight, acrobatics, etc.) and the spectatorial effects of its body spectacles are translated and embodied by Zoë Bell, a stunt double for Lucy Lawless, the New Zealand actor who played *Xena*'s eponymous lead character.

Cinematic and televisual techniques and practices depend on the relationships between bodies in front of and behind the camera: camera operators adjust focus; actors move on cue; lighting and sound professionals are often precariously placed outside the frame to augment and capture the action without becoming a part of it. Each of these techniques (the zoom, the steadicam, "bullet time," etc.) has a unique and often transnational history. The circulation of films and television shows across national boundaries makes possible the reinvention and, in some cases, the translation of film and television techniques in a new and distinct national context. In speaking of these techniques, I refer not simply to cinematography, editing, and mise-en-scène but also the use of special effects, performance styles, and assistive devices, including wires, trampolines, and ratchets (pneumatic devices that pull a stuntie upward, forward, backward, left, right, or in any combination of directions) in the creation of spectacle. Stylistic choices are absorbed and repurposed by media makers the world over. This chapter attempts to address the manner in which historically specific cinematic and televisual techniques can, through translation, be simultaneously dehistoricized and expertly embodied by a stunting star.

In recent years, writing on stunt work has proliferated in film and media studies: Jennifer M. Bean's analysis of the technologies of stardom that produced serial queens like Pearl White and Helen Holmes, Miranda Janis Banks's project on the production contexts of action-centered television programs with female leads, and Jacob Smith's essay on the gendered representation/function of stuntmen in the 1970s.[11] Also, a series of biographies of and collected interviews with stuntmen and stuntwomen have been released in the decades following the surge in low-budget, stunt-driven action films of the 1970s.[12] However, the expert action performer as a repository of translated, genre-specific techniques is a unique focus of this project and is examined in great detail in this chapter in an effort to rescue the stuntie from the shadows of film and media history.

This project is motivated by a desire, as David Bordwell puts it, to "consider how it's possible for certain stylistic patterns to be traced to transcultural processes."[13] I disagree, however, with Bordwell's larger point, in his essay on Chinese film poetics, that film style the world over is based on certain "universal" circumstances, precluding any need for translation, cultural or otherwise. Bordwell contends:

> Those factors include some international norms of film style, in some wide-ranging—I daresay universal—conditions of filmmaking itself. Chinese films, to put it bluntly, are Chinese; but they're also films. And films are a powerful transcultural medium, going not only on local knowledge but also on a range of human skills which are shared across many cultures. . . . If we simply look at films from mainland China, Hong Kong, and Taiwan, we can see, going back quite far, a common stylistic point of departure: the classical continuity system associated with Hollywood since the late 1910s. . . . Parallel to these changes, local film industries around the world developed approximate equivalents of Hollywood's division of labor.[14]

While I agree that form communicates meaning, if this meaning were universal, would it not eliminate the need for the most common procedures of film translation: subtitling, dubbing, and the like? Chinese-language films, according to Bordwell, use the system of classical Hollywood continuity editing to communicate narrative and spatial relationships to audiences. He also believes that national film industries structure themselves in Hollywood's image. In response, I would point out that film industries outside Hollywood evolve under unique circumstances and do not simply act as mirrors to the Hollywood system. For example, the family-run businesses in Shanghai that produced martial arts films during the silent era were premised on distinct models of filial Chinese capitalist development that were not specific to film. Shaw Brothers Studio in Hong Kong is the best example of the overseas Chinese model of a family-run business, as discussed by S. Gordon Redding, in that the studio was taken over by Run Run Shaw as a "benevolent patriarch" to over 1,200 employees. While production was streamlined at the studio, the employees resided in studio dormitories, which reinforced the conception of the studio as a giant family. Redding has identified similar capitalist structures in overseas Chinese business more generally and considers "paternalism, personalism, opportunism, [and] flexibility" the defining attributes of this model.[15] These characteristics underlie the sensibility of the Hong Kong stunt worker community. For its part, the stunt community in New Zealand, as a form of flexibly specialized labor, is not afforded the same labor protections as its American counterpart, which is based on a union-dominated system.[16] Without contractual union restrictions on the number of hours a stuntie can work in a day, or the types of acts that a stuntie is expected to perform, television programs like *Xena* are provided with more coverage and more elaborate body spectacles in a shorter time and on a smaller budget than in US domestic productions. In fact, stunties who perform hazardous stunts are given an "adjustment" to their standard pay (a bonus) when they work in the United States, according to the rules of the Screen Actors Guild - American Federation of Television and Radio Artists (SAG-AFTRA), but New Zealand stunties are not afforded the same protections. In my conversation with Bell, she joked about the marked differences between production contexts, explaining that she was shocked to get her first "adjustment" in the United States because on *Xena* she was given the New Zealand equivalent, "three crates of beer," for performing a physically exhausting partial-body burn in a spinning harness, discussed later in this chapter. The transnational circulation of media forms and the historical dominance of Hollywood in world exhibition markets have not produced a singular universal global production format nor truly universal film and television styles.

Despite my differences with Bordwell, I do agree with him that it is productive to trace film style transnationally (as I address in detail in chapter 4). In particular, the examination of what Bordwell calls a "craft tradition" that is "passed from filmmaker to filmmaker over time" is something I address in the translation of techniques of body spectacle from Hong Kong to New Zealand. As an artisan, the filmmaker has knowledge about what works and what doesn't work. Passed from filmmaker to filmmaker over time, this knowledge coalesces into craft traditions, and these in turn provide schemas, repeated patterns of shot composition, lighting, camera movement, or editing that get the job done.[17] Bordwell's poetics acknowledges that forms have a history. Yet at the same time this poetics seems to be limited to the cinematographic techniques (camera movement, camera placement, lighting, shot arrangement, etc.). Though the wuxia film, or the martial arts film more generally, may be innovative in terms of cinematography and editing, what distinguishes the films generically is embodied technique: wirework-aided flying, acrobatic kung fu, and leaps effected by the use of minitramps.

These techniques, "passed from filmmaker to filmmaker," also have a history, and, owing to the circulation patterns of Hong Kong films, that history is transnational. I am speaking in particular of the combined use of wirework, acrobatics, trampolines, and the bodies of skilled laborers. These techniques are of course amplified by the cinematographic and editing choices of the filmmakers, which commonly involve adjustments in camera speed, alternation of medium close-ups of stars with long shots of stunt doubles in action, the use of blue filters, and the "pause-burst-pause" pattern that Bordwell has identified elsewhere.[18]

A Degraded Art Form: Wire Fu and the Technologized Body

The internationally syndicated television series *Xena: Warrior Princess*, produced in the United States and New Zealand, was inspired by the cycle of new wuxia films made in the late 1980s and 1990s by Hong Kong new wave directors. How the show came to be formed in the image of films like *Bride with White Hair* (白髮魔女傳), *Heroic Trio* (東方三俠), *Dragon Inn* (新龍門客棧), and the *Swordsman* series will be examined shortly.[19] First, it is necessary to trace the history of the wuxia and kung fu genres to which the new wuxia films are indebted and to identify the operating dynamics that have consistently contributed to the discursive erasure of the effort involved in working with wires. The history of the Hong Kong martial arts film can be divided into at least six discrete yet mutually informing periods: the Shanghai-produced fantasy serials (wuxia-shenguai pian or "martial arts–magic spirit film") of the 1920s; the "authentic" physiodynamics of Kwan Takhing in the Huang Fei-hong series of the 1950s; the Shaw Brothers wuxia pictures of the 1960s, populated with high-flying swordsmen and swordswomen; the kung fu films of the 1970s, which (as addressed in chapter 1) either were star vehicles or featured the elaborate group dynamics of a Peking opera–trained troupe; the police/triad cycle of the 1980s and 1990s; and the resurgence of a technologically innovative series of wuxia features in the late 1980s and 1990s, commonly made by directors who had both trained abroad and apprenticed under the Hong Kong action auteurs of decades past. The most readily apparent influences on the wuxia films of the 1980s and 1990s are the special-effects technologies developed in the silent era, the semantic and syntactic elements of the Shaw swordplay films, and the alternating star-making function or coordinated opera troupe dynamic of the 1970s kung fu films.

As Zhang Zhen has eloquently explained in "Bodies in the Air: The Magic of Science and the Fate of the Early 'Martial Arts' Film in China," the earliest incarnation—or what she calls the "pre-consciousness"—of Hong Kong martial arts cinema was a compound genre (wuxia-shenguai pian) addressing the obstacles faced by the knight-errant (*xia*; 俠) and tending toward fantasy.[20] The heroes and heroines of these films could move objects with their *qi* (氣; energy force), fluidly jump from rooftop to rooftop, and perform acrobatic maneuvers while flying through the air. The modernizing mainland Chinese government banned the production of this genre in the early 1930s because of such "superstitious" elements. These elements, which remain key to the action aesthetics of the modern wuxia film, offer an inherently "cinematic" pleasure to audiences, as Stephen Teo notes: "The magical properties of *shenguai* revealed through the technology of special effects formed the chivalric sensibility of wuxia, which fundamentally make the genre a purely *cinematic* attraction. The genre remains relevant to this very day because it exhibits a natural correlation with the film medium—that through the medium of film, it makes the impossible real."[21]

The move to eliminate generic elements showcasing antiquated modes of thought (superstition) is ironic given that it is precisely the use of such technologies (e.g., wires, harnesses, slim female bodies in flight) that marks martial arts films as new and distinctive for non-Chinese spectators. The wuxia, or "martial hero," film was sometimes cast with female actors. Male actors' preference for theater over the degraded art of cinema led to an increase in films with female stars portraying female martial heroes, or *nüxia* (女俠).[22] Several convergent histories permeate the contemporary cinematic manifestation of the Hong Kong martial arts heroine: the woman warrior figures of traditional Chinese literature; the operatic tradition of performance, which is closely intertwined with the rise of Chinese cinemas; the globalized audience address and circulation of the films; and generic shifts in Hong Kong cinema and the implications of these for the star personae and hypertechnologized bodies of martial arts actors.

Though the wuxia film was historically devalued as a vulgar genre, banned as superstitious drivel in the mainland, and labeled low-grade "chopsocky" entertainment in the "West," the wuxia work of certain directors gained the acclaim of the international film festival circuit in the late 1960s. The international releases of Bruce Lee's films in the 1970s led to a global kung fu craze. From the mid-1960s through the late 1970s, Shaw Brothers became the leading producer of Mandarin-language martial arts films, or the "new wuxia pian." The new wuxia pian were films derived from or inspired by the highly successful martial arts serials published transnationally in the newspapers of diasporic Chinese communities in the 1950s and 1960s. Though still relatively inexpensive in comparison to Hollywood productions at the time, these films were produced on budgets that were unprecedented in the history of the martial arts film, in part to compete with Hollywood's shift to high-budget blockbusters. Because Hollywood was also in decline in the 1960s and 1970s, Robert Sklar explains that "the studios became interested only in the motion-picture equivalent of a home run."[23] The studios may have made fewer pictures, but the films they did make had higher production values, making it harder for Hong Kong and other national cinemas to compete.[24] To attract local audiences and compete with these Hollywood blockbusters, Hong Kong films showcased high-flying heroes drawn from wuxia literature.[25] Supported by seemingly invisible cables and harnesses, the limber bodies of skilled performers glided gracefully though the air with swords drawn.[26] While film critics abroad attributed the aesthetic innovations introduced by the genre to several notable auteurs, the technologized bodily display of the on-screen performers may have been the major draw for Chinese audiences. In these decades, select Shaw directors like King Hu garnered the interest of international film festivals.[27]

In the 1970s Shaw Brothers met with its first real local competitor, Golden Harvest, formed by Raymond Chow in 1970. Chow's company had absorbed the vast distribution network of Shaw's main rival in the 1960s, Cathay. As discussed in the first chapter of this book, Golden Harvest also hired many Peking opera stars, causing a transition in the genre yet again, from swordplay films to kung fu films, as Stephen Teo remarks:

> The release of movies such as *The Jade Bow* (Zhang Xinyan and Fu Qi), *Tiger Boy* (Chang Che), and *Come Drink with Me* in 1966 triggered a rash of other *wuxia* movies, and the genre came to dominate the popular imagination of overseas Chinese audiences for the rest of the decade into the 70s, out-grossing and eventually replacing the Japanese samurai movies in the domestic market. The sword fighting wuxia movie had a few more years of popularity in the 70s before it was itself replaced by the kung fu movie. The crunch came in 1971 with the release of Bruce Lee's *The Big Boss / Tang Shan Daxiong*.[28]

Shaw Brothers and Golden Harvest ceased to produce martial arts films in the style of the new wuxia pian in the early 1980s, when both the publication of wuxia literature and theater attendance for the genre declined.

Leon Hunt isolates three stages in the development of martial arts chore-ography beginning from the success of the kung fu film with Western audiences in the 1970s. Key to the first stage (early to late 1970s) was Bruce Lee's "authentic virtuosity," which marked his films as distinct from the swashbuckling and wirework of the Shaw Brothers fare of the 1960s. Hunt uses the term *displacement* in reference to Lee's function as a replacement for the wuxia performers trained in wirework, the skills necessary to manipulate one's own body while air-bound, riding on horseback, and wielding a sword. Hunt argues, "Bruce Lee placed a new emphasis on individual, authentic virtuosity, displacing trampoline-aided stars like Wang Yu and embodying the 'stuntman as hero.'"[29] The skill set acquired by Shaw actors and stunt performers would have renewed importance in the 1990s, when Cantopop stars found work in the new wave wuxia productions. In the second stage of this history (late 1970s–1980s), there was a fascination with the role of the choreographer and the archival function that such filmmakers served in preserving "authentic" martial arts styles on-screen. This phase was characterized by the organization of stunt performers into teams, distinct from the earlier phase embodied by Lee, in which action sequences focused primarily on the individual. Hunt points out that Jackie Chan bridges the gap between the first two stages. Chan's films utilize Peking opera training and dynamically orchestrated group performances. At the same time, his films serve as star vehicles owing to the complexity of the stunts that Chan attempts. In the third stage (early to mid-1990s), the technological accomplishments of the medium were greatly expanded, allowing shots of beautiful Hong Kong starlets and handsome male leads—strung up on wires, flying gracefully through the air—to be intercut with shots of stunt performers. The use of computer-generated effects facilitated the erasure of differences between the skilled actor and the technically adept stunt performer.[30]

Fanboy Auteurs: A Hong Kong Reservoir for *Xena*

I elucidate the production context of *Xena: Warrior Princess* through various means: outlining the fan practices surrounding the show's creation and the intentions of the show's producers, tracing the two forms of communicative translation active in the preproduction and production process of *Xena*, identifying semantic and syntactic genre elements common to the wuxia cycle that are present in the show, and examining the conditions and effects that enabled the production context of the series.

Fueled by overseas Chinese investment, the economic growth that Hong Kong experienced in the 1950s affected the entertainment industry as well. The industry sought to capture not only overseas Chinese investors but also overseas Chinese audiences. The subject matter of Mandarin-language films by MP & GI (Motion Picture and General Investment Co.) and Shaw Brothers appealed to Chinese expatriates.[31] The primary overseas market for Chinese-language films was not non-Chinese consumers. In North America, for example, most films were distributed to movie theaters in local Chinatowns, with little circulation of screening information outside of the Chinese community, or to video stores with no English-language database for their videotapes. Most Chinese-language video stores in the United States, having a limited amount of display space, keep a list of their holdings organized by title (or, in some cases, by star). English-language titles are often not given, and even when alternate English-language titles are listed, the patron must first be familiar with the Chinese title, and the video database's system of organization, to find the title. Chinese-language video stores often structure their inventory in this manner because many of the VHS tapes in the database are illegally dubbed from television and cannot be displayed in the store. The few exceptions to this formula are martial arts films released in urban centers, at art houses, and on college campuses after the success of Bruce Lee pictures in the American market.[32] The breakthrough success of Lee and Jackie Chan with American cinephiles contributed to the migration of American hipsters to Chinese-language video stores in search of hidden martial arts treasures.[33] Cindy Hing-yuk Wong explains that "this initial group of fans is epitomized by Quentin Tarantino: educated filmgoers who appreciate a 'new' style of commercial filmmaking that does not represent the obscurity and/or pretentiousness of art cinema but seems to inject fresh air into a world saturated with Hollywood."[34] The videotapes and laser discs that such English-speaking fans procured and dubbed in the late 1980s to late 1990s were circulated among friends, eventually finding their way to independently run video stores specializing in international cinema genres and auteurs.

Sam Raimi and Robert Tapert, the creators of *Xena: Warrior Princess*, were adored by members of this alternative cine culture as the creators of the cult *Evil Dead* cycle.[35] Raimi and Tapert were also avid consumers of Hong Kong texts and participated in fan practices, not only sharing tapes but ultimately sending Tribune, the company that later held the rights to *Xena*, a mix videotape of martial arts sequences from their favorite new wuxia films as a pitch for the proposed content of the show. Raimi explains, "In fact, when we pitched *Xena*, I made a demo reel of four Hong Kong movies to show the studio the kind of action sequences we wanted to do in the show."[36] Though the phrase *demo reel* was used in this interview, Raimi and Tapert have described this object as a *demo tape* in other interviews. It is much more likely that potential investors (the production company) were shown a *mix-tape*, that is, video of Hong Kong action sequences. Raimi and Tapert were unlikely to have procured film copies of the originals and had such copies edited together because of the slightly less formal means by which Hong Kong prints were distributed in the states (thirty-five-millimeter film cans often remained in the projection booths of Chinatown movie theaters for years) compared to the more organized and regimented Hollywood distribution networks. Video would have been a much more convenient medium for Raimi and Tapert's purposes. In all later discussions about such materials (sending them to each other, to the stunt coordinator, to second-unit directors), video is clearly articulated as the medium of choice.

The initial stage of communicative translation was made in preproduction, as Raimi and Tapert hoped to use the spectatorial effects elicited by Hong Kong wuxia action spectacles to convey the proposed content of *Xena*. This first act of translation was effected by the producers-as-fanboy-consumers before the series had even been scripted. This was an instance of communicative translation because the wuxia film's spectatorial effects—shock and pleasure in the dynamic, air-bound, martial arts body on display—helped define the impetus behind a US television series. That is, the program was funded based on proposed content that would mimic Hong Kong action sequences and their desired spectatorial effects on a smaller scale and a lower budget. Tapert and Raimi pitched and sold *Xena*, not on the basis of narrative content, but rather with recourse to Hong Kong body spectacles. The spectatorial effect of such dynamic visuals on the executives who funded the production of *Xena* was necessary to the large-scale communicative translation of acts of reception common to wuxia films. This act of translation occurred when the spectators at Tribune conceptualized *Xena* as a viable project in relation to the American cinephilic reception of Hong Kong wuxia sequences.

The Hong Kong wuxia model was adopted by *Xena*'s creators and by the company funding the show because both groups felt that the stylized spectacle would attract audiences and allow the production to save money on visual effects, which was not the case in the long term.[37] After the show was picked up for syndication, producers Tapert, Raimi, and Liz Friedman, as well as action consultant David Pollison, consistently delivered new wuxia mixtapes to the show's directors so as to model the series precisely after Hong Kong action sequences from the following films: *Chinese Ghost Story* (倩女幽魂), *Bride with White Hair, Swordsman II, Swordsman III, Heroic Trio, Once Upon a Time in China* (黃飛鴻), *Fong Sai Yuk* (方世玉), and *Ashes of Time* (東邪西毒).[38] *Xena* director Doug Lefler has said of the films, "It was something we felt was sort of like *our private reservoir* that we were going to [in order] to drink from[emphasis added]."[39]

Note that Lefler referred to the aesthetic sensibilities of wuxia films from Hong Kong as a "reservoir" that could be returned to, whenever needed, for narrative and visual content. This reserve was continually refilled by the new films being made in Hong Kong and seemed free for the taking to a select, "private" group of cinephiles who knew where to look. The repository held syntactic, semantic, and spectatorial elements: thematic content, character traits, costumes, stylistic choices, and the ability to elicit in the spectator a visceral reaction to the on-screen body in flight.

From this wuxia-based reservoir, the creators of *Xena* borrowed not only structures of reception or Newmark's reader-effect but also certain key characters and themes corresponding to Newmark's semantic and communicative categories of translation. They wanted the show to focus on revenge motifs and the conflicted swordswoman's search for salvation in a world plagued by warlords and dangerous mythological creatures. These attributes are common to the wuxia serial in both its literary and cinematic forms. Stephen Teo has traced the history of the genre and identifies the following semantic and syntactic elements, all of which were also present in *Xena*: an episodic structure, a "labyrinthine narrative," romance subplots, allegiances forged between protagonists in the service of the greater good, heroes who come to the defense of old masters, and a cliffhanger structure. Teo adds, "The execution and satisfaction of vengeance (*baochou* 報仇) underlies the growth of the hero or the heroine, leading to the final resolution where justice prevails, and law and order are restored in the fractious world of the martial arts."[40] The presence of a labyrinthine narrative and alliances formed for the greater good suited the structure of the long-running series and allowed for crossover episodes with the producers' other series, *Hercules: The Legendary Journeys*.[41] As the shows participated in a singular narrative universe (referred to as the "Xenaverse" by fans), the presence of shared characters and revenge plots also facilitated interlocking shooting schedules and alleviated strain on the production budget.

Both *Xena* and its predecessor, *Hercules*, were filmed in New Zealand for US production and distribution companies and are examples of flexible specialization. Local crews handled both first- and second-unit production, the second unit being the primary crew for stunt work. Local actors filled both primary and supporting roles (e.g., Lucy Lawless/Xena vis-à-vis warlords, villagers, and extras). This scenario helped to minimize costs and was prompted by New Zealand's "film-friendly" policies as promoted by Film New Zealand. According to Bruce Babington, Film New Zealand's policies held that offshore productions like *Hercules* and *Xena* could benefit from the nation's varied topography in the form of "the extraordinary variety of the New Zealand landscape (its 'English Summer lanes, Welsh hillsides and forest . . . Cretan and Grecian coastlines', as well as 'Fantasy landscapes') . . . and the experience, 'competitive crew costs' and adaptability of New Zealand technicians."[42]

The producers of both series quickly made use of the "fantasy landscapes" as well as the "adaptability of New Zealand technicians." They requested that stunt coordinator Peter Bell (no relation to Zoë Bell) and his crew re-create on location in New Zealand the wuxia action sequences that the creative team had put together on the mixtapes of Hong Kong films. This is a second instance of communicative translation, as Bell had to perceive the spectatorial effects prompted by sequences of bodily spectacle and attempt to approximate these with the resources available to him in New Zealand. New Zealand film crews had been trained in the British system and did not have much experience with Hong Kong–style wirework. Hiring Hong Kong technicians and choreographers and flying them to New Zealand would have defeated the purpose of low-cost offshore production. The New Zealand stunt team had experience with pratfalls (short falls or stumbles), high falls, full-body burns, explosions, ratchets, air rams (low-power catapults), and stunt driving. Since Hong Kong filmmakers were not employed to assist with stylization, Peter Bell had to work from the mixtapes he was given, using the resources at hand in New Zealand. Bell studied the action sequences and developed makeshift wire rigs to approximate the on-screen action. Bell's stunt teams worked analogously to the Hong Kong system, with a group of men in charge of lifting a person (usually a woman) on the other end of the wire rigs. However, unique to this Kiwi-style wire fu were multibeat fight and wirework sequences. These complexly choreographed moments of seemingly violent bodily contact were staged in advance of filming. In contrast to the production of wuxia body spectacles, in Kiwi-style multibeat stunts, the stunt actors in the rigs were in charge of their own harnesses, and the action choreographer did not always maximize his control of the action. Such multibeat fight/wire sequences in *Xena* were distinctive in that a large number of stunties participated in each "attack." Multiple combatants per beat are not as common to Hong Kong action sequences, with the exception of sequences choreographed by the Jackie Chan Stunt Team. The style of these numbers on *Xena* was facilitated by both the structure and the pay scale of the New Zealand stunt industry. Zoë Bell spoke to the distinction between Kiwi-style wire fu and Hong Kong practices as she experienced it the first time she tried to put on her harness on the set of *Kill Bill: Vol. 1*. She had started to attach the harness by herself, as was the custom on *Xena*, and she was quickly descended on by six members of Yuen Woo-ping's stunt crew. Bell described the process, explaining that she felt like the car in a raceway pit stop.[43]

By the time production wrapped on *Xena*, New Zealand had a dedicated stunt team trained in a Kiwi–Hong Kong hybrid of wire fu techniques. The producers and directors were doubtful that the first- and second-unit crews, who had trained for eight years, would find work at the close of the series.[44] As it happened, New Zealand's cultural policies—which had encouraged international coproductions, offshore production, and native filmmaking practices—generated profound interest in shooting television, digital projects, and large-scale features in the region.[45] Many of the crew members from *Xena* found work on other television series (as discussed in chapter 4) and on Peter Jackson's *Lord of the Rings* trilogy, a film franchise that created a similar new national repository for computer-generated effects and animation talent in New Zealand.[46]

The "Air Sense" of Zoë Bell

The production context of every television show or film that requires stunts makes unique demands on the trained stunties assigned the task of generating body spectacles: Pal's (Lassie's) perilous swim in the San Joaquin River, trapped in an upsurge of current in *Lassie Come Home*; Wayne Michaels's dangerously close seven-hundred-foot bungee jump off of a dam in *Goldeneye*, during which he reached one hundred miles an hour; and Debbie Evans's (doubling Carrie-Anne Moss) motorcycle race against the flow of freeway traffic in *The Matrix Reloaded*, as seen in figure 3.1.[47] The distinguishing requirements of *Xena*'s production context were the low-budget re-creations of scenes from Hong Kong new wuxia films and a tight schedule. Such conditions, which closely mimicked deliberate-practice training, accelerated the development of stuntwoman Zoë Bell's marketable skill set.

3.1 Debbie Evans (doubling Carrie-Anne Moss) performs masterful motorcycle work in *The Matrix Reloaded*.

The marketing and accumulation of new skill sets based on newly acquired bodily dispositions and lived experiences can lead to a successful stunting career. Most activities at which a stunt performer is physically adept or even merely proficient become profitable, but Bell's training on set and continually evolving bodily disposition have produced a distinctive trajectory that can be mapped from *Xena* to *Kill Bill*, both of which were marked by a visual symmetry to Hong Kong–style cinema body spectacles and prompted by cinephilic fanboy sensibilities.[48]

The degree of preparation and the skilling process necessary to film acting have long been a concern for star studies. However, the labor that occurs *before* the moment of production has not been examined in relation to the stunting star. The discourse on training in film, and its importance to the actor's craft, is of paramount importance to my project. Actors' established training regimens have been scrutinized by the press and academics alike for traces of the performance's means of production (this is particularly true of method actors). The assumption that actors hone their craft through years of training and self-discipline contributes to the belief on the part of both audiences and scholars that these actors intend for their actions to be perceived in a particular fashion; that is, trained actors have authorial intent and they create characterization, as opposed to unskilled actors, who merely impersonate. While Barry King disputes that the actor is an author, he also admits that, "notwithstanding this fact, the romantic myth of the author has readily and voraciously fastened itself to the world of performance by a facile, but plausible extension of the literary conception of the author to that field."[49] The specific attributes of a performance are perceived by the audience as a mode of authorial intent on the part of the actor. The performance may be viewed as evidence of the intellectual and affective contribution of the actor in question. The same audience assumption does not hold true for stunt actors. Audiences do not tend to recognize the spectacles supplied by stunt performers as evidence of the complex cognitive operations of the stunt actor. However, the stunt actor also prepares for each part through deliberate-practice training for months or years in order to adapt to the spectacular task at hand. These same stunt actors must not only learn to manipulate their bodies but also acquire the mental fortitude required to control normal impulses and avoid panic during dangerous situations, such as falling from great heights (e.g., high falls), being lit on fire (full-body/partial-body fire burns), and standing in the path of a moving vehicle (car hits). In my discussion with Bell, she revealed that even the most seasoned stuntie must trust in her training and the competence of her crew in order to deactivate the body's instinctive reticence to jump from the top of a building (in the film *Catwoman*) or stand in the path of a fast-moving car (in the "Send in the Clones" episode of *Xena: Warrior Princess*).[50] The training history of a stunting star is marked both on their body and in their performance, as is the case with Xena's stunt double, Zoë Bell.

Xena's Other Half

Zoë Bell began her career as a stunt double on *Xena* in 1997, when she was nineteen years old, after doing some background action for *Amazon High* and stunts for *Xena*.[51] The distinction between being credited with "stunts" and acting as a "stunt double" is determined by whether the stuntie is the action counterpart of an identifiable character who has a history of sustained narrative development. Bell had been working with *Xena*'s stunt team for approximately six months on the show before she was approached to act as a stunt double for Lucy Lawless.[52] Bell acted as the primary stunt double for Lawless (there were multiple doubles, each with their own specialties) from the fourth to the sixth and final season of the show, from 1998 to 2001.

Doubling the show's lead required a singular skill set. Bell had been trained since childhood in gymnastics and tae kwon do before becoming a stuntwoman, and the bodily disposition that she developed in her training in each can be witnessed by the keen observer of *Xena*'s action sequences.

Identifying that history is a productive enterprise when one considers the importance of the mental and corporeal conditioning process through which stunt actors prepare to embody spectacle. Stunting, as a distinct form of spectacle, is produced by and consists of the body of the skilled performer in motion. Stunting star Zoë Bell both performs and becomes spectacle in much the same fashion as the silent-era stars discussed by Jennifer M. Bean and Zhang Zhen.[53] As Zhang explains, "The 'techniques of the body' in the 'martial arts-magic spirit' film constitute a particular 'habitus' in which the body is both the medium (instrument) and a new focus of a cultural practice."[54] For Bell, a stunting star working in the martial arts genre, her body is both the instrument through which spectacle is manifest and the spectacle itself.

The process of becoming a bodily spectacle is enhanced by cinematography, editing, costuming, computer graphics, and other special effects, as seen in figure 3.2, in which Bell is suspended in flight, dressed in a red kimono, and set on fire. In this shot from the episode "A Friend in Need, Part 2," technical enhancements serve three mutually beneficial functions for the performer's status as a virtuoso in the creation of the body spectacle.[55] First, the isolation of the performer via visual cues or blots in the mise-en-scène is often accomplished via elaborately designed, colorful costumes. Such tactics give the object the power to attract the eye, as the object is distinguished from the background, acting as a "stain in the visual field," or blot.[56] Second, the perceived danger is amplified through proximity to precarious situations such as full-body or partial-body burns. Third, the assistive devices that lend the bodily spectacle a superhuman quality are digitally erased (the postproduction team removed the wires visible in figure 3.2 before the episode's release).

In becoming a body spectacle, Bell performs and becomes the third act of communicative translation in the production and reception of *Xena*. Her bodily disposition is a congealed artifact of generic translation. This translation is communicative in that, in her labor as a stunting star, Bell becomes the captivating image reminiscent of Hong Kong wuxia sequences. Bell's function is to approximate both the semantic underpinnings (costume, movement, etc.) of the Hong Kong new wuxia film and also the spectatorial effects prompted by the dynamic visuals common to the action sequences of this genre. To be effective, the communicative translation of the spectator effects (the mesmerized spectator, the jerk reaction, etc.) of new wuxia action sequences necessitated a specific skilling process for Bell, who was simultaneously an expert laborer and a visual effect. In trying to approximate

3.2 Zoë Bell is harnessed, lifted, and lit on fire after being covered in flame-retardant gel in the *Xena* episode "A Friend in Need, Part 2."

the spectacular images of Hong Kong wuxia films, action choreographers trained Bell to fly, kick, and twirl through the air on a rigged harness while dressed in revealing and elaborate costumes. Such stunts required prior deliberate-practice training in gymnastics and martial arts but were visually enhanced by cinematographic techniques and Bell's new training regimes in wirework.

For stunt performers, the required training for becoming a bodily spectacle necessitates its own erasure. For this reason, a knowing spectator who wants to see the stunt actor made invisible in a hypervisible action sequence must be familiar with the history and distinctive individual signatures of stunt performers. To identify Bell's presence on-screen, the spectator must look for sequences requiring a higher degree of risk and search out moments of accelerated motion in which Lawless's face is not clearly identifiable, while discerning markers of Bell's individualized difference: her eyes, nose, wig, physique, and, most significantly, history of training. Bell's foundation in tae kwon do is readily apparent in many of the fight sequences from *Xena* in the last three seasons. When delivering a kick, Bell tends to position her hips at a forty-five-degree angle to the floor with her knee quickly raised and her body turned ninety degrees. In tae kwon do, this is referred to as a *yeop chagi* (옆 차기), or, more simply, a side kick. This stance is manifest in most of Bell's frontal-attack kicks, and she frequently uses it to step on an opponent's chest to perform Xena's trademark flip, aided by wires and a harness. The stance also helps Bell to balance when delivering flying side kicks, *idan yeop chagi* (이단 차기), on a wired harness because the weight is shifted to a triangulated pattern between her upper body, her waist, and both of the wires. Bell's bodily disposition toward flexibility, achieved by her deliberate-practice training in tae kwon do and gymnastics, is glaringly apparent in her flawless execution of martial arts action on screen.

As noted above, Bell's grounding in gymnastics is markedly identifiable in all flying sequences with Xena's signature flip, facilitated by a wired harness and a minitramp, but is most apparent in the high-bar flip in the episode "A Friend in Need, Part 1."[57] Xena needs to save a burning village by flipping her way to the water tower and climbing it. Lawless, the actor who plays Xena, is visualized initiating a jump to a high bar. The shot cuts to a medium close-up of Lawless's upside-down face, hands presumably on the bar as she is about to use it to gain leverage for an airborne maneuver (see figures 3.3–3.4). The scene continues with a long shot of Bell, who performs a handstand into a backward giant, eyes wide open. A backward giant is a gymnastic maneuver in which the performer swings her fully extended body 360 degrees while grasping a bar, facing forward. The sequence is intercut with shots of the actor who plays another lead role, Renée O'Connor (Gabrielle). O'Connor and her stuntwoman approach the water tower via a balance beam routine. The *Xena* stunt sequence closes with a close-up shot of a smiling Lawless and an extreme close-up on Bell's hands for the release. Bell developed her "air sense"—her ability to manipulate her body in flight—during her early years of training as a gymnast. *Air sense* is a stunt industry term for the dexterity and elegance of air-bound performers. As Bell has remarked in interviews, her air sense was honed on the set of *Xena* when she had to master the art of graceful flight while attached to a harness that gave her more thrust but limited her movement: "If there's any kind of flipping or twisting . . . it's hard enough to do that stuff on your own steam but sometimes it's even harder on wires because you have to avoid the wires. You have to make it look like the wires aren't there and the timing is not just me but it's me and the six guys on the other end of the wire that are pulling me . . . and the camera."[58]

The physical requirements of wirework eliminate a large percentage of the populace from even attempting flight. Effective use of wires makes sev-

3.3 Zoë Bell flips and performs a handstand on the high bar in the *Xena* episode "A Friend in Need, Part 1."

eral requirements of the body on display: the subject must be light; have strong back, leg, chest, and abdominal muscles; and (most commonly) have a background in the physical domain of acrobatics, martial arts, or dance. In addition, the performer must be patient while in discomfort and unafraid of heights and must display the requisite air sense to generate a graceful spectacle. While, in the course of my research, I have encountered countless critics, academics, and fans who decry wirework as the effortless trickery of unskilled performers, I have yet to meet one who can fulfill most of these requirements. Far from being a simple aid to spectacle that anyone can effectively utilize, a wired harness rig requires physical mastery if the profilmic event is to be camera-worthy. Wirework does not simply require training on the part of the individual stunt actor. The sequence preparation as a whole is cued to the needs, choreographic style, character traits, and technological appointments of individual productions.

3.4 Lucy Lawless's face is intercut with Zoë Bell's body spectacle in the *Xena* episode "A Friend in Need, Part 1."

Kill Bill: Disposition as a "Bodily Accent"

Bell's bodily disposition is constantly evolving; not only does it show signs of her gymnastics and tae kwon do training, but her wuxia wirework and fight sequences on *Xena* subsequently informed her disposition as well, making her the ideal candidate for Quentin Tarantino's wuxia-inspired series, *Kill Bill*. When asked about the manner in which her combat performance changed for *Kill Bill*, Bell addresses both her history in bodily disciplines and the need to adjust her mind-set to control the specificities of her bodily articulation of spectacle:

> I have a base in gymnastics, I was pretty decent at gymnastics when I was a gymnast, I'm no longer a gymnast. I was pretty decent at martial arts when I was a martial artist, I'm no longer a martial artist. I'm now a stunt person. . . . So, in terms of shifting my style, it had to be very conscious for me, because fighting Xena-style had become very instinctive and unconscious. So, I had to be really conscious of every time I let go and got into the fight in *Kill Bill*. I sort of reined myself in and reminded myself that I was a *wushu* expert or a samurai expert and not a warrior princess.[59]

Many of the stunt sequences for *Kill Bill* were shot in China, under the tutelage of choreographer Yuen Woo-ping, who came to prominence as a martial arts director in Hong Kong in the 1970s. Bell had to attempt to remove traces of Xena from her performance as she adjusted to the Hong Kong style of harness work, but the bodily disposition gained on *Xena* was never fully eclipsed. Peter Bell's team had been compelled to construct rigs that could mimic the motions of Hong Kong performers in the wuxia films of the 1980s and 1990s. Since the martial arts film was not historically rooted in New Zealand, the style of rigging, the set-up time, and the individual re-quirements of the stunt performer were unique to the new Kiwi-style wire fu techniques. Kiwi-style wire fu was prompted by and tended toward com-municative translation of the effects that Hong Kong wuxia sequences have on the spectator. It was developed within tight budgetary constraints and through trial and error on the part of the stunt performer. This process of trial and error was physically demanding and often painful or injurious and, as such, mimicked the strategy of learning through failure and repetition common to expert performance. The use of expert stunt performers trained in martial arts, dance, and gymnastics facilitated the speedy production of Hong Kong–style action design on *Xena* at a lower cost. The money that the production company saved on *Xena* by shooting the show offshore in New Zealand allowed for a full-time second unit, a scenario that is extremely uncommon in US television production. The use of New Zealand's varied topography for first-unit shoots often required the second unit to set up rigs outdoors in a less controlled environment than is common for Hong Kong productions. The show's shooting schedule required the stunties to work quickly and manage their own equipment. Each was in charge of outfitting their own harness before being attached to the rig.

In Hong Kong, after decades of assisting stars and starlets in their efforts to take flight, the system for wirework is more streamlined and controlled by the choreographer and his team. In my discussion with Bell, she recounted the first time she was expected to do wirework on the set of *Kill Bill*. As she tried to strap herself into her harness, which she had been trained to do on her own on the set of *Xena*, she was pounced on by Yuen Woo-ping's stunt team and in seconds was harnessed and attached to the rig.[60] The unique scenario of second-unit production in *Xena* and the Kiwi translations and reworkings of Hong Kong wuxia techniques had made Bell the ideal stuntie to double Uma Thurman for *Kill Bill*, but the process of working with Hong Kong–based martial arts choreographers also required adjustments on Bell's part. For expert stunt performers, training is a lifelong process, and the artists accumulate skills that transform their bodily disposition. In the global cinematic and televisual production marketplace, the expert stunt performer's body spectacles are increasingly marked by their participation in translatable texts; one could conceptualize the bodily disposition of such experts as attaining a new bodily "accent" in each instance of translation. That working bodies have histories, and that such histories can be read in the comportment of subjects, is a fundamental principle of forensic anthropology. Performing the same action repeatedly has identifiable effects on biomechanics, effects known as *occupational markers*.[61] Training regimes and injuries have marked effects on comportment, and the traces of such histories can be read as accents in the biomechanical tendencies of laboring bodies.

This continually evolving, accented physical style can easily be observed in Bell's performances in Tarantino's *Kill Bill* series. Like *Xena*, both films borrow from a similar reservoir of action technique, Hong Kong wuxia and martial arts films of the 1960s and 1970s.[62] The traces of earlier modes of deliberate-practice training (gymnastics, tae kwon do, wirework and falls for *Xena*) have been inscribed in Bell's ever-evolving habitus. Bell's "restored behaviors" can be clearly identified in the *Kill Bill* series.[63] In the King Hu–style inn sequence in *Kill Bill: Vol. I*, shot on a soundstage at the Beijing Film Studio in China, Bell's somatic repertoire is enhanced—which is to say that it becomes more apparent and is transformed—by the wire rig design, the spatial arrangements generated by large-scale set construction and composition that allow for more lateral body movement. The Beijing set provided unique circumstances and distinct conditions of production, which greatly contributed to the specific articulations of body spectacle. The "Showdown at House of Blue Leaves" sequence from *Kill Bill: Vol. I* was designed on a soundstage large enough to allow for fluid movement and the seamless incorporation of expertly designed wire rigs. Both the style of movement and the rig design on *Xena* and on the Beijing Film Studio set diverged widely. As discussed above, Kiwi-style wire fu on *Xena* was often accompanied by a certain degree of trial and error, as demonstrated in Amanda Micheli's 2005 documentary on Bell and stuntwoman Jeannie Epper. The documentary provides a rare glimpse into the second-unit production practices of *Xena*. The Kiwi stunt crews were incredibly adept at rig construction, but the demands of the production schedule and the learning curve for production design influenced by Hong Kong action meant that Bell sometimes spent hours in her harness trying to get the desired results from faulty rigs. Bell's patience and deliberate practice with devices that misfired, forced a shift in her center of balance, and sometimes caused (minor) injury helped her to masterfully execute the wire-bound numbers in the "Showdown at House of Blue Leaves" sequence with a graceful fluidity of movement. Bell's muscular coordination, honed on the set of *Xena*, and her comfort with multiple-combatant, multibeat fight scenarios are readily apparent in the completed scene in which Bell faced off against seventy-six Chinese stunt performers.

Bell's performance in this scene is marked with visual cues to her history of learned dispositions: gymnastics, martial arts, and her work on *Xena*. Close scrutiny of the scene in slow motion allows for Bell to be easily identified based on her markers of difference from Thurman: her slightly curly wig, her height (Thurman is four inches taller than Bell), and her bodily disposition. Close-ups and medium shots of Thurman about to perform an action, her face clearly visible, are matched with long shots of Bell in motion, in the standard intercutting strategy for stunt work. Thurman wields her sword with a reticence that is absent in Bell's performance, and she closes her eyes as flying weapons and debris approach her face (figure 3.5). Some fans have noticed the marked difference in bodily display; as thirty-year-old fan Eileen C. explained, "I did watch a slow motion action sequence in *Kill Bill*. It was in the final fight against the crazy eighty-eights. I paused during the leap to the railing. Zoë stepped on a sword and soared to the second story in the restaurant. It was exhilarating. I paused because it was great. I knew dorky Uma Thurman couldn't perform the magical leap."[64] Stunt performers and martial artists are trained to keep their eyes open so as to allow for more maneuverability and to maintain better control over objects approaching the face. Bell, in contrast to Thurman, executes moves with precision and without identifiable fear, as when she completes a wire-aided back flip reminiscent of Xena's trademark maneuver remarked on earlier in this chapter (figure 3.6). The expansive "Blue Leaves" set allowed for maximum fluid lateral movement and acted as a catalyst for the production of a series of elaborate body spectacles.

The Hong Kong–style rig construction, choreography, and vast spatial dimensions of the "Blue Leaves" set provided the conditions of production for a body spectacle that simultaneously was informed by Bell's bodily disposition and also transformed this disposition. The dance-like attack sequence in which Bell's skills were cast against those of the Yuen Woo-ping Stunt Team required greater timing and precision than did many of the combat scenes on *Xena*. While fights on *Xena* commonly involved multiple combatants, foes generally approached Xena one at a time. While not necessarily less difficult, the fight scenes on *Xena* had simpler choreography than the "Blue Leaves" sequence by virtue of the scale of the set, the average number

3.5 In *Kill Bill*, Uma Thurman's bodily disposition is clearly distinct from Zoë Bell's: Thurman closes her eyes when objects approach her face.

3.6 In *Kill Bill*, Zoë Bell executes a flip common to her work on *Xena*.

of performers, and a more restricted use of camera movement. Tarantino's use of overhead camera placement made it simpler for Bell to double Thurman and execute movements without covering her face, making longer takes of continuous action possible. A primary example of this shooting strategy is visible in the one-to-many fight on the illuminated glass dance floor. Bell drops to the ground, spinning and kicking, sword in hand, as the overhead camera captures the continuous action. Bell's movement is visible in full as the camera alternates between overhead shots and composition with extremely low camera heights. The arrangement of movement, the shot composition, and the shot duration are distinct from Bell's work on *Xena* and thus required more attention to comportment. The physical demands of the production context for *Kill Bill* affected Bell's style and would inform the more graceful articulations of body spectacle in her later work.

The Star-Making Functions of *Double Dare* and *Death Proof*

> The first time [that I saw Bell] was the TV show *Xena*, but I didn't know
> who she was because she was a stunt double. Second time was *Kill Bill 1
> and 2*, but the same as the first, didn't know her. It was *Death Proof* that
> made me notice that I had been "seeing" Zoë for a long time.
> —RUTH LIZARDI, "ZOË BELL FAN SURVEY"

The construction of Zoë Bell's body spectacles in *Xena* and the *Kill Bill*
series is examined in great detail in the documentary *Double Dare*, a film
about Bell and stunt double Jeannie Epper, Lynda Carter's double on *Wonder Woman*.[65] The behind-the-scenes numbers have a star-making function
in that they expose the labor involved in the production of Bell's body spectacles. The documentary considers the life-changing consequences of *Xena's* finale for Bell. The film combines narrative sequences of Bell's struggle
to find employment with footage of Bell's stunt work on the sets of *Xena*
and *Kill Bill*. The film opens with shots of *Xena's* second-unit crew examining and adjusting the wire rig, followed by shots of Bell preparing for a
partial-body burn on a rotating harness, which is fastened so tightly that
Bell lets out a giggle as the harness constricts around her pelvic area. She
is outfitted in layers of flame-retardant long underwear and strapped into
a specially designed harness with two central rings set on ball bearings to
produce a 360-degree rotation effect. A preliminary lift is attempted on the
special harness, and whereas an untrained performer would lose balance in
a harness, flailing about and rocking back and forth, Bell maintains perfect
form and seems nonplussed by the dangerous stunt she is about to attempt
for the first time. Bell is then seen dressed in *Xena's* bright red kimono, a wig,
and a pair of leather gloves that she dips in a clear gel before smearing the
substance on her face. The gel is a flame-retardant substance used by stunt
people. It will burn, but it takes longer to ignite than skin alone. The bottom
of the costume is sprayed with flammable liquid, and Bell gives the crew a
wink to let them know she is ready for the stunt. The kimono is ignited, and
Bell is pulled forward across the set as she spins. The burning spiraling red
fabric fills the screen, and as she reaches the end of the set, the conflagra-
tion is extinguished. Mechanical, computer-generated, optical, and bodily
spectacles are defining characteristics of action-oriented film and television.
Xena, as a commodity, relied on Hong Kong–style body spectacle from the
development phase (mixtapes) through to the final episode. The opening
scene of *Double Dare* exposes the production context of *Xena's* translated

spectacle, stripping the commodity of one of its most valued fetishes. This exposure positions Bell as an expert stunting star; that is, the film makes the labor of her body spectacle readily apparent to the spectator. Both narrative and number inspire identification with Bell as she is depicted as a charming, lighthearted daredevil with a strong work ethic, a sentiment echoed by Tarantino's 2007 exploitation genre film *Death Proof*, in which Bell plays a character similar to herself.

In *Death Proof* Bell is "Zoë the Cat," a Kiwi stuntwoman desperate to take a high-speed ride on the hood of a 1970 Dodge Challenger. Like *Double Dare*, this film had a mythmaking function in that narrative claims were made as to the character's invincibility that were amplified by the body spectacle of Bell on the hood of a speeding muscle car as it was rammed by a murderous driver (see figures 3.7–3.8). This sequence required Bell to spend two weeks of the shooting schedule on the hood of the car. Her bodily disposition as a stuntwoman had to be adjusted to this unique dual role as stuntwoman and star.[66] Serving both roles required that Bell change some of her habitual posture. Tarantino showed her some takes that were otherwise perfect but had one major flaw, the lack of the star's face. After years of doubling for other actors, Bell had a habit of turning her face away from the action.[67] Bell quickly learned to keep both her face and her body in full view while secured to the car with a safety cable, a precaution that did not keep her fully protected from harm, as explained by Kevin Conley:

> But even with the cable, the danger to Bell in the scene was real. Unlike amateurs in the copycat videos, she was hooked to a car that was being continually spun out or rammed from behind or sideswiped—if her car blew a tire or slid off the road into a rollover, she was toast, a genuine risk that a normal *actress* (that is, one with no stunt experience) would never be allowed to take. And Tarantino could mount a camera inside the car so that audiences could see what she was feeling while this happened. "If I'm doing another action movie," Tarantino told me, "it would be almost foolhardy not to put Zoë in it, because you get so much."[68]

Death Proof may not have revealed the conditions of production for the car chase or Bell's performance, but, like *Double Dare*, the film generated interest in Bell as a unique kind of star. In two surveys I conducted with Bell's online fan community, 60 percent (twenty-seven) of the forty-five respondents identified *Death Proof* as the film that sparked their interest in Bell. Robyn, a twenty-two-year-old female fan, responded to a question about the most memorable Bell action sequence with the following comment: "The

3.7 Zoë Bell's face is visible while she is attached to the hood of a 1970 Dodge Challenger in *Death Proof.*

3.8 Zoë Bell clings to the car's hood as it is rammed from behind.

car chase in *Death Proof* [was the most memorable], because after watching it, I was in a full body sweat, and it was one of the greatest car chase scenes in cinematic history." Multiple respondents explained that watching Bell in *Death Proof* made them seek out her other work.[69] The stunting star, as an expert laborer, participates in body spectacles that are constructed by camerawork and editing so as to maximize facial visibility in long shot. The facial visibility of the stunting star confirms the authenticity of the performance and reinforces the dangerous nature of the stunt.

In the wake of *Kill Bill*, Bell gained the public recognition of her skill set necessary to any understanding of her status as a virtuoso, which is to say, Bell developed a fan community. In my surveys of Bell's fan community 29 percent explained that their first knowledge of Bell's work as a stuntwoman

3.9 Zoë Bell completes a midair flip during a high fall on *Catwoman*.

was gained though exposure to the documentary *Double Dare*.[70] Lisa S., a twenty-four-year-old from San Francisco, commented, "After seeing Zoë [lit] on fire in *Double Dare* I looked her up on IMDb and rented a lot of her movies to try to spot her. I even watched . . . *Catwoman* and the fall gave me chills. It looks so good; it could be CGI." The stunt that Lisa S. referenced is a 220-foot fall attached to a descender cable—a mechanical device that allows a harnessed stunt worker to fall at a controlled rate of speed—during which Bell doubled for Sharon Stone (see figure 3.9). In the scene, from the film *Catwoman*, Stone's character, Laurel Hedare, is fighting with Catwoman and falls out a window, plummeting to her death. Bell shot the long exterior fall in around three takes, dressed in white so that she could easily be spotted against the building and the sky.[71] It is telling that Lisa found the body spectacle so phenomenal that to her the image appeared good enough to have been computer generated. This reception of the scene may be linked to the increase in computer-simulated body spectacles in the action genre in the past twenty years, such that Lisa used that standard as a measure for spectacles generated by living bodies. Bell's air sense in the scene, as she flips in midair and speeds to the ground, is so impressive as to seem synthetic. The fall was shot in three segments with a short drop to an air mattress on set, a 220-foot fall for the exterior shot, and a short jump for the conclusion of the action. The "chilling" effect of the scene may have been amplified by the use of a wide-angle lens and extreme long shot, making the fall seem farther than it was. The knowledge of Bell as a stunting star animates the reception context of some fans, making visible the labor involved in the creation of her body spectacles.

Toward a Transnational History of the Stunting Star

Bell's work on *Xena*; the documentary on her early career, *Double Dare*; and her starring role in *Death Proof* have helped to bring about the recent resurgence of the stunting star. The history of the stunting star dates to the performers in American silent action-adventure serials of the 1910s and 1920s, as detailed by Jennifer M. Bean.[72] These films featured heroines who jumped from the top of moving trains, scaled high buildings, and performed a variety of maneuvers on horseback. The female stunting star also has a long history in India, where "Fearless Nadia" (Mary Ann Evans) disarmed her opponents with a whip in the 1930s through the 1960s. In China, 1920s wuxia films featured a high-flying wuxia woman (Qian Siying, Hu Die). The female stunting star has been a long-standing figure in Chinese-language filmmaking since 1925 owing to the generic longevity of the martial arts film. In the United States, the rise of the star system both necessitated the use of trained stunt doubles in the 1920s to ensure the safety of the star as a precious studio-owned commodity and relegated stunt performers to background action.[73] The shift away from the stunting star was also brought about by the transition to narrative-driven films after the slow decline (though not eclipse) of the "cinema of attractions." In fact, one of Tom Gunning's key points is that the cinema of attractions transformed into the cinematic tendency toward spectacle (in certain genres) and that narrative and attractions have become codependent.[74] The studio system as an institution, the star system as a marketing device, and the rise of the narrative feature forced the conspicuous decline of the stunting star in the United States. A brief resurgence of what Jacob Smith calls the "stunt man as hero" occurred in the low-budget action films of the 1970s, a time when the studio system failed, the star system broke down, and the exploitation film, with its preference for spectacle over narrative, was all the rage.[75]

Even though the stunt-heavy exploitation cycle of the 1970s may have brought stuntmen into the limelight, the majority of stunt performers stayed hidden from view, known only to connoisseurs of the exploitation genre. Before the widespread use of the VCR, fans could follow the work of individual stunt artists by paying close attention to the credits and searching for reports on stunt injuries in trade papers. In earlier decades, however, stunting fans did not form the same technologically linked communities that the spread of new technologies has enabled: the internet unites fans and communicates shared interests and adoration; video-sharing websites like YouTube isolate spectacular stunting feats; DVDs and high-definition technologies allow fans to better observe and decode the hidden faces of corporeally adept stars and provide behind-the-scenes material. While the technological developments that make the resurgence of the stunting star a possibility may be easily identifiable in the case of Bell, it is her similarity to the US stars of the 1910s and 1920s as well as her training in Kiwi and Chinese wuxia pian techniques that makes her a curious and charismatic object of study.

Like certain female stars of silent-era action-adventure serials who performed their own stunts, Zoë Bell serves a dual cinematic purpose, which I call a *narrative function* and a *material function*.[76] All well-developed characters have a narrative function, that is, the character's role in the development of the story and the effect this has on the spectator. The narrative function of any identifiable character lies in the degree to which their actions act as a catalyst for the story's development. This narrative function often adheres to the film star who plays diegetic characters. These stars also serve a material function, a corporeal contribution to the production, by virtue of their presence in front of the camera. The narrative function of a character often has a profound effect on the conditions of that star's material function. For example, Xena's narrative function in many early episodes is to rescue Gabrielle, her "female traveling companion," from harm, and the screen time that such endeavors required caused Lawless to spend very long hours on set, mimicking the fight choreography of the stunt actors in the service of performing her material function, her presence on set.

In contrast to the simultaneous material and narrative functions served by stars, stunt performers, some of whom have become popular in their own right, most often have only a material, nondiegetic function, namely, the stunt actor's physical performance as connected to a profilmic event. Stunties do not generally provide a narrative function, as they are not often given speaking roles that lead to character development. All actors and extras visible in the finished product fulfill a material function simply by having their likenesses captured by the camera; however, the spectator has a special relationship to the material function of certain stars and to stunting stars in particular.[77] This special relationship is fostered by the recurring presence of these stars and stunt performers in spectacular kinesthetic displays. Watching Fred Astaire and Ginger Rogers dancing in roller skates in the long-take sequence of *Shall We Dance* or seeing Bell's face clearly visible in long shot as she rides on the hood of a speeding car in Quentin Tarantino's *Death Proof* provides a spectatorial thrill quite distinct from the pleasures derived from knowing that Lawless was present on the *Xena* set to deliver lines for the camera.[78] As a stunting star, Zoë Bell occupies a unique position. On the one hand, the charismatic stunting star stands in stark contrast to other stunt performers because the stunting star is a known entity with a star text and other generic associations. Therefore, the corporeal existence of the stunting star as body spectacle is marked for viewers and may produce feelings of proximity or provoke more intense identification. On the other hand, the material function of the stunting star, which is not primarily based on broad audience recognition, leads to an acute connection with spectators that can more easily produce what Linda Williams has dubbed a "jerk reaction."[79] Bell's training as a double for Lucy Lawless helped her to prepare for her dual function as a jeopardized body. She has alluded to this in interviews: "I've sort of been acting for ten years without realizing it. . . . If you're not performing, not convincing the audience you're in jeopardy, and in pain or angry, then no one's going to engage with what you're doing."[80] This dual function distinguishes her from stars who do not perform their own stunts and from stunt performers who are not well known to the public.

Bell's rise and the return of the stunting star were made possible by the translation of a Chinese genre (the martial arts film) into a new national media context, facilitated by the cinephilic practices of the show's producers and New Zealand's cultural policies, which encouraged offshore production. *Xena*'s production context forced three acts of communicative translation: the sale of *Xena* as a compilation of Hong Kong wuxia sequences in preproduction, the reception and re-creation of these sequences by stunt coordinator Peter Bell, and the living embodiment of Zoë Bell performing and becoming a body spectacle. Zoë Bell's work on *Xena* prepared her for the material conditions of the *Kill Bill* set, though her bodily disposition was also transformed by the unique circumstances of working with a Hong Kong–trained choreographer, his stunt team, and the formal tendencies of Quentin Tarantino. Bell's status as a virtuoso was cemented by the star-making functions of her performances in *Double Dare* and *Death Proof*, as each film helped to establish a reception context in which Bell's narrative functions could be appreciated and her material functions could be mapped. The bodily disposition of the stunting star is a distinct marker of cultural histories of technique, translated and mediated by the exigencies of the global media marketplace. As I hope to have demonstrated, the bodily dispositions of expert stunting stars like Bell betray a complex history of translation.

FOUR

HONG KONG ACTION IN TRANSIT / The Postmillennial Stunt Craftwork of Chad Stahelski and Dayna Grant

This chapter posits a transnational approach to Hong Kong–style action media as a sensibility *in transit*—not as a sensibility in transition between a knowable origin point and a predictable terminus, but as a mode in constant motion in and between localities, an interstitial amalgam made of bodies and machines in a perpetual state of reformation, a style on the move. This movability was produced by a cinema in crisis, a "culture of disappearance," a flexible media workforce in motion, and the cross-border circulation and fervid reception of a cinema on fire.[1] As evidenced in the preceding chapters, Hong Kong–style action swiftly moved beyond the borders of the special administrative region (SAR), swelling in intensity in the mid- to late 1990s and early 2000s and spreading far and wide but not necessarily with equal impact. The previous chapters have looked at the effects of this movement via analyses of individual expert action performers; in this final chapter, we put on a wider lens and consider a more expansive approach. While we examine the work of Hollywood stuntman, coordinator, and stunt team founder Chad Stahelski as well as New Zealand stuntwoman, coordinator, and stunt work educator Dayna Grant in greater detail than the work of other expert performers in the final pages of this chapter, the larger goal of this chapter is to expand our analytic framework to consider the wide-scale effects of Hong Kong–style action on stunting craftwork in communities of practice operating in and across various national media contexts. In this final installment of *Experts in Action*, we return to Hollywood and New Zealand to better address why Hong Kong–style action thrives—or, more accurately, finds a greater facility of translation—in specific production contexts.

While transnational media flows and shifts in aesthetic traditions have at times been traced to a single film or television program, a single director, a single performer, or a single audience, such arguments are (at best) narratives of convenience. The movement of films and television programs, laborers, equipment, and media beyond borders requires mechanisms that tend to follow the well-worn paths of least resistance. Location-based financial incentives, trade policies, distribution patterns, migratory labor streams, and consumption histories sculpt this course. These processes produce media texts, objects, and personalities that seem to appear fully formed as pioneers. Neither Jackie Chan nor Bruce Lee introduced mediated versions of Chinese martial art forms to the English-speaking world, *Xena: Warrior Princess* was not the first Western television program to feature a female protagonist skilled in Asian martial arts, and Thailand was not the first Asian country to market its own Hong Kong–style action variant with an eye toward the global box office. Chan's late 1990s Hollywood coproductions, the action choreography for *Xena*, and the rise of new Thai action cinema are not worthy of study because they are originary (as they are not) but because these examples operate as tipping points most relevant in relation to the conditions that preceded their emergence and the effects on US, New Zealand, Thai, and other communities of stunting practice that followed. Shifts in performance traditions happen because expert action performers and film and television aesthetics work in transit, and technique and training are in a consistent state of flux because of this medial state of transnational industrial operation.

This chapter asserts that Hong Kong action aesthetics function in transit and beyond the realm of the singular influence of creative individuals. Experts in action work in teams that have been effected and affected by the transnational influence and circulation of Hong Kong–style action techniques and aesthetics. These same experts share the body knowledge they accumulate in transit with communities of practice in specific national production contexts. With these concerns in mind, I visited members of stunt communities of practice in the United States, the United Kingdom, Ireland, and New Zealand to assess, among other things, the conditions of national and transnational stunt production and the effects of Hong Kong–style action aesthetics in distinct but networked stunt communities, each with their own production cultures, labor structures, and regulatory frameworks.

This chapter first positions Hong Kong–style action in transit (as a collection of techniques, technologies, workers, and production structures) in relation to common and similarly aligned scholarly approaches to transnational media and transnational Hong Kong action cinema. Following this, the chapter delineates the similarities in regulatory and production contexts that facilitate (e.g., flexibility, off-site production, limited oversight) or hinder (e.g., strict division of labor, training and regulation of stunt communities) the replication or reimagining of Hong Kong–style action in other geographic contexts. Third, I posit the specific contributions of this style to transnational stunting traditions and craftwork. And, last, this chapter examines the work of stunt team labor in Hollywood via an analysis of the work of both Chad Stahelski and his 87eleven Action Design team and stuntwoman Dayna Grant and her team on the New Zealand–produced horror-comedy television program *Ash vs Evil Dead* in order to historicize the effects of Hong Kong–style action in transit on stunting craftwork.[2]

Action in Transit

In the wake of the increasing Western circulation of Hong Kong cinema, stars, directors, and choreographers in the 1990s, film and media studies scholars took note, and the field of English-language transnational Hong Kong cinema studies experienced its own millennial tipping point. In the flurry of scholarly activity that attended the rise in circulation of Hong Kong aesthetics in the 1990s, three monographs made lasting contributions on the subject of transnational action: David Bordwell's *Planet Hong Kong: Popular Cinema and the Art of Entertainment* advanced a formal-analytical framework that dissected the unique characteristics of Hong Kong action cinema; Esther Ching-mei Yau's anthology, *At Full Speed: Hong Kong Cinema in a Borderless World*, addressed the pace of production and consumption of transnational Hong Kong cinema; and Meaghan Morris, Siu Leung Li, and Stephen Chan Ching-kiu's collection *Hong Kong Connections: Transnational Imagination in Action Cinema* provided a lens through which to view the transnational histories of Hong Kong action cinemas.[3] These books delineated the unique qualities of action films from the SAR, and this chapter owes them a scholarly debt—my consideration of Hong Kong–style action in transit revitalizes these books' thematics: speed, border crossing, a return to form and greater attention to numerous tipping points in the transitional history of Hong Kong–style action in the context of transnational stunt labor.

Bordwell's *Planet Hong Kong* calls for closer attention to formal analytics and proclaims a cross-cultural approach premised on the universality of popular cinema. Bordwell's book aims to demystify the means by which premillennial Hong Kong cinema achieved international popularity by creating films that were simultaneously artful and entertaining. Bordwell discounts the degree to which his position as an outsider might lead to a culture-blind analysis because popular cinema is "designed to cross cultural boundaries" and, he argues, is more dependent on images than on spoken language.[4] While we should never discount our relative geopolitical and cultural positions as informing our analytic processes, Bordwell's contention that many Hong Kong films were designed for both foreign and domestic consumption is, of course, accurate. His detailed analysis of editing patterns and cinematographic decisions is profoundly productive in that he outlines formal similarities and distinctions between Hong Kong and Hollywood action style. *Experts in Action*, and this chapter in particular, like *Planet Hong Kong*, lays bare the formal properties of action style and addresses the extent to which style crosses borders, but it does so to a slightly different effect and with an emphasis on the labor necessary to produce stylistic innovation.

Published within a year of *Planet Hong Kong*, another key text contending with the transnationality of Hong Kong film, Yau's anthology, *At Full Speed*, positions Hong Kong cinema "as a highly visible component of changing world styles" premised on an intensified speed of production and consumption.[5] This chapter addresses the worldliness of this "visible component" in great detail by historicizing style in relationship to the flow of stunt craft traditions through networked production contexts. The third book to transform the field of Hong Kong action scholarship, Morris, Li, and Ching-kiu's collection *Hong Kong Connections*, addresses the historical circumstances of Hong Kong action cinema's transnational appeal. In the introduction to the collection, Morris initiates a critical call to arms to which this chapter, and *Experts in Action* as a whole, is a willing and enthusiastic response: "The vicissitudes of this wildly inventive, commercially hybrid geo-political imaginary of combat (and the force of *Ong-bak's* riposte to its impact in Thai cinema) suggest a historical depth to the transnational invocation and contextually complex uptake of the Hong Kong action 'model' that students of intercultural dialogue and cross-cultural media circulation, as well as of film industries, national film cultures, and their relays in domestic, regional, and global popular cultural formations, might want to investigate more closely."[6] To probe the depths of the transnational appeal and adaptability of the "Hong Kong action model," I propose that we approach action design from the perspective of stunt labor, and to best accomplish this task, we must yet again reconsider what specifically we mean by the term *transnational*. It has been over a decade since the last of these books was released, and in that time the concept of "Chinese cinemas" has been reworked and redefined, and the term *transnational* has been contested but also elaborated on as a series of microprocesses.

Some scholars have suggested that the term *transnational* may have outlived its usefulness to discussions of Chinese-language mediascapes (and of media more generally). Though scholarship on transnational media proliferates at an ever-increasing rate to keep up with the vagaries of academic fashion, often very little ground is gained, and the subfield of transnational media studies at times resembles an amorphous blob devouring every media object in its path with even the vaguest hint of national difference. If you will allow me the sin of overgeneralization, transnational media studies is divided into scholarship that addresses transnational film and television without defining the stakes of transnational analysis and scholarship that engages with the concept of media transnationality in great detail, proffering new frameworks through which to understand modern globalized media relations and relationships. This second type of scholarship provides us with key terms that have clarified and delineated the boundaries of the transnational as an episteme, for example, *accented cinema, the new international division of cultural labor, media contra-flows, poly/translocality*, and *assemblages*. Hamid Naficy describes films made by diasporic and exilic subjects using artisanal production models, in opposition to the design of dominant cinema, as "accented" and identifies recurrent thematics, including displacement, interstitiality, and synesthesia, among many other attributes.[7] Naficy's reconception of diasporic and exilic production practices might seem less applicable to popular Hong Kong–style action media, but one must certainly consider action design techniques inherited from the production practices of Hong Kong choreographers working abroad as accented. Additionally, Toby Miller, Nitin Govil, John McMurria, and Richard Maxwell's coinage, *the new international division of cultural labor,*, advanced transnational media scholarship in prioritizing the discussion of flexible labor in any discussion of globalized media and the shift in Hollywood production and postproduction models.[8] Daya Kishan Thussu proposes the term *contra-flow* to describe the mobility of media as a form of "reverse traffic" against the stream of US-dominated media production while also calling into question the effectiveness of contra-flows from the periphery against seemingly insurmountable competition from the United States.[9] Though Thussu might characterize Hong Kong–style action production as a "subaltern flow" or as part of "Easternisation," the coimbricated relationship between Hong Kong and Hollywood action media production in the 1990s and beyond suggests a more complex directionality than dominant and contra flows, and as we will see, any examination of the mobility of Hong Kong–style action in transit must approach movement through a convoluted and complex network.

We have learned so much since Sheldon Hsiao-peng Lu's field-changing characterization of mainland Chinese, Taiwanese, Hong Kong, and diasporic Chinese films as "transnational Chinese cinemas" in 1997.[10] Recent scholarship has expanded on this work by proposing alternative frameworks that accommodate the wealth of articulations, models, and structures that constitute Chinese-language media. While we may have come to accept the transnational as a more specific framework through which to view globalization, the term *transnational* still fails to directly address relationships of production, distribution, marketing, exhibition, and reception with a specificity that somehow remains universally applicable across borders and media forms. As the production, circulation, and afterlives of media objects have become increasingly transnational, now is not the time to abandon this scholarly paradigm. This is our moment to contend with the transnationality of media, not as an amorphous blob swelling to a state of ubiquity, but as a set of specific and yet highly differentiated operations of power (on bodies) needing to be contextualized and historicized. While this book introduces conceptual frameworks to better understand the specific transnational operations of power in each of its case studies (e.g., risk economies, Hong Kong action cinema as a mode, communicative translation, a craftwork in transit within networked communities of practice), this project draws heavily from the amazing work that has already been done by other scholars; in particular, this chapter relies on previous interventions in the field by scholars who have addressed transnational labor conditions and proposed useful frameworks for analysis, such as Nitin Govil, Sylvia J. Martin, and Ying-jin Zhang.

Stephen J. Collier and Aihwa Ong propose the term *assemblage* as a way to more specifically navigate the structural transformations of culture in relation to globalization. They argue that "as global forms are articulated in specific situations — or territorialized as assemblages — they define new material, collective, and discursive relationships. These global assemblages are sites for the formation and re-formation of what we will call . . . anthropological problems."[11] Collier and Ong position the assemblage as a more specific way to address transnational flows that have technological, political, and ethical implications for the biological and social life of humans. Nitin Govil adapts Collier and Ong's term to media economies as he finds it far more specific to the "dynamic associations" of industries, financiers, markets, and individuals than the evacuated term *globalization* when discussing the shifting and circuitous relationships between Hollywood and Asian economies.[12] Following Govil, Sylvia J. Martin describes "the varying configurations of local production and transnational conventions, the uprooted media workers . . . as media assemblages."[13] Media assemblages, defined by Martin as cross-cultural collections of practices, workers, and production structures, a common effect of transnational media flows, are an operational dynamic of Hong Kong–style action in transit. Martin already elaborates effectively on the specific conditions of Hong Kong stunt labor in her book *Haunted: An Ethnography of the Hollywood and Hong Kong Media Industries*, treating stunt labor as an anthropological problem. Simultaneously borrowing from Martin's approach and expanding on it, this chapter considers the effects of the cross-border flow of techniques and individual workers on stunt labor collectives as media assemblages.

Yingjin Zhang provides the endlessly generative neologisms *translocal* and *polylocal* to describe cinema production and distribution practices. Grand-scale media production is polylocal in that it requires large labor forces working in different localities (often production hubs problematically dubbed "creative cities"). Production and distribution are also translocal in that relationships between geographic locations require systematized coordination, and projects move through distinct but networked localities at various stages of the process between preproduction and release. Zhang illustrates the function of his approach to Chinese cinema as a historical method not confined by linearity: "Chinese cinema as translocal practice strives . . . 'to capture multiplicity, not totality — perspectival insight, not empyrean oversight,' as well as to 'construct a history without closure, one that can be entered through many points and can unfold through many coherent, informed, and focused narrative lines.'"[14] A consideration of Hong Kong–style action in transit not only relies on Zhang's spatial lexicon for transnational media production but also inherits his nuanced approach to history as spatialized, networked, and entangled.

As addressed in the previous chapters, the Hong Kong film industry collapsed in the mid- to late 1990s as a result of numerous factors including the geographic flexibility of above-the-line Hong Kong film industry talent (the movement of Hong Kong stars and directors first to Hollywood and later to mainland China), the effects of the SARS (severe acute respiratory syndrome) epidemic on exhibition, the funding shortfall caused by the Asian financial crisis and the forcing out of the triads by the Anti-Triad Ordinance, the looming threat of the 1997 handover to China, and the rise of Chinese coproductions after the Mainland and Hong Kong Closer Economic Partnership Arrangement. As each of the preceding chapters makes clear, as local cinema production plummeted, Hong Kong–style action aesthetics resurfaced translated and transformed in other geographic contexts. The production context of these transformative processes can take many forms including assemblage, translocal arrangements, and communicative translations of "a cinema without a nation, a local cinema with transnational appeal."[15] The paradigms of assemblage, translocality, polylocality, and the New International Division of Cultural Labor are integral to the operation of Hong Kong–style action in transit because each is an effect of the circulation and stratification of non-nation-specific labor forces. Communities of stunting practice are networked far beyond the boundaries of individual nation-states or even regional media production contexts, and this network incorporates diverse and expansive performance traditions that predate cinema, including martial arts, gymnastics, acrobatics, circus arts, rodeo, and Wild West shows.

Hong Kong–style action operates transnationally to the extent that it has influenced and altered, through acts of translation and the effects of assemblage, the craftwork of stunt communities of practice in various regions, but this operation is not uniform or complete. There was not a unilateral rollout of Hong Kong–style action globally after 1994; transnational media flows are rarely that organized. Hong Kong may have been a transnational media industry from its inception, but it took changes in exhibition markets, legal and illegal video circulation, state-sanctioned soft-money funds, regional economies, and cultural policies for Hong Kong–style action to go global. Such processes are never equal or synchronous and, as such, are rarely truly global. Hong Kong–style action has infiltrated various communities of stunting practice through various means (assemblages with Hong Kong workers, translocal productions aimed at communicative translation, and tactical attempts to address Chinese audiences), but the aesthetics and techniques associated with Hong Kong action cinema of the 1980s and 1990s flourish most in very specific contexts with not only a history of producing this style of action but also flexible structures of production that closely mimic those operative in Hong Kong during the 1980s and 1990s.

Production Contexts in Transit

The following pages identify the historical and industrial conditions for action design both in Hong Kong and in other localized production contexts that have inherited or closely approximated Hong Kong action style. Three craftwork contexts had the greatest effect on both the techniques and the aesthetics of action design in the SAR: local craft traditions, the observation of foreign craft techniques and tools in transit, and the adaptation of craft techniques deduced from the importation and circulation of foreign films in Hong Kong. The absence of intense regulatory frameworks and the lack of collective bargaining arrangements for stunt personnel, actors, and choreographers led to a comparatively intensified speed of production and a flexible labor structure, which Sylvia J. Martin has demonstrated is still common to Hong Kong media productions.[16] Such conditions foster an improvisational work environment in which experts are forced to draw from their training histories in stunt work and other corporeal craft traditions, experiment through a (seemingly dangerous) trial-and-error process that mimics deliberate-practice activities, and, in so doing, generate distinctive and captivating body spectacles.

Hong Kong–style action design for films of the prewar period adapted techniques from other local craft traditions, including martial arts, Cantonese opera, Peking opera, gymnastics, and the circus. Bryan Chang explains that two of the most easily identifiable performance traditions to influence Hong Kong action design are northern and southern opera techniques and martial arts. He explains that, following the influx of opera and martial arts techniques into the wuxia shenguai pian, or "martial arts-magic spirit films," a skill set developed for film production, and a professional class of action designers emerged in the process:

> As opera personnel began to gain a foothold in the staging of combat, martial artists from various disciplines gravitated toward the industry. The first group recruited en masse was the "dragon–tiger stuntman." They base their craft on either opera moves or Chinese martial arts, producing fight scenes that addressed the illusionary nature of the film.

What they provided were in fact performing techniques cured specifically for the camera, either distilled from experience or simply invented by novices who adapted quickly to filmmaking. A profession began to materialize.[17]

Opera contributed what Yung Sai-shing refers to as an "actor-oriented" engagement with the performer's skilled body, a type of virtuoso reception context. Hong Kong action aesthetics emphasize movement, and the framing and editing privilege the actor's skilled body in motion.[18] In addition, not only did the first *dragon-tiger stuntmen* (*longhu wushi*; 龍虎武師), an early industry term for expert on-screen fighters, more commonly originate from opera, as discussed in chapter 1, but the four primary Peking opera academies established in Hong Kong after 1949 (the China Drama Academy, Spring and Autumn Drama School, Eastern Drama Academy, and Chung Wah Drama Academy) produced the most accomplished and prolific choreographers, stunt performers, and action stars to work in the local industry.[19] The Hong Kong action style inherited acrobatic movement, timing, and group dynamics from the opera, and, as Chang argues, "movement-pause" and "extend-withdraw" posturing from various Chinese martial arts traditions:

> Movement and pause for example. In single unit encompasses the start of movement to the pause of movement. An exchange lasting a few seconds to over a minute, comprises a series of units, with which combatants are engaged in offenses and defenses as well as movements and pauses. The exchanges in turn function as units in linear deployment of action, punctuated by withdrawals, which are in fact units of pauses, involving resumption of breathing patterns and/or the posing to prepare for the next strike. Linked together, the alternating exchanges and withdrawals make up a fight scene.[20]

These techniques, adapted from martial arts craft traditions of sparring and forms training, generate both the rhythmic patterns and the physio-dynamics of the complex multibeat combat structures most common to Hong Kong–style action design in transit. As Craig D. Reid explains, Hollywood action choreography historically (before the influx of talent from Hong Kong) favored "beginning-end edits" that showcased the start of a motion (for example, the film star's fist is propelled through the air toward a face with the actor's visage clearly visible) and the anticipated completion of that motion (a stuntman's face receiving the full impact of the punch).[21]

Many contemporary US film and television fight scenes now follow the staging, pace, framing, and editing traditions of the "movement-pause" and "extend-withdraw" style common to Hong Kong. The practice is now so common that even a fantasy action television program like *Game of Thrones*, produced in Northern Ireland, follows the same combat format; as stunt coordinator Rowley Irlam explains, "Generally, as you attack you move forward and as you defend, you move back."[22] Post-*Matrix* and post-*Xena*, there is a much greater emphasis on a performer's range of movement and an increase in "series of units," termed *fight beats* in stunt communities of practice, that performers must memorize and articulate.[23] Though stunt communities of practice outside of Hong Kong have absorbed and adapted these techniques that originated in Chinese opera or martial arts training and have integrated them into transnational film and television action aesthetics, the flow of craft tools and technique is not unidirectional.

Hong Kong stunt communities of practice borrowed instruments and methods from the in-transit stunt laborers and teams with whom they came into contact, and they also designed new accouterments and strategies to reproduce special-effect designs they observed in foreign imports. As foreign film production increased in Hong Kong from the postwar period to the present, Hong Kong stunties, choreographers, and riggers observed and assimilated stunt craftwork and tools from these production communities in transit, including the most regularly available and practical form of safety equipment used in most stunt industries today: the cardboard box. Local stunt teams witnessed the use of cardboard boxes as a mechanism to offset the impact from a fall when the 1965 French comedy-adventure film *Les tribulations d'un Chinois et Chine* was filmed in Hong Kong.[24] Hong Kong action director Chan Siu-pang (陳少鵬) explains, "Before, when we shot people jumping off the second or third floor, there would only be straw and bedding beneath. After *Les Tribulations* brought cardboard boxes here, we began to use cardboard boxes."[25] Large quantities of cardboard boxes are readily available at low cost in major shipping hubs and port cities, and the transnational circulation of media labor as well as the push toward a flexible specialization model furthered the adoption of this staple of stunt industry protective equipment in all large-scale polylocal and translocal production hubs. Chan clarifies that Hong Kong stunt workers borrowed the tool from the French and that when the US production *The Sand Pebbles* was shot in Hong Kong, the crew used more technologically advanced air cushions as fall protection, but the Hong Kong stunt team favored the lower-budget cardboard box option.[26] The prohibitive cost of advanced devices like air cushions, along with the degree to which Hong Kong film production budgets operate on a per-film basis without a separate account for larger purchases that can be factored into a studio's overhead, means that to this day cardboard boxes are still preferred to and more trusted than advanced air-cushion technology in Hong Kong stunt communities of practice.[27]

While identifying the history of stunt craftwork is a project to which all scholars of action media should be finely attuned, fixing or fixating on the moment of origin or crossover for the transnational flow of stunt craft is less productive (and also less possible) than identifying the means by which the tools, skills, and techniques spread in relation to media laborers in transit. Prominent action directors like Chan Siupang and Tong Kai (唐佳) disagree on how cardboard box rigs became standard stunt equipment in Hong Kong. While Chan argues that Hong Kong stunt crews borrowed the technique from French crews working locally in Hong Kong, Tong claims to have imported the use of box rigs into Hong Kong after watching stunt crews use them abroad.[28] The instant of adoption is unlikely to be fixed in this murky chronology because, as other authors have demonstrated, invention and adaptation are processes with multiple points of origin and intersecting trajectories. Stunt craftwork is best historicized through an analysis of the conditions that led to recombinant expressions of tool and technique, as in many other networked histories of media production. The operational dynamic of laborers in transit enabled this exchange of technique and continues to foster narratives of discovery. The cardboard box rig is common to stunt communities of practice in Hong Kong, Hollywood, New Zealand, Ireland, the United Kingdom, South Africa, France, and countless other countries because of the postwar new international division of cultural labor that Toby Miller and colleagues identify.[29] Though much of the capital accumulated on the backs of media laborers flows in predictable directions, craft knowledge and tradition do not. Not all craftwork pathways originate, flourish, or terminate in Hollywood.

The movement of stunt labor through major communities of stunting practice is not the only means by which technique has moved between localities. Adaptation, addressed in chapter 3 of this book in the form of communicative translation, can be a definitive practice for particular stunt communities. Though Hong Kong action design is well regarded for a commanding use of wirework, Hong Kong's most highly regarded wire rig designer adapted techniques he observed and deduced from the Hollywood film *Superman*.[30] Tsui Hark (徐克), a director-producer commonly known as the "Steven Spielberg of Hong Kong" owing to his emphasis on special effects and his integration of special-effects craft techniques from Hollywood, instructed his action design team to watch *Superman* as inspiration for wirework rig design, as action director Fung Hak-on (馮克安) explains: "Tsui Hark made us watch many films for reference. We played *Superman* (78) shot by shot to study how the wire is used. How come Superman can soar into the skies, descend to put the woman down, say goodbye to her and fly away in one continuous action? We've finally discovered the secret when we rewound the tape—on freeze frame, we could tell that a metal rack was used."[31]

The observation and analysis of action design techniques from *Superman* helped Hong Kong stunt craft workers to redesign their wirework rigs to allow for more elaborate movement without an overreliance on cheat cuts. Eventually, Lee Kwan-lung (李坤龍), as part of a props division, working in collaboration with the stunt team, designed a wire rig using a mobile metal rack system that allowed for the fluid and dynamic movement associated with the modern wuxia film.[32] The close relationship between stunt workers and the props department (sometimes known as *art direction* or the *art department*) in most production contexts has greatly facilitated adapted stunt craft techniques. Much like the preproduction context for action design for *Xena: Warrior Princess*, Hong Kong action design teams did not learn all techniques through direct observation. There is a tradition of avid viewership of technique, via screening and detailed analysis of action design in scenes from films and television programs, as a learning tool in many stunt communities of practice. Through this process these communities are indirectly exposed to craft techniques from other communities and localities. These techniques are reconstructed through trial and error and adapted based on available resources and the bodily dispositions of local experts within that stunt craft community.

Sylvia J. Martin's illuminating ethnographic research into the stunt industry in Hong Kong, as well as the volume of interviews with action choreographers published by the Hong Kong International Film Festival, provides rare insight into the conditions of stunt labor production in the SAR and the transnational history of techniques employed by action design teams there in relation to regulatory structures, worker protections, and the movement of stunt craft in transit. Martin's subjects repeatedly characterize "flexibility" as a primary characteristic of Hong Kong media production owing to the post-Fordist production environment, which both encouraged and necessitated improvisation. She positions this flexibility in opposition to the rigidity of Hollywood production contexts, which have a strict division of labor, with job titles and regimented duties reinforced by contractual obligations. Martin points out that her informants "attributed the industry's success to its 'openness' and its colonial economic policies of laissez-faire, especially when contending with vague and restrictive stipulations imposed by Chinese authorities and ministries."[33] She expounds that such colonialist policies were designed to foster the growth of "right-wing companies" like Shaw Brothers.[34] Great Britain's laissez-faire approach to the Hong Kong film industry encouraged an increase in production but offered no protections for the labor force that facilitated it.

The lack of government intervention is not the only regulatory distinction between Hollywood and Hong Kong; the structure (and aid in gainful employment) provided by long-standing guilds and trade unions incubated particular craft practices. Martin explains that the historical union presence in Hollywood effected a labor environment that is anathema to Hong Kong stunt workers (and other production personnel) and that while the latter's lack of protection leads to a contingent work environment, her research subjects "were shocked at the degree to which people's jobs are defined and protected in Hollywood, many of them citing the preferred 'flexibility' of the Hong Kong film and television industry—in which, ostensibly, any group of people do 'whatever it takes' to get things done—as a much more commonsensical and practical approach."[35] The flexible production environment in Hong Kong, in which tasks and labor relations are not contractually mandated, made it possible for Hong Kong action designers and stunt choreographers to control cinematography and editing for action scenes in a manner that was uncommon in Hollywood. Some Hong Kong action designers like Yuen Woo-ping could work around the regimented Hollywood system as a stunt laborer in transit without union allegiances owing to the confusion and concealment created by off-site production: "I didn't join any of the unions because most of the films I was involved in weren't shot in America. *The Matrix* was shot in Australia. After four months of actor training in the States, we all headed to Australia to shoot. I didn't have to join any local Australian unions. As for *Kill Bill*, that was shot in China, definitely no unions there."[36]

The off-site production of these films meant that Yuen could hide in plain sight. Working with Quentin Tarantino and the Wachowski sisters, who were enamored of his Hong Kong oeuvre, Yuen had close to the same authority to determine camera placement, movement, and editing that he has in Hong Kong. Hong Kong action designer Stephen Tung Wai (董瑋) was surprised by the limited control afforded to fight choreographers and stunt coordinators in Hollywood. He was informed that second-unit directors would have control over the finished product and that he would need to join the Directors Guild of America to be afforded the same degree of respect and input that he had come to expect on set in Hong Kong: "When I arrived in Hollywood to work, I asked for control over shot angles and editing, otherwise my best work wouldn't surface. But they have their system, and in the end, they advised me to join the Directors Guild. This way, I could work as a '2nd unit director' and shoot Hong Kong style."[37] As more Hong Kong action directors worked in transit in Hollywood productions at the close of the past millennium, Hong Kong stunt craft traditions moved with them. Though Hong Kong stunt workers were forced to either adapt to or circumvent the rigidity of Hollywood's division of labor, their very presence transformed Hollywood stunt craft. The techniques and tools common to Hong Kong stunt communities of practice are evident not only in the United States but even more readily in other localities that mirror the flexibility of the Hong Kong media production context.

Craftwork/Communities of Stunting Practice

While the earlier pages of this chapter addressed the effects of location-specific industrial labor processes on stunt work, the following pages delineate the parameters of Hong Kong–style stunt craft beyond the borders of the SAR. They do so, first, by positioning stunt work as a craft and in relation to communities of stunting practice, which are affected by expert performers and craft traditions in transit, and, second, by identifying specific types of stunt craft as effected by these same experts and traditions in transit.

Stunt labor is best classified as *craftwork*, an underanalyzed designation for below-the-line labor in both media industries and live-performance traditions. Mark Banks has used the term *craftwork* "not just to refer to the common *specific* crafts (such as woodworking, jewelry-making, ceramics, embroidery and the like) but more broadly to describe *an input of the industrial labour process* and the attitude or mind-set that configures that labour."[38] Following Banks, I contend that stunt work develops its own craft traditions based on both location-specific industrial labor processes and the movement of stunt workers in transit. It is through homegrown and imported (and also adapted) craftwork that identifiable "localized" stunt craft traditions emerge. I hesitate to call such traditions *glocal* as that is too broad a term to address the specific pathways and networks through which these techniques circulate, and there are dominant techniques from specific regions (Hong Kong, Hollywood, etc.), but those techniques are not universal and are routinely displaced. Nor are these practices simply translocal, as the flow and transformation of stunt craft exceed the relationships between polarized creative cities. The means by which stunt craft becomes localized is certainly exemplary of the media assemblage paradigm favored by Martin and Govil, but any in-depth consideration of stunt craft as transnational forces us to contend with histories of craftwork that far exceed the temporal and spatial confines of "media" as a useful delineation, as stunt craft lineages can be traced to live-performance traditions beyond the scope of any media paradigm.

The Craftwork of Stunt Work

It is key to contextualize the ways in which craftwork has historically been defined as well as the degree to which craftwork as a model operates in the current division of labor common to many media industries. Doing so allows us to not only better frame stunt work as craft but also identify the inherent biases in the division between "artistic" and "craft" screen labor, which have resulted in an absence of historical and theoretical work on stunt communities in film and media studies. The degree to which stunt work has been positioned as craft, as well as film and media studies' internalization of the cultural logics of the division of labor in media industries (which relegate craftwork to a lower position than artistic work), has resulted in approaches to action that are more concerned with stars (as images or texts) and directors (as progenitors of form and theme) than with the work of action design. Such approaches, so common to action film and television studies, regularly obscure the labor of the stunt worker, stunt team, and stunt coordinator. As Richard de Cordova points out, performance analyses need to be genre specific: "The ways that different genres circumscribe the form and position of performance in film is an important and underdeveloped area in genre studies."[39] One of the failings of many previous approaches to performance in action film and television is that they neglected to address the performance of action with any specificity to action design and instead addressed performance in action much as the field would any other genre. This tendency in action media analysis could be rectified by greater attention to stunt craft. Banks argues that "analysis of craft labour is necessary, then, partly to avoid overestimating the contribution of the artist to the production of cultural goods (a common trait amongst proselytizers of the 'creative' labour process), but also because craft is itself significant in the context of the range of often hidden (nonartistic) labour tasks that make up cultural and creative industries production."[40] While I would actively contest any distinction between "craft" and "artistry," many media industries certainly operate on this distinction, and the field of film and media studies has most assuredly spent a good deal of our history romanticizing the work of the artist as an individual worthy of analysis, even if done in the service of deconstruction.

Banks outlines a general history of craft labor that also aligns with the developmental history of Hollywood stunt communities of practice, including the formation of hierarchically structured workshops with experts, intermediates, and novices in attendance.[41] He considers the workshop model a defining element of modern cultural work, explaining that, "in craft production, control over conception, design, and manufacture of a cultural good is possessed by an individual or small groups of workers, operating at close quarters in 'workshop' conditions. In cultural industries, this is both prevalent and necessary."[42] Though the workshop model was displaced by industrial capitalism in favor of the assembly line of factories, the workshop persisted in other forms and became an operational framework of trade guilds and unions. Though many Hollywood studios operated on a Fordist model of production common to industrial capitalism, in the early years of this system many film craft workers banded together to form unions; as Michael Curtin and Kevin Sanson explain, "Craft also served as the most pervasive principle for labor organizing during the 1930s when actors, set dressers, and carpenters each aligned themselves with unions or locals that were identified with particular job categories."[43] The early labor collectives operated on the traditional craft workshop model, which has remained a common element of the stunt craft in Hollywood, Hong Kong, New Zealand, the United Kingdom, Ireland, and South Africa as well as many other countries. This workshop model is a fundamental framework of stunt team work and greatly contributes to the spread of technique when expert members of the team acquire skills in transit. The workshop model, which unites experts, intermediates, and novice stunt performers, makes possible the transmission and adaptation of stunt craft traditions and specializations from other geographic locations because expert stunt performers may operate in teams but a flexible labor market keeps them on the move, constantly looking for new work.

A second key characteristic of craft labor that is also an inherent property of stunt labor is the tendency of the stunt personnel for a film, television show, commercial, or live performance to remain unnamed and unrecognized by stars, directors, and studio publicity machines. This depersonalization has been an operational logic of craftwork since antiquity according to Richard Sennett: "Archaic craftsmen experienced a kindred impersonality; [they] were frequently addressed in public by the names of their profession. All craftsmanship, indeed, has something of this impersonal character. That the quality of work is impersonal can make the practice of craftsmanship seem unforgiving."[44] Craftspeople were known by their occupation and not by their proper name. Their work was seen as interchangeable with that of any other craft worker with an identical title. The tendency to see craft laborers as interchangeable and to withhold their names is still common to media industries and particularly insidious in its operation in relation to stunt labor. Within stunt communities, experts who have demonstrated their skills consistently and with increasing complexity of execution are hired by stunt coordinators based on their reputations and are often known entities, because, as Curtin and Sanson point out, "craft identities fostered standards of excellence and achievement within each job category, and they provided a context for workers to pursue recognition from managers and colleagues."[45] Though stunt performers need and desire to distinguish themselves within their peer group in a transnationally competitive labor market, their work regularly remains publicly unheralded through a depersonalization process that is designed to both highlight and embellish on a star's physical contributions to stunt work and fight choreography. While stars will sometimes mention that stunt doubles work with them, they rarely name these performers and commonly take credit for the work of their stunt doubles. In numerous interviews with stunt workers in different national contexts, I was told that having stars take credit for your work is an expected, if disappointing, part of the job and that through experience stunt workers learn to remain silent about the practice if they wish to continue working in their chosen profession.

Communities of Stunting Practice: Not Art versus Craft

We must strive to make visible the contributions of individual stunt laborers and stunt teams, to name them, and to introduce the nomenclature of stunt craftwork to the field of film and media studies. Identifying these performers, collectives, and techniques allows both aesthetic analyses and histories of action design to begin to bring into view the people and topics previously unobserved and underserved by action studies. Such content includes the transnational flow and adaptation of stunt craft technique, commonly effected by the movement of expert stunt performers in and between communities of stunting practice (or workshops) within and beyond their home countries. Though the workshop model is a productive way to envision and historicize the social dynamics and collective labor processes of craftwork, an additional useful designation to describe these groups is *communities of practice*. As Maureen Guirdham explains, "A community of practice is a collection of people who engage on an ongoing basis in some common endeavor. Organizational communities of practice bring together people with common work-related interest and knowledge from across distributed units and locations of organizations."[46] Though seemingly similar to the craft workshop, the concept of communities of practice—developed by Jean Lave and Etienne Wenger to explain how learning happens in communal settings—is key to understanding the extent to which the national landscape for stunt craftwork is transformed by communal learning environments.[47] Of primary importance to this process are two factors: the presence of a slightly shifting group of novices, intermediates, and experts (drawn from the workshop model) in each community of stunting practice and the degree to which these communities are both plural and networked within transnational media production contexts. Communities of practice are not intrinsically limited by gender, race, or national origin, though they can be extrinsically limited by the biases of institutionalized hiring practices within craft traditions.[48] The movement of stunt workers between communities of practice facilitates shared technique, and as members of individual stunt communities of practice climb the ranks from novice to expert, they have a greater effect on the education of newer members of the group. Through this process stuntman Chad Stahelski introduced techniques he had learned in Hong Kong to the US stunt craft market, and stuntwoman Dayna Grant shared the Kiwi-adapted Hong Kong–style wirework techniques she learned on *Xena: Warrior Princess*.

A plenitude of phrases have been proffered to define laborers working in film, television, and new-media industries: *cultural laborers, creative laborers, knowledge workers, cognitive workers, media makers,* and so on. Each of these always-imperfect terms factionalizes the labor force within and beyond those working in media industries, and each holds its own political resonance within the field of film and media studies. We can avoid many of the pitfalls of the dialectics inherent in the use of these terms (cognitive vs. corporeal, knowledgeable vs. unskilled or deskilled, creative professional vs. culture industry pawn) by focusing on the specificities of training and by employing the concepts of experts and expertise. Identifying individual members of the labor force and groups of workers as experts (or novices) does not replicate the factionalism that divides workers of the world into mental or physical laborers, as such divisions (regardless of any attempts at nuance made by certain authors) both replicate the ideological underpinnings of the division of labor inherent to neoliberalism and perpetuate a scientifically false dichotomy. All human and animal workers are hired for and rely on their cognitive abilities, all human and animal workers have an embodied relationship to work, and all human and animal workers are trained before and during acts of labor.

While the legal, financial, and nonunionized or unionized structures of industrial production may be location specific and deterministic for craft, stunting craftwork occurs in transnational media economies that privilege flexible specialization, with skilled laborers locally trained and/or geographically mobile. The transnational nature of the production process and the movement of individual laborers in search of work produce stunt communities of practice rooted in local traditions (e.g., training, workshops, teams, guilds, techniques, domains of physical expertise) but also influenced by labor forces and individuals in transit that introduce, teach, and adapt techniques from stunt communities of practice in other locations. As demonstrated earlier in the chapter, Hong Kong stunt craft techniques have been inherited and adapted from other traditions in transit and have also influenced stunt craft technique elsewhere in the world through the movement of Hong Kong stunt laborers abroad to work in US, UK, Irish, and New Zealand productions. One of the great misconceptions regarding the influence of Hong Kong action aesthetics abroad after 1997 is that Hong Kong–style action films and television programs all stem from direct Asian involvement, either produced in Asian countries or produced in the United States with Hong Kong action choreographers. However, as the influence of Hong Kong stunt craft grew after the 1997 handover through the networked transnational system of stunt labor in transit, Hong Kong action aesthetics began to dominate production in localized media industries far removed from Hong Kong, such as in Auckland, New Zealand, and became more common in Hollywood productions without Hong Kong laborers. Martial arts, broadly defined as structured forms of corporeal training for combat, sport, and performance, have been common since the early days of American cinema, in particular in boxing films. Nevertheless, the particular style of fight choreography (more fight beats per shot); the power of the action choreographer/stunt coordinator and stunt team to influence cinematography, editing, and mise-en-scène; and the increased, innovative, and flexible use of wirework rigs are decidedly new Hong Kong influences on transnational stunt craft. The two greatest turning points in this modern history are linked to the production of *The Matrix* in Australia with an in-transit stunt team led by Yuen Woo-ping and, as stated in chapter 3, the production of *Xena: Warrior Princess* in New Zealand. The commercial success of both of these productions had long-standing effects on both the transnational visual economy for stunting and fight design for film and television and the careers of at least two expert stunt performers trained on these sets: Chad Stahelski and Dayna Grant.

Expert Stunt Craft in Context: Chad Stahelski and Dayna Grant and the Function of Action Previz

Hollywood and New Zealand stunt communities of practice introduced new stunt craft techniques adapted from and influenced by working alongside Hong Kong fight choreographers in the years following *Xena*'s communicative translation of Hong Kong–style action design and the transnational production and wide release of *The Matrix*. The incorporation of these techniques, such as the implementation of *previz* (also spelled *previs*) videos, featuring extended multibeat fight sequences with complex choreography, led to an industrial preference for experts trained in martial arts and intersectional bodily domains, as well as the redistribution of the division of creative labor for action sequences. The networked nature of stunt communities of practice meant that these techniques were shared and circulated under workshop models, through individual film productions and recurring television series and through the "stunt schools" and stunt team–sponsored workshops that have materialized in many media production hubs in the past five to ten years. I acquired information about stunt communities, individual stunt workers, and training procedures via a series of conversations with stunt industry professionals in the United States, New Zealand, the Republic of Ireland, and the United Kingdom between 2015 and 2017.

The term *previz* has historically been used in US film and television industries to identify artifacts as varied as storyboards, animatics (animated storyboards), and primitive computer-generated effects sequences designed as templates or prototypes for sequences that are later reworked with higher production values. All forms of previz operate as proof of concept and make clear not only the feasibility of complex choreography on a budget but also the degree to which the team who developed the previz is trained for the task at hand and can distinguish their work from that of other craftspeople. An action design previz is created during the preproduction stages of a film, television program, or video game, and the term that it originates from, *previsualization*, covers a wider range of genres and is most commonly used in US film and media industries to indicate a computer-generated low-fi prescription for the manner in which character and object movement, lighting arrangements, and camera placement might operate in a scene. Christopher Cram explains the most common uses of previsualization in Hollywood as such:

> At its most basic level, though, previs is used as a tool for complicated visual effects sequences to determine where the camera will be, what it will see, and what components in the frame will be digital. It is most commonly rendered at a resolution that looks like simplified video game animation—shapes are made of polygons, animation seems "blocky," etc. The actual building of all the digital objects (*assets*) and animation in the previs might be done at a visual effects company under the direction of the vfx supervisor, or it may be done by a company that specializes exclusively in previs.[49]

Previsualization is often used for scenes that require complex staging, need digital effects to be added later, or are underserved by their descriptions in the script. Action design is rarely described in a script in any detail; screenwriting craft very rarely intersects with stunt craft, so the two do not share the same language and, as such, operate in different descriptive registers. As Cram explains, a screenplay's description of the action design may be limited to the two-word combination "they fight."[50] Stunt previz videos translate the action design into a discernible register for directors, cinematographers, editors, art directors, and actors.

One of the Hong Kong–style action craft tools that has infiltrated stunt communities of practice outside the SAR through the transnational function of assemblage is the use of previz fight videos featuring elaborate action choreography complete with blocking, decisive camera placement, and well-timed cuts to emphasize the skill of an individual stunt performer, stunt team, or action choreographer. In my conversation with Cale Schultz, the operational director and a member of 87eleven Action Design, he identified the influence of Hong Kong director and choreographer Yuen Woo-ping's use of previz for the action design of *The Matrix* as a primary means by which the tool infiltrated stunt communities of practice in the United States. Schultz described how Chad Stahelski worked as Keanu Reeves's stunt double on *The Matrix*, which allowed him to observe and later absorb Yuen's previz craft practice into his own repertoire of technique. Schultz addressed Stahelski and his partner David Leitch's relationship to Yuen's stunt craft techniques on *The Matrix* films as a culture of indebtedness that further informed a lifelong education in martial arts and stunting:

> A lot of that choreography was [Yuen] Woo-ping, but Chad doubled Keanu for all of those movies so, he worked very closely with him [Yuen]. Dave was also in the second and third one, I think. I know he doubled Agent Smith quite a bit and did other stunts. So, for them to learn through him [Yuen] and to develop, it is always a learning style. It is always picking up more, and more, and more, because they were also trained at the Inosanto Academy through Dan Inosanto, who was Bruce Lee–associated. So, Bruce Lee was very invested in learning and taking what you can use and discarding the rest, and that is how they have grown in development. That has always been their mind-set.[51]

Stahelski teamed with Leitch to form the internationally renowned US stunt collective 87eleven in 1997, and Schultz explains that their use of the previz post-*Matrix* helped to influence the adoption of the craft tool from Hong Kong as an industry standard that is now expected from stunt communities of practice in the United States:

> I think *The Matrix* was a big breakthrough film, and I feel like the movie that really brought martial arts choreography to the forefront. Because there is plenty of the Hong Kong stuff, and the Bruce Lee stuff that has been going on forever, but, like I said, it was never widely accepted here. And then when that [*The Matrix*] came out, it was kind of revolutionary.... And that is really how we have developed into monetizing this place because before David and Chad would use this place, and all the guys would kind of volunteer, and they would do a previz for a movie that they really want to get. . . . Maybe with the script, maybe without the script, we make a fight. . . . And then we might get the movie based on that. But once people started seeing that product, they started asking for that in advance, like "I want you guys, and I want you to do this fight," and then we said, "Here is what it is going to cost." And so that was a way in which we started bringing in money on a higher level for that [previz work]. Which is great, because now directors and producers are seeing the value of that product up front, in a way that they never did before. And if you give us eight weeks and a decent budget, we can previz your entire movie

for you. And it will look, if the guys were in wardrobe, you would basically have your movie.[52]

During the period that Schultz identifies, post-2010, it became more common for individual stunting collectives, stunt performers, and coordinators working in Hollywood to develop, deliver, and circulate action previz videos to market their work and demonstrate their work-readiness in a manner that was more easily readable to directors and producers than the presentation of simple stunt reels for individual performers. Stunt reels—compilations of a stunt performer's dynamic fights, burns, falls, crashes, and wirework—were previously the industry standard and a common accompaniment to any performer's résumé. In the shift toward previz videos as a marketing tool, the emphasis has changed to foreground the individual performer's ability to learn complex choreography, act for the camera, and operate as part of a collective. Previz videos better facilitate the marketing of stunt workers as teams and also call into question the traditional attribution of creative labor on set, which has long been reinforced by misconceptions about directorial control perpetuated by film and media studies scholars and critics.

Previz design in stunt communities of practice in the United States is remarkably similar to Hong Kong director and choreographer Yuen Woo-ping's previz craftwork for *The Matrix* in that the fights are elaborately staged with multiple points of contact and fully or partially articulated movements as well as blocking suggestions, fully or partially staged mise-en-scène, and considered approaches to camera placement and movement. Even casual viewers of *The Matrix* who have no prior training in action design can recognize the similarity of Yuen's previz for *The Matrix*'s "dojo fight," with performances by stuntmen Lee Tat-chiu (李達超) and Tiger Hu Chen (陳虎), to the finished product starring Keanu Reeves and Laurence Fishburne. The movement, gestures, camera placement, and editing are nearly identical. We can see the stuntmen move, with Lee Tat-chiu using a low, wide stance similar to tiger-crane style, demonstrating a wushu black dragon recovery (a flip or "kip-up" in which the legs are positioned in the air and spun to generate the momentum to stand). We can see both Lee and Tiger Hu Chen performing aerial kicks in "Hong Kong harnesses" with two wires attached, one on either side of the hips, to allow for greater lift and maneuverability than that allowed by the harnesses typically used to make Hollywood superheroes take flight, which are more rigid and require at least four points of contact with the actor's body to hold them aloft (figures 4.1, 4.2, and 4.3). The stuntmen accentuate each movement with the practice Craig D. Reid has

4.1 Stuntman Lee Tat-chiu performs a low, wide stance to the right of the frame in a previz fight for *The Matrix*.

identified as YEBET, or "YEll Before Each Technique," to assist with the timing of impact and reaction.[53] Action choreographers in Hong Kong have a revered status on set, which allows them greater input into direction and cinematographic decisions than is common in Hollywood. In Hollywood the division of labor is decidedly more rigid, as Sylvia J. Martin has explained in her comparison of on-set labor in both contexts: "The environment of a Hollywood set is generally more controlled, particularly if filming is at a studio, with executives dropping by to keep an eye on things. Multiple Hong Kong directors and producers describe their production style's flexibility as an advantage and distinctly 'Hong Kong.'"[54] In Hong Kong the choreographer is respected as a sifu, or master, and that same privilege was extended to Yuen during his work on *The Matrix*, most likely owing to the directors' desire to create a Hong Kong–style action aesthetic even though they lacked US and Australian stunt performers who had worked exclusively in that specific métier. Yuen was given more leeway and power to inform creative decisions than the Hollywood system generally allows choreographers because the Wachowskis were out of their depth.

4.2 Stuntman Lee Tat-chiu demonstrates a wushu black dragon recovery to the bottom left of the frame in a previz fight for *The Matrix*.

From observing Yuen's process on *The Matrix*, Chad Stahelski developed similar techniques for previz craftwork, which he introduced to the 87eleven stunt team (which he cofounded with David Leitch), including multibeat longer-take choreography, a staging environment meant to replicate the mise-en-scène of the finished production (approximated with cardboard boxes), decisive camera placement, and a shooting location that maximized the capacity for elaborate wirework rigs. If we examine 87eleven's previz for *Serenity*, we can see that the staging approximates the mise-en-scène they will use for the finished film, complete with mock stairs, as well as tables and a bar constructed from stunt pads (figure 4.4).[55] The sparse aesthetic of the set in a previz is meant to convey the size and the shape of the space to allow for blocking. This space is normally a minimalist staging ground for action in which many walls and obstacles are replaced with cardboard boxes, which do double duty as both an approximation of set design and protection for stunt performers. Stuntwoman (and former champion kickboxer) Bridgett Riley, doubling for Summer Glau, descends the stairs, and stuntmen and stuntwomen act as extras. Camera movement and framing are very similar to the finished scene, and blocking and choreography remain analogous. Much

4.3 Stuntman Tiger Hu Chen flies in for an aerial kick on a dual hip pick point "Hong Kong harness."

like the previz, the finished version of the fight in the film begins with stunt-men being kicked by Glau (her face visible) in a three-beat fight sequence facilitated by her dance training (figure 4.5). The more complex maneuvers in the scene are performed by Riley, who replicates her movements from the previz, albeit with a mise-en-scène with far greater production values. The air-bound flips made possible by Riley's training and her dual pick point harness appear like supernatural abilities attributable to the character in the finished product, with the wire rig digitally removed from view (figure 4.6). A "pick point" is a secured loop on a harness designed to accommodate wire rigging. The number and placement of pick points and the variation in har-ness design contribute to the mobility and directionality of the performer. The stunt team made adjustments between the previz and the final version of the scene owing to the actor's bodily disposition and her familiarity with deliberate-practice training. Glau's dance training aided her in the slow but precise execution of longer sequences of fight beats, and the preplanning established by the previz made it easier for her to work with the 87eleven stunt team so that her face could be visible more often than is common for actors participating in action scenes. The 87eleven Action Design team has

4.4 For the previz of a fight scene in which stuntwoman Bridgett Riley (left) doubles Summer Glau for *Serenity*, the 87eleven training facility is outfitted with wooden stairs, a padded bar on the right, and tables with patrons on the left to mimic the planned mise-en-scène.

become very well known for their ability to train actors and integrate them into complex multibeat fight sequences using previz work and on-site training, as evidenced by the behind-the-scenes footage for *John Wick* and *Atomic Blonde*.[56] The trajectory of previz adoption from Hong Kong to Hollywood via the work of 87eleven is demonstrably direct, from Yuen to Stahelski, but the same stunt craft tool has taken a more circuitous route in other contexts.

While on the *Ash vs Evil Dead* set in Auckland, New Zealand, during production for season 3 of the television program in May 2017, I observed and conversed with Dayna Grant, stunt coordinator Stuart Thorp, members of the stunt team, and lead actor Lucy Lawless, and I also toured the set. Grant was the stunt co-coordinator and also worked as Lawless's stunt double. Grant started in the New Zealand stunt industry as a horse-riding stunt double for Lawless on *Xena: Warrior Princess* and later became one of Lawless's main stunt doubles for the show. Grant has since worked as a stunt double for Charlize Theron in *Mad Max: Fury Road*, which was shot in Namibia; for Tilda Swinton in *The Chronicles of Narnia: The Lion, the Witch and the Wardrobe*, shot in New Zealand; and for Rhona Mitra in *Underworld: Rise*

4.5 Actor Summer Glau executes the first part of this three-beat fight sequence by kicking the stuntman to her left. Her face is clearly visible.

4.6 Stuntwoman Bridgett Riley lends the River Tam character supernatural flair by flipping in her wired harness. The wires are erased in postproduction and do not show in the finished scene from *Serenity*.

of the Lycans, also shot in New Zealand.[57] Like all expert stunt performers, Grant has been training in bodily disciplines from a young age: she started training in horseback riding, dancing, and gymnastics from the time she was a toddler and added additional disciplines later in life:

> Horses, I could ride before I could walk. I used to get tied to the saddle when I was six months old. We lived on a farm. My dad used to just tie me to the saddle and would go on big cattle drives and stuff like that. I was doing that, and then we had a rodeo, and I did a bit of that. Gymnastics, my mom, we owned the gym club, so I did gymnastics from when I was tiny, little. And then I started dance when I was five. So I've always done something.[58]

According to Grant and other members of the *Ash vs Evil Dead* stunt team, the use of previz videos became more common in Kiwi stunt communities of practice after *The Chronicles of Narnia: The Lion, the Witch and the Wardrobe* was filmed on location in New Zealand, and the technique has since been integrated into local television production practices.[59] Grant witnessed the practice being used firsthand and participated in some of the earliest uses of previz in New Zealand, as she was Swinton's stunt double for the film. While on the *Ash vs Evil Dead* set, I witnessed two stunt previz videos being shot, as well as observed and discussed other structures of production with members of the stunt team and Lawless.

I watched the stunt team create and adjust two wire rig stunts and witnessed their previz process in action. In the first stunt, Grant, doubling Lawless, performed a stair fall from a second story through a breakaway foam banister designed by the art department, flipping through the air in the harness and landing on stunt pads on the staircase. During a trial-and-error process, they discussed how Grant could perfect the flip in the confined space by using a rolling bridle rig so that she could be jerked by the wires and spin her body without becoming tangled in the wires. A "rolling bridle" or "wide rolling bridle" rig gives the stunt performer the freedom to twist at the hips instead of having pick points fixed on both sides of the hips. This device would provide Grant with the freedom of movement necessary to avoid bashing her head on the stairs. She was fully outfitted in a helmet and pads but informed me that the helmet would not remain part of her ensemble during production, as she would be wearing a wig to better approximate Lawless's character Ruby and so would have less protection. Grant worked with the stunt team to get the trajectory correct so that she would have enough time to flip once before landing on the stairs, which was difficult in the confined space of the staircase. She was outfitted in a women's jerk vest full-body harness at the time and had to ice her leg in between attempts because she had injured herself by slamming her leg into the banister on the side of the staircase. While she set up the stunt, a team of wire pullers assembled out of view while her stunt team shot the stunt on their phones. The footage was edited together, and Grant sent it to the senior members of the production team. Later I watched as the team tested a wire rig for a high school hallway fight between one of Bruce Campbell's stunt doubles, Raicho Vasilev, and a stuntman doubling for Ray Santiago as Pedro. For both Grant's stair-fall stunt and the high school fight, the stunt team shot the scenes and edited them together on mobile devices—planning both static framing and mobile shots. Grant informed me that the previz videos were sent through a networked video database that is accessible to high-ranking members of the cast and crew. The previz videos are sent to the second-unit director and to any senior member of the crew who will need to be involved in the final version of each stunt. The videos are also sometimes sent to the actors who will be working with the stunt team so that they can study the movement of their doubles or the fight choreography. As stunt co-coordinator, Grant had control over the finished previz, which suggests camera placement and/or movement, the movement of figures, blocking, and editing.

Given the speed of television production and the advancements of networked digital circulation of production material, previz videos function as a necessary form of shorthand communication with different departments and as a training device; they hold more weight than mere suggestion. The previz informs the senior production personnel and the actors of the most dynamic and studied approaches to fight scenes and stunt work, as drawn from the knowledge base of the coordinator's years of training and craftwork in the industry. Previz videos operated on the set of *Ash vs Evil Dead* as a shorthand that assisted the stunt team in communicating with other production personnel, but the videos also exemplified the considered opinion of the stunt coordinators as experts, a criterion of value in a flexible fast-production context in which safety facilitates efficiency. Both Grant and Lawless confirmed that the videos and the one-on-one martial arts fight training that the stunt team provided (in a section of the *Ash vs Evil Dead* studio that Lawless showed to me, which had protective equipment and cardboard boxes designed to mimic the mise-en-scène) streamlined the production process and helped the cast and crew to deliver more dynamic action scenes than would normally be possible on a television schedule and budget. Grant explained:

> I watch her, and we kind of talk about it as well. We watched each other. She might, if I shoot the fight first, she'll kind of watch and do what I do a little bit. Or I'll watch, because her character [Ruby]—there are two different forms of her character: one where she's mortal and one where she's immortal. So there's different movement and different sells. [A *sell* is a dynamic movement that makes it appear as though an object has made an impact.] In the fight that we're doing down here, she's immortal, so the sells are very minimal and when she gets hit in the face, there's nothing. In this one she just gets blasted four times, body blown to pieces, hole in the head. You know, almost, it's nothing . . . and we talk about it. I'll go, "How do you think we should do this? I'm thinking it's a small sell." And she'll

go, "Yeah, yeah," and we'll rehearse, and I'll see how she moves when I teach her the fight, and I move like her. I think it's just like a dancer with the dance mimicking their movement and what they're doing, and the little quirks that they do.[60]

This skilling process was further accelerated by Grant and Lawless's familiarity from having worked together on the set of *Xena: Warrior Princess* and Lawless's dance training, which eased her memorization of complex multibeat fight arrangements owing to her nimbler motor skills and previously acquired cognitive strategies for movement training. As Lawless noted, her time on *Xena* was the most effective action training:

> When I was doing *Xena*, I was warmed up all the time because we were doing fight sequences and I was twenty years younger. Now, thermally it's cold, muscularly it's cold, and you can hurt yourself doing the slightest little movement. If you're selling the stunt and you get slapped in the face, that could ruin your life for a month. In terms of gentle warming up, I take it much more seriously. I take care of myself much better now. Otherwise, it's a lot of muscle memory. I learn things on the fly. In fact, I'm quite irritated if we come in three days early to learn a fight which I can learn in ten minutes. Then you take another ten minutes and you learn it again. That space between the first time we learned and the second time, you're getting it into your working memory. It's quite short. I don't want three days because by then I've totally forgotten it. I don't know, *Xena* was pretty great training because it was all day, every day. . . . It's not hard. These fights are so small compared to what we used to do on *Xena*. There're way less than twenty moves. We don't have time to improv. We have to mesh to be really efficient. . . . It was hard for me at first because I was black and blue for two years. I was never good at sports. I was never interested in sports. [But now it is] so much easier, because getting punched in the face for two years gives you quicker reflexes.[61]

The previz becomes a template that assists the cast and crew in reproducing the complex arrangements designed by the coordinator in a quick and controlled manner to limit the precarities of the production process because the process has been rehearsed, perfected, blocked, and framed in advance for the desired effect.

When we examine the completed version of the stair-fall scene, which aired as part of a longer fight sequence in the "Tales from the Rift" episode of season 3 of *Ash vs Evil Dead*, we can see that the camera placement is

identical to the placement suggested by the phones used to film the previz.[62]
A camera placed at the top of the stairs captures Grant crashing through
the breakaway banister (figure 4.7), and a second captures the initial impact
of Grant's body on the stairs (figure 4.8) and her forward roll (figure 4.9).
A trial-and-error approach, so common to deliberate-practice training, was
key to the design of this action set piece. It is clear, based on the results of
the finished scene, that the wire rig and harness could not compensate for
the lack of clearance. Grant propels herself backward through the banister
but cannot flip 360 degrees owing to the lack of space and instead completes
a 180-degree flip, with her hands bracing the impact of her head on the stairs
(figure 4.8). Without the helmet and much of the protective gear used for
the planning and previz creation, Grant uses her years of training in stunt
craft to protect her head from injury, both in the initial impact on the stairs
and in the following shot, in which she tumbles forward at an angle that allows her to tuck her head in toward her body and use her elbows and hands
to brace herself for impact and control the speed and direction of the roll
(figure 4.9). These five seconds of screen time, with Grant's face consistently
shielded from view by her blonde wig and her arm, required a couple hours
of preparation and a lifetime of training. As an expert stunt worker and a
stunt coordinator, Grant has decades of experience working both within
the New Zealand stunt community and transnationally as a highly regarded
stunt double for high-profile actors on big-budget productions.

Grant's position as an expert stunt worker and coordinator and Lawless's years of fight practice and weapon work for *Xena* facilitated more dynamic fight scenes than are possible in most other thirty-minute television
programs. While Grant's familiarity with Lawless's body and performance
styles, from being one of her stunt doubles for *Xena*, certainly aided in this
endeavor, the use of previz videos as well as the training room to prepare
the actors for fight scenes engendered an environment in which all long-
term cast members were far more prepared to fight on-screen than most
action actors. The end result was that the fight scenes on *Ash vs Evil Dead*
were structured similarly to Hong Kong film fight scenes from the 1980s and
1990s: multiple beats per shot, fighting styles reminiscent of Eastern martial art forms, elaborate wirework, and, most shockingly, the actors' faces in
plain view of the camera without the aid of performance-capture technology. While extended martial arts fight scenes are more common to action
television programs post-*Xena*, very few thirty-minute programs would have
the capacity to stage complex fight scenes, but the presence of a dedicated
stunt team coordinated by three expert stunt performers (lead stunt coor-

4.7 In a scene from *Ash vs Evil Dead*, Dayna Grant, the stunt co-coordinator and stunt double for Lucy Lawless, crashes through a breakaway banister.

4.8 Dayna Grant lands headfirst on the stairs, bracing for the fall with her hands, while doubling Lucy Lawless in *Ash vs Evil Dead*.

4.9 Dayna Grant uses stunt craft techniques to protect her head during a forward roll down the stairs in *Ash vs Evil Dead*.

dinator Stuart Thorpe with the assistance of stunt co-coordinators Dayna Grant and Tim Wong), the networked video database for sharing previz videos, and the fight training room were also far beyond the norm for most programs. The television program *Ash vs Evil Dead* may be categorized as a horror-comedy hybrid, but, as clearly demonstrated by its production resources, the show operated in the action mode. Much as in *Xena*, the stunt work and fight design for *Ash vs Evil Dead* did not imagine Hong Kong action films as competition, but the show did engage many of the aesthetics common to Hong Kong action cinema: wirework, longer-shot multibeat fights, canted angle shots, and innovative uses of mobile camera. In fact, the off-kilter framing, fast-moving steadicam and tracking shots evoking the point of view of evil forces, and disproportionate uses of blood are elements that became more common to Hong Kong cinema after Tsui Hark adapted these techniques from Sam Raimi's film *The Evil Dead* when producing *A Chinese Ghost Story* (倩女幽魂), released in 1987.[63] As the film *The Evil Dead* was source material for *Ash vs Evil Dead*, and the show inherited much from Hong Kong action traditions, it appears as though the cycle of transnational intertextual references has come full circle. The similarities between Hong Kong action aesthetics of the 1980s and 1990s and *Ash vs Evil Dead* may also stem from the flexible creative labor markets and the related do-it-yourself philosophy of their production contexts.

If we compare the fight scene that follows the stair fall in the narrative context of the show—which was actually shot the night before—we can see that both Lawless and actor Dana DeLorenzo showcase spirited combat form in front of the camera. Both women sell each impact, and DeLorenzo, in particular, demonstrates that her character (Kelly) is in excruciating pain (figure 4.10). During my interviews Lawless and Grant each stated that De-Lorenzo delivered a particularly enthusiastic performance; both indicated that DeLorenzo took the fight training and previz sample very seriously as she prepared for the scene, to the point that both Grant and Lawless were possibly a little sore from the staged fight a day later.[64] Lawless and Grant also indicated that they watched each other's performance and movement to make the fight and stunt scenes as harmonious as possible.[65] Given that both Lawless's and DeLorenzo's faces are visible during much of the fight (figure 4.11), it becomes difficult to distinguish between Grant's and Lawless's on-screen performance, but the trained eye can see that Grant is most commonly substituted for Lawless during wirework sequences, such as a crash into the fireplace (figure 4.12); for ratchet pulls (in which a wire is centrally attached to the back of the harness and forced backward with pneumatic pressure), employed, for example, to demonstrate the strength of a shotgun blast (figure 4.13); and with jerk rigs (in which one wire is attached to the harness and pulled by hand) for lesser impacts (figure 4.14). Grant indicated that she performed these stunts differently depending on whether she was doubling Lawless as the human version of her Ruby character or the supernatural version, who was more impervious to pain and regenerated quickly.[66] When doubling the supernatural version of Ruby (as seen in figures 4.7–4.9 and 4.12–4.14), Grant held a solid stance while being pulled through the air, yanked to the ground, thrown into the breakaway fireplace, or, in the case of the fall discussed earlier, slamming headfirst into the stairs. The dynamism of Grant's performance is echoed by the demonstrable complexity of the fights delivered by the actors she helped to train.

Previz production is an in-transit stunt craft tool inherited from the Hong Kong tradition and has increasingly become an industry standard in multiple linked transnational media production markets. There are two distinct types of action previz videos: the first, like those of 87eleven or the *Ash vs Evil Dead* stunt team, operates as a template and visual instruction manual for production on set. The second variety is increasingly displacing the stunt reel as a marketing tool for stunt teams and individual stunt workers. This second type of previz is designed to secure employment and to demonstrate the screen-readiness of the team or individual by showcasing not only

4.10 Actor Dana DeLorenzo sells the impact of Lucy Lawless's attack.

4.11 The faces of Dana DeLorenzo and Lucy Lawless remain visible and identifiable for much of the fight sequence.

4.12 Dayna Grant crashes into the fireplace while doubling for the supernatural version of Lucy Lawless's Ruby.

4.13 Dayna Grant doubles for Lucy Lawless during a ratchet pull simulating the impact of a shotgun blast.

4.14 Dayna Grant is jerked backward, simulating the impact of a gunshot on Lucy Lawless's supernatural Ruby character.

their dexterity but also their innate understanding of working with the camera. Because of the circulation of previz stunt craft from Hong Kong to the United States and the networked stunting communities of practice in many media production hubs around the world, the previz has become the industry standard, and stunt craft now includes cinematographic prowess and editing skills. Irish stuntwoman and coordinator Eimear O'Grady indicated as much during our conversation:

> It's now become a really big thing [in Ireland since 2015]. So there are stunties my age [in their thirties] who have been jumping, leaping, doing all those things, and wondering, "What do I do now?" So a lot of them are doing editing courses. And they are really jumping into that and thinking, "Right, this is where I need to go because it's a nice job, and I can still be involved in the action, and I know all of the little angles and things." And so that's now become a career choice as well.[67]

Action previz construction has been fairly standardized across different national media production contexts though this stunt craft tool did not appear in all production communities simultaneously. Many stunt communities of practice trace the appearance of previz in their home production context to an individual film or television program. These films or shows, which are always off-site international coproductions, expose stunt performers to stunties from other communities of stunting practice. The movement of technique between these networked communities produces an international standard and set of expectations. Action previsualizations have become the means by which stunt communities of practice make their craftwork legible to producers and directors. Additionally, incorporating this tool has given stunt teams more input into the way in which their work is filmed and edited.

The geographically wide-reaching effects on production hierarchies that have been fostered by the circulation and adaptation of previz as a form of expert opinion are the by-product of in-transit stunt craft traditions emanating from Hong Kong. The addition of previz videos to stunt craft traditions in various networked transnational media industries alters the landscape for action design aesthetics in at least three ways: it initiates a shift in the required skill set for stunt performers to include cinematography, editing, and direction of actors; it makes possible complex multibeat martial arts fight scenes that more seamlessly integrate stunt performers and actors; and it alters the production hierarchy to more closely mimic the flexible arrangement of on-set labor in Hong Kong, with the stunt coordinator/action designer's input functioning as a form of expert opinion because "experts are more successful at choosing the appropriate strategies to use than novices."[68] Michelene T. H. Chi describes a collection of attributes that can commonly be used to distinguish expert performance from the work of novices or apprentices, which includes the selection of strategies as well as the detection of features invisible to novices. These characteristics of expert performance, which are shared by stunt industry professionals like Chad Stahelski, Dayna Grant, and Eimear O'Grady, help them to differentiate the style and complexity of action design they can provide and offer a more steadfast guarantee of safety on set.

The Transnational Art of Craft

The success of *Crouching Tiger, Hidden Dragon* and *The Matrix* ushered in a sea change in postmillennial US action aesthetics, but the transition to complex, multibeat martial arts fight scenes and elaborate wirework design cannot be distilled to any one industry decision or individual locality. As Curtin and Sanson explain, "Unlike an integrated assembly line, motion picture production is a large-scale industrial enterprise that is distinguished by the collaborative production of prototypes, each one the outcome of thousands of creative choices."[69] In a transnational production environment in which laborers form media assemblages, and craft traditions are passed through the in-transit circulation of expert laborers with training in both local and transnational communities of stunting practice, no historical transition in action design is simple or linear. Histories of media industry craftwork are circuitous and networked, but the in-transit circulation of expert laborers has determinant effects on this evolution. Action design is a combination of choreographed trained expert and novice bodies in motion, camera placement and movement, lighting, costume, set design, and editing decisions. Thinking about action forces us to recognize the past failings of film and media studies as a discipline focused on "great artists." Media labor, like most labor, is collective. These techniques also operate in transit in that they are in a constant state of transition within and beyond national communities of stunting practice, as expert stunt workers remain flexible in their pursuit of work, and the composition of communities continually evolves. We must examine the effects on experts in action beyond the individual and look in greater detail at stunting communities of practice in order to assess the conditions of production in specific localities. This process involves speaking to stunt workers, stunt coordinators, trainers, and stunt team operations managers, as well as observing them in the planning stages and in context.

The training process for stunt workers does not simply include the ten years or more commonly spent learning gymnastics, jujitsu, wushu, tae kwon do, dance, or a wide variety of intersectional physical domains but also the time spent working in transit in networked stunt communities of practice all over the world. The deliberate practice and eventual mastery of stunt craft techniques that are learned in transit enable greater employment opportunities and expedite the flow of these techniques into the local media industries linked most closely to those expert performers. In a competitive media marketplace, expert stunt performers draw on this long history of training and retraining and through that process adapt and transform the art and craft of transnational action aesthetics.

NOVICE AND
EXPERT PERFORMANCE
— A CALL TO ACTION

The opening ceremonies of the 2008 Beijing Olympics were almost universally lauded for their ornate spectacle; the coordinated interplay of bodies, objects, and effects; and the direction of mainland Chinese filmmaker Zhang Yimou.[1] The four-hour event featured over fourteen thousand performers: dancers, musicians, acrobats, and athletes. The ceremony opened with 2,008 drummers beating their glowing *fou* drums in a choreographed countdown with astonishing precision, followed by the musicians singing, moving, and playing the glowing drums in unison. The event included an illuminated scroll with images synchronized to the movements of wire-bound bodies floating just above the surface of the scroll. While each of these performers participated in dazzling displays of dexterity and endurance that linked body and screen, questions arose as to the authenticity of other special effects. The televised ceremony showcased an impressive fireworks display of footprints in the sky above the Bird's Nest stadium. These illuminations in the night sky were later revealed to be "fake"; that is, they were computer generated and not the actual fireworks seen by those in attendance.[2]

Two contradictory discourses circulated about the 2008 opening ceremonies in Beijing in reference to the series of effects presented in the program: the spectacle of the "real" performers as a remarkable phenomenon and the spectacle of the fireworks as a synthetic pleasure, a form of on-screen trickery. The body spectacles of the performers were noted to include "more dazzling wirework than *Crouching Tiger, Hidden Dragon*," and host Matt Lauer exclaimed that the event was "a cinematic blockbuster in real time."[3] In these comments we can recognize a disdain for the mediated effects of cinematic spectacle as opposed to the authenticity of the live event, and it is particularly humorous that the representative of the mediating process (the television host) would make such comments. The live event showcased real bodies, as opposed to the film *Crouching Tiger, Hidden Dragon*, the cinema as an art form, or the "faked" fireworks, all of which operated as two-dimensional illusions. The devaluing of the computer-generated fireworks as fake because they were not identical to those seen by crowds at the stadium privileges liveness at the expense of the real labor of the technicians, who spent countless years training and one year creating the fifty-five-second effects sequence. These discourses on the ills of screened culture are telling: more than simply reinforcing the perception that life's most important moments happen with the television turned off and outside the confines of the movie theater, such statements ignore the labor inherent in all spectacle production.

The two-dimensional pleasures of film and media spectacles are always made possible by the labor of three-dimensional bodies, and in this respect screened spectacles are not distinct from live events. One of the primary concerns of this book has been to identify the ways in which expert labor makes spectacle possible, but an analysis of the reception of the 2008 opening ceremonies reveals the shortcoming of this project. Much like those commentators who privileged the performers' visibility and liveness over the screened object, this book has primarily been concerned with high-profile experts in film and television action over other expert laborers and forms of performance. The strategies for studying expert performance used in this book are, of course, more broadly applicable to craft traditions within and beyond screened culture. The first two chapters of this manuscript focus strongly on the labor of high-profile stunting stars, and the last two chapters make the transition from stunting star to the contributions of expert stunt coordinators and the collaborative nature of spectacle production. Most action stars do not do their own stunts, and most stunt performers do not ascend to coordinator positions, and yet most working stunt performers are experts. Most expert stunt workers, like laborers in other craft traditions, are well known only to other members of their intersecting communities of practice. Additionally, the labor performed by expert stunt workers is, as demonstrated in previous chapters, hypervisible in the form of body spectacle and made invisible by the discursive erasure of stars, directors, and studio publicity engines more inclined to credit the star with the performance of the stunt worker. Stunt work is invisible labor within the parameters delimited by Winifred R. Poster, Marion Crain, and Miriam A. Cherry because, as they contend, "the term *invisible* may also refer to the visual act of not seeing the workers or not understanding that they are performing work."[4] More recently, there has been a major historical shift in action spectacle production that has as yet gone unnoticed in film and media studies. This shift extends the invisibility of expert action labor and warrants further scrutiny: the digital erasure of common markers of identity for stunt workers. The labor of identifiable stunt workers has always been hidden in some fashion, and their work discursively erased by the claims of directors and stars, but a new defining element of postmillennial action work is the complete digital erasure of the stunt worker's face from their work via performance capture. Since 2014, it has become common industry practice in most major film production markets to replace the faces of stunt performers with those of stars. Stunt labor is increasingly harder to map because the working body is digitally rendered unidentifiable—or is it? If we apply the techniques used in this book to the expert performance of relatively unknown stunt workers who have been made less visible through both digital and discursive erasure, we can make their work legible.

Kung Fu and the Invisibility of Labor

Though the phrase *kung fu* has come to be associated with a Chinese style of martial arts (wushu), or for many in the West is synonymous with *all* martial arts, the original meaning of the Chinese phrase *gong fu* can be loosely translated as "skilled effort."[5] Each chapter of this book has dealt with the specifics of training regimes, styles, and skill sets connected to distinct martial arts practices. However, all of the expert action performers discussed in this book are unified in their practice of gong fu. That is, on-screen displays of incredibly impressive skilled effort in various forms characterize the action experts analyzed in this book. However, I feel that future film and media studies research on expert performance should not be limited to investigating the skilled efforts of laboring bodies that are hypervisible and discursively legible. In my final attempt to make screen labor apparent, I want to demonstrate the applicability of expert analysis to the body spectacles of lesser-known stunt workers. If one function of this project has been to reveal the labor involved in the production of spectacle, examining the working conditions of less visible second-unit performers would be a logical transition. All of the performers discussed in previous chapters create hypervisible body spectacles that are linked to distinct skilling processes. I want to expand the analysis of the expert in action to spectacles of the concealed laboring body.

Though screened culture is regarded as a decidedly visual pleasure, most screen labor is invisible to audiences, or at most semivisible. Although many (but not all) screen laborers are credited with their work, industry and academic discourses on screen labor have long redistributed the credit for visible work, attributing it to directors and stars. For example, not all stunt workers appear in the credits of Hollywood productions. The Screen Actors Guild - American Federation of Television and Radio Artists, the union representing both stunt workers and the actors for whom they double, has a regulation allowing members of the stunt team to be excluded from the closing credits beyond a set quota.[6] In recent years, production studies scholars have made it a point to illuminate the contributions of the bulk of screen laborers, those who work below the line. However, these scholars face an uphill battle given the substantial literature on stardom and the auteur, which still maintains that these figures have proprietary standing in the creative process, superseding the rest of the screen workforce. Analysis of the gong fu, or skilled effort, of most of the screen labor force is still a pressing need. Even as ethnographic and historical work in production studies rescues individual and collective groups of screen laborers from obscurity, media industrial discourses persist in crediting directors and stars with the contributions of other workers. While the work of art directors, editors, and camera operators is credited on-screen, is increasingly covered by production studies scholarship, and is highlighted in craft-specific periodicals aimed at their communities of practice, the discursive erasure of their labor by the predominating industrial and academic discourses makes their work (and that of many below-the-line laborers) semivisible. Poster, Crain, and Cherry explain that invisible labor can be conceptualized on a spectrum and that the visibility of labor is conceptual, in that discourse may operate as an extension of power to discredit the work of certain laborers. They explain:

> One might consider these *semivisible* types of labor. Either the worker or the work is unrecognized. The invisible labor may be central or peripheral to the occupation, and the number of viewers may vary from a few to many. These jobs may have commonalities with visible labor in that they are located in the public sphere, physically identifiable, and formalized on the books. However, they are devalued socially, politically, and economically in ways that subordinate them relative to visible labor. It is this contradictory nature of invisibility within visibility that we seek to tease out.[7]

The work of below-the-line screen laborers who are listed in the credits of film and television programs and discussed in craft publications is semivisible in that their work is identifiable but disregarded or obscured in publicity materials consumed by screen publics. Their work is also only semivisible in that classes continue to be taught and books written on directors and stars, while making no effort to examine the collaborative nature of media production environments. It is possible and, I would argue, necessary to uncover the work of all members of the screen labor force along the spectrum of visibility. Though this conclusion treads familiar territory (e.g., stunt work, Hong Kong–style action design, martial arts training), we can, of course, extend the discussion of expert craftwork to a variety of laborers along this spectrum and to labor and performance more generally, outside the boundaries of screen work.

An analysis of the semivisible second-unit labor necessary to spectacle production could be applied to a variety of genres, because action set pieces are not limited to action as a genre. You can find action design in film and television medical dramas, comedies, and even musicals. Increasingly, however, many US film and television productions in the superhero genre tend toward Hong Kong–style action aesthetics in terms of both fight choreography and wirework design. This is due to three factors: the rise of the superhero genre under Marvel Studios; the in-transit circulation of Hong Kong–style action techniques in stunt communities of practice, as described in chapter 4; and the success of action design teams like 87eleven and their compatriots in getting consistent work. Hong Kong–style action design is common to segments of the Marvel Cinematic Universe, the television programs *Daredevil* and *Luke Cage*, and other Marvel Studio properties.[8] This conclusion identifies structural differences in the choreographed movement of stars and professional stunt doubles via an analysis of the "May vs. May" fight sequence in the "Face My Enemy" episode of Marvel's *Agents of s.h.i.e.l.d.*[9] The distinctions between star and double are blurred both through editing and cinematography and through the discursive erasure of the labor of the stunt double when a star's claims to do their own stunts are circulated by the popular press. This project incorporates research on expert performance to make visible the mediating mechanisms that distinguish expert and novice performance in the action genre, including deliberate practice in martial arts and/or other intersectional forms of bodily practice like gymnastics and dance. As demonstrated in previous chapters, expert stunt performers call on their histories of training when they learn and practice choreography and are able to store longer sequences of action beats than amateurs, who struggle with memorization and comportment. Action genre actors like Ming-na Wen commonly undergo very short periods of bodily training in which they are required to memorize very small chunks of choreographed action in order to manufacture on-screen credibility. In contrast, stunt doubles like Samantha Jo are required to draw on their decade-long training (in this case in the Chinese martial art wushu), as well as to memorize and actualize a series of complex choreographed chunks. The function of this book's performance analysis is threefold: to shed light on the material and mediatized histories of below-the-line action production, to promote further discussion of expert performance in film and media studies, and to recruit scholars for further research on expert performance and invisible labor.

Most action stars and actors who star in action series make claims about their commitment to doing their own stunt work, although, as explained in chapter 1, insurance contracts and occupational safety regulations prevent them from doing so. In previous decades, a scholar could watch an action scene slowly to identify moments when the actor's face was not visible and accurately assume the action was being done by a stunt double, but newer technologies have rendered those observational tactics useless. Stunt performers now regularly face the camera head-on during some of their most dynamic fights. Stunties' faces are now digitally erased using performance-capture technology, as tracking markers are placed on their faces to allow the star's facial expressions to be superimposed. Modern stunt doubles exist on the edge of cinematic visibility, given that performance capture lends credence to action actors' false claims by matching their faces to stunt workers' laboring bodies. This practice reinforces Poster, Crain, and Cherry's point that invisible labor is not easy to define because "dynamics of visibility . . . may serve to obscure and even misrepresent those being viewed."[10] The frontality of performance made possible by emerging digital technologies can provide a more immersive reception of an action star's body spectacle, but that corporeal presence and disposition belong to another performer. In contradistinction to Roland Barthes's remark on Greta Garbo's on-screen presence and the centrality of her visage that "a mask is but a sum of lines; a face, on the contrary, is above all their thematic harmony," the action star's face sutured to the body spectacle of the expert action performer is perceived as thematically harmonious when it is in reality just a sum of dots aligned and reconfigured to mask their labor (figure C.1).[11]

With a little training in the mechanics of stunt production and in the disposition created by training in specific martial arts or intersectional disci-

C.1 Performance-capture markers appear as dots on the faces and bodysuits of stunt double Zoë Bell (right) and actor Cate Blanchett (left). Bell's actions were matched to Blanchett's face in *Thor: Ragnarok* (2017).

plines, scholars can differentiate between novice and expert performance in action scenes even when stunt workers' faces have been digitally erased. This process is necessary if we wish to make more visible the labor of stunt workers whose work has been hidden by the discursive practices of promotional materials and by cutting-edge computer-generated techniques. Expert studies pioneer K. Anders Ericsson has explained that differences between experts and novices should not be attributed to differences in intellect or perceived natural talent but rather to distinctions in both the type of training and the period of training because "systematic differences between experts and less proficient individuals nearly always reflect attributes acquired by the experts during their lengthy training."[12] In short, the spectacle of the imposed face of the nonstunting action star can be torn from the seams of the body spectacle because, as demonstrated in each chapter of this book, expertise leaves discernible marks.

The two major mediating mechanisms that distinguish amateur and expert performance in choreographed action scenes are the number of fight beats a performer can chunk and the degree of difficulty and precarity of each movement. According to the publicity material circulated via interviews with stunt double Samantha Jo and star Ming-na Wen, "they got a chance to really focus on this fight on weekends, in between scenes, whenever there was a free moment."[13] Wen trained with Jo for two weeks off and on to prepare for the May-versus-May fight, which was then shot in three days. Actors commonly train with stunt doubles for fight scenes, and although actors with dance and martial arts backgrounds, like Wen, are reportedly easier to train, they are not stunting experts, and their performance is limited to short fight beat sequences with limited complexity in the finished product. All of the publicity material for this scene implies that Wen fought Jo, but in fact the complex and high-fight-beat-count sequences were done by Jo and stuntwoman Tara Macken, who is never mentioned in any of the literature. Wen's face was performance-captured, or *p-capped*, onto both stuntwomen, and the stuntwomen shifted roles between Agent 33, in the silver dress, and Agent May, in lingerie. Jo, who was a member of the Canadian national wushu team at the Beijing Olympics and won a bronze medal at the 2007 World Wushu Championships in Beijing, was tasked with the most complex aerial maneuvers, and Macken, who was trained in ballet, played a secondary role. Both Jo and Macken are able to use their previous deliberate-practice training in bodily disciplines to deliver high-beat sequences, and Wen is left with the tertiary role in the choreography, with simple one- to three-beat sequences. As described above, the scene in which Wen seems to play two roles required two stunt doubles, and yet Macken's role in the production is never discussed in publicity materials so as to make it seem as though Wen was involved in the precarious action to a much greater degree than was the case. Jo's interview with *Entertainment Weekly* bears this glaring omission (which she could have alluded to in a segment the reporter excluded via an ellipsis): "From the vision of Kevin Tancharoen, the director, to the execution from Garry, who was our second unit director and our action director, to Tanner, who made things as safe and smooth as possible, to Matt who choreographed punch for punch, to Ming and I performing it . . . it's such a collaborative effort."[14] While viewers are led to believe that Wen is doing her own stunts, two stuntwomen did the bulk of the labor, and one was never publicly acknowledged. We can, however, given our knowledge of form and training for wushu, clearly delineate Jo's contributions and identify fight beats in which Jo is working with Macken and not Wen based on the precarity of the fight beats. There are two beats that were turned into GIFs and circulated in mass quantities by fans of this series, the double drop kick (figure C.2) and the jump off the table (figure C.3), both of which were performed by Jo and Macken. In the double drop kick, we can easily identify both Jo's wushu training and the effect that training has had on isolated muscle groups. Because Jo was a wushu performer who specialized in forms (as opposed to sparring), her quadriceps muscles are more developed than

C.2 Samantha Jo executes the double drop kick.

C.3 Samantha Jo jumps from a table and performs a butterfly twist; the move from this fight is most often shared as a GIF online.

either Macken's or Wen's, and the knee-to-chest jumps that she repeated during her early wushu training prove useful in actualizing this maneuver. Jo can consistently obtain more lift from her jumps and is able to deliver a kinetic performance when she jumps from the table to effect a variation of a butterfly kick twist (an air-bound kick with a 360-degree spin) while slamming Macken's head into the table. Macken's ballet training provided her with coordination and made her accustomed to pain as an expected element of performance, but Jo's wushu training is what makes it possible to produce this fight beat sequence without using a wire-harness rig because she can generate her own lift and momentum for the twist.[15] The interviews and publicity photos make Jo's labor semivisible and Macken's much less so. The performance-captured image of Wen's duplicated face opened a discursive opportunity to publicly acknowledge the work of two lesser-known stunt doubles, but the pull to aggrandize the star in place of the stunt worker is too strong in US action productions. Technologies of stardom in the form of interviews, behind-the-scenes featurettes, and performance-capture techniques operate to cement the public perception that action stars do their own stunts. If these technologies are to be believed, all action stars are stunting stars, but the mechanisms for identifying and discussing expert performance proffered in this book make it possible for us to not only prove otherwise but reconceptualize transnational histories of craft labor and laborers.

The distinguishing quality of the body spectacle of contemporary stunt labor is the manner in which the spectacle of the star's face obscures the labor of the skilled expert body for most spectators. The unknown expert stunt worker shares many of the characteristics of the performers discussed in this book (training regime, spectacle production, endurance of physical discomfort, etc.). The body spectacles analyzed in this project are closely connected to visible star bodies. The spectacle of the action star is, in the eyes of most viewers, seemingly divorced from the physical labor of the stunt worker. In chapter 3, on stuntwoman Zoë Bell, I argued that Bell's labor was obscured in the act of becoming a spectacle. This attribute is shared by all stunt workers, but the work of the below-the-radar stunt performer sheds light on an area of concern for further research, the separation of the star as object from the labor inherent in stunt production. One of the topics touched on by this book has been the work of second-unit crews and the off-screen labor required for the production of spectacle. The last chapter, on stunt coordinators, attempted to shift attention toward such issues, but the topic should be addressed in much greater detail.

Approaching stunt workers as experts and studying stunt communities of practice makes it possible for film and media studies scholars to not only identify the material conditions under which action aesthetics are realized but also map the transnational flow of technology and technique and historical shifts in practice while simultaneously making stunt labor more apparent and fighting the discursive strategies of technologies of action stardom. To make stunt work more legible, we must first speak to stunt workers and stunt communities of practice about the conditions of production for their labor.[16] This process also requires research on the training histories of individual performer, interviews with stunt workers and actors, on-set observation, visits to training facilities, and firsthand material engagement with the stunt production process, but most of these techniques require access to the industry and considerable research funding. For scholars of action design without these resources, the first step is to become as fluent as possible in craft language, performance technique, and the terminology used to discuss comportment and movement within the bodily disciplines evident in a performer's training. If we wish to call ourselves experts in action, we must learn how to identify the work of action with greater precision than ever before.

Not the End: A Call to Action

As explained in the introduction of this book, the function of expert action analysis is not simply to discuss a unique group of performers, trained in bodily disciplines and harnessed as special effects. More important, this project was designed to force a methodological shift in work on action, labor, and transnational media production in cinema and media studies. This methodological transition is characterized by more detailed research into technologies of the expertly skilled body. The expert performance formulation is an attempt to recondition star theory, shifting from the persistent fascination with the star as a text or an image to a detailed analysis of the star in relation to culture industries, as a precariously positioned working body.

Each succeeding chapter of this book has moved the discussion further away from Hong Kong cinema as an industry and toward Hong Kong action as a mode in other national media contexts. The first chapter dealt with Peking opera–trained performer Jackie Chan in relation to Hong Kong genre history, the structure of the studio system, and US labor restrictions. The second chapter examined the effects of the Asian financial crisis on the film industries of Hong Kong and Thailand. This chapter also addressed the aesthetics of astonishment associated with the virtuoso reception context of Thai martial artist Tony Jaa. The next chapter examined Hong Kong martial arts cinema as a mode operating in *Xena: Warrior Princess*. In this chapter I considered how *Xena*'s use of a wuxia aesthetic affected the laboring body of Kiwi stuntwoman Zoë Bell. The final chapter expanded the book's discussion of action design to predominant stunt workers and coordinators operating in linked stunt communities of practice. This chapter also demonstrated the value in conceptualizing transnational media histories in relation to workers and craft traditions in transit. Each of these case studies has moved us further from Hong Kong action cinema as a set location and generic designation, toward Hong Kong as a national cinema effect: Hong Kong's biggest star, Jackie Chan; a Thai martial artist who found success in the martial arts genre modeled after the artifacts of the declining Hong Kong film industry; a New Zealand gymnast trained to imitate Hong Kong–style wirework; and, finally, action coordinators Chad Stahelski and Dayna Grant as instrumental in the adoption of Hong Kong–style action aesthetics and techniques within flexible media workforces in motion. Action is not a genre; as Paul Willemen's research proves, the category was initially used to describe a potential audience for video sales.[17] If we limit analysis of action to the genre and medium known as the action film, we are letting preconceived notions about genre cloud our vision. If we approach action from the perspective of labor, it is a mode of production and audience address that is informed by historically shifting techniques indebted to processes of assemblage, spectatorship, direction, and experimentation. Action is a mode common to many genres, media forms, and sites of live performance. If we look beyond the martial arts film, beyond the action film or even action television as a genre, we find action in commercials, medical dramas, and even Renaissance fair combat. There are traditional places we might look for Hong Kong–style aesthetics, and with each chapter this book has moved further afield from Hong Kong proper: to Hong Kong in Hollywood, to Hong Kong's influence in Thailand, to Hong Kong's translations in New Zealand on a wuxia television program with a white female protagonist. Action is transnational, translocal, transmedia, and transgenre and exceeds the narrow boundaries of screen work. The bulk of the action labor force is at best semivisible, so there is much work left to be done.

This book is a tactical deployment of expert performance studies designed to unify some of the concerns of screen studies and production studies. The techniques used in this book to discuss expert performance in action could easily be extended to further analyses of location-specific and transnational craft and performance techniques within and beyond media industries. My first inclination was to try to repair star theory from within the discipline of film and media studies. However, it is simple to write about film stars, and it is disingenuous to analyze screen labor without acknowledging that most work in film and television production is not done by stars. Though most of the performers discussed in this book are headliners, most spectacle production is done by second-unit performers, effects artists, safety captains, animal actors, and a host of others. The success of the action stars and expert stunt workers discussed in this book is effected by spectacle production as a collaborative act. If one project of this book has been to make screen labor more visible, then further studies on expert performance should consider the collective effort necessary to produce phenomenal body effects.

Introduction

1. *Game of Death*, directed by Robert Clouse and Bruce Lee, action choreography by Bruce Lee and Sammo Hung Kam-bo (Hong Kong: Golden Harvest; Los Angeles: Columbia Pictures, 1978).

2. *The Way of the Dragon* (*Meng Long Guo Jiang*; 猛龍過江), martial arts direction by Bruce Lee (Hong Kong: Golden Harvest and Concord Production, 1972).

3. Note on personal names: The use of non-European names in this volume follows the standard practice in East Asian studies. Chinese and Korean names are listed with the family name first and the given name second. The only exceptions to this practice are for individuals who are known internationally by their stage names.

4. *Enter the Dragon* (*Long Zheng Hu Dou*; 龍爭虎鬥), action choreography by Sammo Kam-bo Hung (Hong Kong: Golden Harvest and Concord Production; Los Angeles: Warner Brothers, 1973).

5. Esther Ching-mei Yau, ed., "Introduction: Hong Kong Cinema in a Borderless World," in *Full Speed: Hong Kong Cinema in a Borderless World* (Minneapolis: University of Minnesota Press, 2001), 1–3.

6. Poshek Fu and David Desser, introduction to in *The Cinema of Hong Kong: History, Arts Identity*, ed. Poshek Fu and David Desser (Cambridge: Cambridge University Press, 1990), 4.

7. Meaghan Morris, "Introduction: Hong Kong Connections," in *Hong Kong Connections: Transnational Imagination in Action Cinema*, ed. Meaghan Morris, Siu Leung Li, and Stephen Chan Ching-kiu (Durham, NC: Duke University Press; Hong Kong: Hong Kong University Press, 2005), 12–13.

8. Morris, "Introduction," 13.

9. Jean Lave and Etienne Wenger, *Situated Learning: Legitimate Peripheral Participation* (Cambridge: Cambridge University Press, 1991); and Etienne Wenger, *Communities of Practice: Learning, Meaning, and Identity* (Cambridge: Cambridge University Press, 1999).

10. *Xena: Warrior Princess*, created by Rob Tapert and John Schulian, action choreography by Peter Bell and Shane Dawson (United States and New Zealand: Renaissance Pictures and Universal Television), aired September 15, 1995–June 18, 2001 (syndicated).

11. William Lowe Bryan and Noble Harter, "Studies on the Telegraphic Language: The Acquisition of a Hierarchy of Habits," *Psychological Review* 6 (1899): 345–75.

12. K. Anders Ericsson, "The Acquisition of Expert Performance: An Introduction to Some of the Issues," in *The Road to Excellence: The Acquisition of Expert Performance in the Arts and Sciences, Sports, and Games*, ed. K. Anders Ericsson (Mahwah, NJ: Erlbaum, 1996), 1–50; and George Miller, "The Magical Number Seven, Plus or Minus Two: Some Limits on Our Capacity for Processing Information," *Psychological Review* 63 (1956): 81–97.

13. William G. Chase and Herbert A. Simon, "Perception in Chess," *Cognitive Psychology* 4 (1973): 55–81.

14. Richard Schechner, *Between Theater and Anthropology* (Philadelphia: University of Pennsylvania Press, 1985), 35–116.

15. Timothy A. Salthouse, "Effects of Age and Skill in Typing," *Journal of Experimental Psychology: General* 113, no. 3 (1984): 345–71.

16. Julietta Singh, *Unthinking Mastery: Dehumanism and Decolonial Entanglements* (Durham, NC: Duke University Press, 2018), 2.

17. Singh, *Unthinking Mastery*, 6–7.

18. Singh, *Unthinking Mastery*, 2.

19. Singh, *Unthinking Mastery*, 7.

20. Pierre Bourdieu, *Distinction: A Social Critique of the Judgment of Taste*, trans. Richard Nice (Cambridge, MA: Harvard University Press, 1984), 97–256.

21. Chris Shilling, "Physical Capital and Situated Action: A New Direction for Corporeal Sociology," *British Journal of Sociology of Education* 25, no. 4 (2004): 473–87.

22. Paul Metzner, *Crescendo of the Virtuoso: Spectacle, Skill, and Self-Promotion in Paris during the Age of Revolution* (Berkeley: University of California Press, 1998), 2–11.

23. Judith Hamera, "The Romance of Monsters: Theorizing the Virtuoso Body," *Theatre Topics* 10, no. 2 (September 2000): 147.

24. Hamera, "Romance of Monsters," 147.

25. Hamera, "Romance of Monsters," 147–51.

26. Bourdieu, *Distinction*, 170.

27. Bourdieu, *Distinction*, 562n2.

28. Bourdieu, *Distinction*, 190.

29. This difference was noted, in a different context, by Steve Fore in the contrast he draws between Jackie Chan and Arnold Schwarzenegger, the difference between adroit versus beefcake bodies. See Steve Fore, "Jackie Chan and the Cultural Dynamics of Global Entertainment," in *Transnational Chinese Cinemas*, ed. Sheldon Hsiao-peng Lu (Honolulu: University of Hawai'i Press, 1997), 239–62.

30. Bliss Lim, *Translating Time: Cinema, the Fantastic, and Temporal Critique* (Durham, NC: Duke University Press, 2009), 188.

31. Michele Hilmes conducts a similar project, investigating the relationships and points of convergence between US and UK radio and television histories. See Michele Hilmes, *Network Nations: A Transnational History of British and American Broadcasting* (New York: Routledge, 2011).

32. Meng-yang Cui, "Hong Kong Cinema and the 1997 Return of the Colony to Mainland China: The Tensions and the Consequences" (master's thesis, University of Bedfordshire, 2007), 30.

33. Ubonrat Siriyuvasak, "The Ambiguity of the 'Emerging' Public Sphere and the Thai Media Industry," in *The New Communications Landscape: Demystifying Media Globalization*, ed. Georgette Wang, Jan Servaes, and Anura Goonasekera (New York: Routledge, 2000), 105–6.

34. Yue-zhi Zhao, "Whose *Hero*? The 'Spirit' and 'Structure' of a Made-in-China Global Blockbuster," in *Reorienting Global Communication: Indian and Chinese Media beyond Borders*, ed. Michael Curtin and Hemant Shah (Urbana: University of Illinois Press, 2010), 172.

35. Sylvia J. Martin, *Haunted: An Ethnography of the Hollywood and Hong Kong Media Industries* (New York: Oxford University Press, 2017).

36. *Kill Bill: Vol. 1*, directed by Quentin Tarantino, action choreography by Yuen Woo-ping, Sonny Chiba, Keith Adams, and Ku Huen-chiu (Los Angeles: A Band Apart, Super Cool ManChu; New York: Miramax Films, 2003); *Kill Bill: Vol. 2*, directed by Quentin Tarantino, action choreography by Yuen Woo-ping, Sonny Chiba, Keith Adams, and Ku Huen-chiu (Los Angeles: A Band Apart, Super Cool ManChu; New York: Miramax Films, 2004); and *Death Proof*, action choreography by Jeff Dashnaw (New York City: Dimension Films, Weinstein Company; Austin: Troublemaker Studios, Rodriguez International Pictures, 2007).

37. *The Matrix*, directed by Lana and Lilly Wachowski, action choreography by Yuen Woo-ping (Los Angeles: Silver Pictures, Village Roadshow Pictures, Groucho II Film Partnership, and Warner Bros., 1999).

38. *Ash vs Evil Dead*, produced by Robert Tapert, stunt coordination by Stuart Thorpe, Dayna Grant, and Tim Wong (United States and New Zealand: Renaissance Pictures and Starz!), aired October 31, 2015–April 29, 2018, on Starz.

Chapter 1: Risky Business

1. Chris Berry and Mary Farquhar, *China on Screen* (New York: Columbia University Press, 2006), 47.

2. Zhang Zhen, *An Amorous History of the Silver Screen: Shanghai Cinema, 1896–1937* (Chicago: University of Chicago Press, 2005), 99–100.

3. Yung Sai-shing, "Moving Body: The Interactions between Chinese Opera and Action Cinema," in *Hong Kong Connections: Transnational Imagination in Action Cinema*, ed. Meaghan

Morris, Siu Leung Li and Stephen Chan Ching-kiu (Durham, NC: Duke University Press; Hong Kong: Hong Kong University Press, 2005), 29.

4. Yung, "Moving Body," 26.

5. Bryan Chang, "Sculptures in Motion: The Mind, Body and Spirit of Hong Kong Action Cinema," trans. Ranchos Cong, in *A Tribute to Action Choreographers: A 30th Hong Kong International Film Festival Programme*, ed. Li Cheuk-to (Hong Kong: Hong Kong International Film Festival Society, 2006), 16.

6. Chang, "Sculptures in Motion," 16.

7. Yung, "Moving Body," 25–27.

8. Bey Logan, *Hong Kong Action Cinema* (New York: Overlook, 1996), 9–11.

9. Joshua Goldstein, *Drama Kings: Players and Publics in the Re-creation of Peking Opera, 1870–1937* (Berkeley: University of California Press, 2007), 1.

10. Hector Rodriguez, "Hong Kong Popular Culture as an Interpretive Arena: The Huang Fei-hong Film Series," *Screen* 38, no. 1 (Spring 1997): 1–24.

11. Rodriguez, "Hong Kong Popular Culture," 9.

12. I. C. Jarvie, *Window on Hong Kong: A Sociological Study of the Hong Kong Film Industry and Its Audience* (Hong Kong: University of Hong Kong Press, 1977). 59–61.

13. K. Anders Ericsson, Ralf T. Krampe, and Clemens Tesch-Römer, "The Role of Deliberate Practice in the Acquisition of Expert Performance," *Psychological Review* 100, no. 3 (1993): 363–406; Benjamin Samuel Bloom, "Generalizations about Talent Development," in *Developing Talent in Young People*, ed. Benjamin Samuel Bloom (New York: Ballantine Books, 1985), 507–49; and Janet L. Starkes et al., "Deliberate Practice in Sports: What Is It Anyway?," in *The Road to Excellence: The Acquisition of Expert Performance in the Arts and Sciences, Sports and Games*, ed. K. Anders Ericsson (New York: Psychology Press, 2014), 81–106.

14. Stefan Degner and Hans Gruber, "Persons in the Shadow: How Guidance Works in the Acquisition of Expertise," in *The Politics of Empathy: New Interdisciplinary Perspectives on an Ancient Phenomenon*, ed. Barbara Weber (Berlin: Lit, 2011), 103.

15. Hans Gruber et al., "Persons in the Shadow: Assessing the Social Context of High Abilities," *Psychology Science Quarterly* 50, no. 2 (2008): 239.

16. Ericsson, Krampe, and Tesch-Römer, "Role of Deliberate Practice."

17. Edwin A. Locke and Gary P. Latham, *A Theory of Goal Setting and Task Performance* (Englewood Cliffs, NJ: Prentice Hall, 1990); and Gruber et al., "Persons in the Shadow."

18. Ericsson, Krampe, and Tesch-Römer, "Role of Deliberate Practice," 366–67.

19. Richard Schechner, *Between Theater and Anthropology* (Philadelphia: University of Pennsylvania Press, 1985), 19.

20. Li Ruru, *The Soul of Beijing Opera* (Hong Kong: Hong Kong University Press, 2010), 56.

21. Schechner, *Between Theater and Anthropology*, 35–36.

22. Elizabeth Halson, *Peking Opera* (New York: Oxford University Press, 1966), 8–11; and Jackie Chan, *I Am Jackie Chan: My Life in Action*, with Jeff Yang (New York: Ballantine Books, 1998).

23. Yao Hai-shing, "Martial-Acrobatic Arts in Peking Opera," *Journal of Asian Martial Arts* 10, no. 1 (2001): 24–26.

24. Vivian Sobchack, *Carnal Thoughts: Embodiment and Moving Image Culture* (Berkeley: University of California Press, 2004), 288.

25. J. Goldstein, *Drama Kings*, 37–38.

26. Colin Mackerras, *Peking Opera* (New York: Oxford University Press, 1997), 6; and Chan, *I Am Jackie Chan*, 25–119.

27. Mary Farquhar, "Jackie Chan: A New Dragon for a New Generation," *Journal of Chinese Cinemas* 2, no. 2 (2008): 144.

28. Farquhar, "Jackie Chan," 143.

29. Craig D. Reid, "Fighting without Fighting: Film Action Fight Choreography," *Film Quarterly* 47, no. 2 (Winter 1993–94): 32.

30. Reid, "Fighting without Fighting," 33.

31. Reid, "Fighting without Fighting," 34–35.

32. Reid, "Fighting without Fighting," 35.

33. *Rumble in the Bronx* (*Hung Fan Ou*; 紅番區), directed by Stanley Tong Gwai-lai, action choreography by Stanley Tong Gwai-lai and Jackie Chan (Hong Kong: Golden Harvest Productions, 1995); *Rush Hour*, directed by Brett Ratner, action choreography by Jackie Chan, Muhammed Ali Kesici, Terry Leonard, Chung Chi-li, and Sam Wong Ming-sing (New York: New Line Cinema; Los Angeles: Roger Birnbaum Productions, 1998); *Rush Hour 2*, directed by Brett Ratner, action choreography by Jackie Chan, Muhammed Ali Kesici, Ed McDermott II, Conrad E. Palmisano, and Scott Richards (New York: New Line Cinema; Los Angeles: Roger Birnbaum Productions, 2001); and *Rush Hour 3*, directed by Brett Ratner, action choreography by Jackie Chan, Bradley James Allan, Eddie Braun, Philippe Guegan, Michel Julienne, and Conrad Palmisano (New York: New Line Cinema; Los Angeles: Roger Birnbaum Productions, 2007).

34. Reid, "Fighting without Fighting," 30.

35. *Police Story* (*Jingcha Gushi*; 警察故事), directed by Jackie Chan, action choreography by Jackie Chan, Danny Chow Yun-gin, Benny Lai Keung-kuen, Fung Hak-on, Mars, Paul Wong Kwan, and Chris Lee Kin-sang (Hong Kong: Golden Harvest, 1985).

36. *Jackie Chan: My Stunts* (*Cheng Long: Wo De Te Ji*; 成龍:我的特技), directed by Jackie Chan (Hong Kong: Jackie Chan Group and Media Asia Films, 1999).

37. Lauren Steimer, "Jackie Chan Fan Survey" (online survey), May 5, 2009.

38. *Drunken Master II* (*Zui Quan Er*; 醉拳二), directed by Lau Kar-leung and Jackie Chan, action choreography by Lau Kar-leung and Jackie Chan (Hong Kong: Golden Harvest, Hong Kong Stuntman Association, and Paragon Films, 1994).

39. Lauren Steimer, "Jackie Chan Fan Survey" (online survey), November 15, 2015.

40. Golden Harvest cast Mui, a successful and respected film star, because the studio was packing films with multiple stars in the early 1990s to secure more funding. *Drunken Master II* was a high-budget film with comparatively stunning production values, and the film did phenomenally well at the box office.

41. Steimer, "Jackie Chan Fan Survey," November 15, 2015.

42. *Drunken Master*, directed by Yuen Woo-ping, action choreography by Yuen Woo-ping and Hsu Hsia (Hong Kong: Golden Harvest and Seasonal Film Corporation, 1978).

43. Yung, "Moving Body," 30.

44. Schechner, *Between Theater and Anthropology*, 19.

45. *Police Story 4: First Strike* (*Jingcha Gushi 4: Zhi Jian Dan Ren Wu*; 警察故事4:之簡單任務), directed by Stanley Tong Gwai-lai, action choreography by Stanley Tong Gwai-lai and Jackie Chan (Hong Kong: Golden Harvest Company, New Line Cinema, Paragon Films, and Raymond Chow, 1996).

46. Yao, "Martial-Acrobatic Arts in Peking Opera," 27.

47. *Project A* (*'A' Ji Hua*; A 計劃), directed by Jackie Chan, action choreography by Sammo Hung Kambo and Jackie Chan (Hong Kong: Paragon Films, 1983); and *Safety Last*, directed by Fred Newmeyer and Sam Taylor (Culver City: Hal Roach Studios, 1923).

48. Steimer, "Jackie Chan Fan Survey," November 15, 2015.

49. *Armour of God* (*Long Xiong Hu Di*; 龍兄虎弟), directed by Jackie Chan and Eric Tsang, action choreography by Liu Karwing (Hong Kong: Golden Harvest, 1987).

50. *Police Story 3: Supercop* (*Jingcha Gushi 3: Chao Ji Jing Cha*; 警察故事3: 超級警察), directed by Stanley Tong Gwai-lai, action choreography by Mak Wai-cheung, Dang Tak-wing, Hi Honchau, Chan Man-ching, Sam Wong Ming-sing, Stanley Tong Gwai-lai, and Ailen Sit Chun-wai (Hong Kong: Golden Harvest and Golden Way Films, 1992).

51. *Who Am I* (*Wo Shi Shei*; 我是誰), directed by Benny Chan and Jackie Chan, action choreography by Jackie Chan (Hong Kong: Golden Harvest Entertainment, 1998).

52. A total of forty-one respondents out of sixty-nine made this claim. Lauren Steimer, "Jackie Chan Fan Survey," May 5, 2009; and Lauren Steimer, "Jackie Chan Fan Survey" (online survey), October 3, 2009.

53. Steimer, "Jackie Chan Fan Survey," October 3, 2009.

54. Steimer, "Jackie Chan Fan Survey," May 5, 2009.

55. Aaron Anderson, "Violent Dances in the Martial Arts Film," *Jump Cut: A Review of Contemporary Media* 44 (Fall 2001), http://www.ejumpcut.org/archive/jc44.2001/aarona/aaron1.html.

56. Steimer, "Jackie Chan Fan Survey," November 15, 2015.

57. Robert Stam, "Introduction: The Theory and Practice of Adaptation," in *Literature and Film: A Guide to the Theory and Practice of Film Adaptation*, ed. Robert Stam and Alessandra Raengo (Malden, MA: Blackwell, 2005), 7.

58. Stephen Fore, "Jackie Chan and the Cultural Dynamics of Global Entertainment," in *Transnational Chinese Cinemas*, ed. Sheldon Hsiao-peng Lu (Honolulu: University of Hawai'i Press, 1997), 252–54.

59. Jennifer M. Bean, "Technologies of Early Stardom and the Extraordinary Body," *Camera Obscura* 16, no. 3 (2001): 9–57.

60. Sylvia J. Martin, *Haunted: An Ethnography of the Hollywood and Hong Kong Media Industries* (New York: Oxford University Press, 2017), 111.

61. Peter A. Marshall, telephone conversation with the author, September 2015.

62. Marshall, telephone conversation.

63. Marshall, telephone conversation.

64. Richard Nixon and other Republicans did not support this act and substituted a more corporation-friendly version than the initial bill proposed by Senate Democrats, but the Democrats were able to push the Senate bill through with minor revisions before President Nixon signed it. See James D. Hodgson, "Enactment of OSHA Required Ingenious Compromises and Strategies," *Monthly Labor Review* 111 (1988): 41–43; John Mendeloff, *Regulating Safety: An Economic and Political Analysis of Safety and Health Policy* (Cambridge, MA: MIT Press, 1979); and Benjamin W. Mintz, *OSHA: History, Law, and Policy* (Washington, DC: Bureau of National Affairs, 1984).

65. Eugene Hartwig, "New Directives in Collective Bargaining," in *American Labor Policy: A Critical Appraisal of the National Labor Relations Act*, ed. Charles J. Morris (Washington, DC: Bureau of National Affairs, 1987), 258–62.

66. David Weil, "If OSHA Is So Bad, Why Is Compliance So Good?," *RAND Journal of Economics* 27, no. 3 (Autumn 1996): 618–19.

67. US Department of Labor, Occupational Safety and Health Administration, "Walking-Working Surfaces," *Occupational Safety and Health Standards*, 1910:28, accessed June 19, 2020, https://www.osha.gov/laws-regs/regulations/standardnumber/1910/1910.28; and US Department of Labor, Occupational Safety and Health Administration, "Duty to Have Fall Protection and Falling Object Protection," *Occupational Safety and Health Standards*, 1910.28, accessed June 19, 2020, https://www.osha.gov/laws-regs/regulations/standard number/1910/1910.28.

68. Product placement has also been a necessary means of financing projects, but it is less relevant to my argument because, while companies may prefer an on-screen proximity between star and product, these arrangements have less to do with the need for insurance. For a short time, hedge funds became a popular alternative for film financing, but with low returns and the financial crisis, they have waned in popularity. See Janet Wasko, "Financing and Production: Creating the Hollywood Film Commodity," in *The Contemporary Hollywood Film Industry*, ed. Paul McDonald and Janet Wasko (Malden, MA: Blackwell, 2008), 51–53.

69. *Rush Hour; Shanghai Noon*, directed by Tom Dey, stunt choreography by Yuen Biao (Burbank, CA: Touchstone Pictures; Los Angeles: Spyglass Entertainment, Birnbaum/Barber

Productions; Hong Kong: Jackie Chan Films, 2000); and *Shanghai Knights*, directed by David Dobkin, action choreography by Jackie Chan, Bradley James Allan, Steve M. Davison, Chung Chi-li, and Jaroslav Peterka (Burbank, CA: Touchstone Pictures; Los Angeles: Spyglass Entertainment, Birnbaum/Barber Productions, All Knight Productions; Hong Kong: Jackie Chan Films, 2003).

70. Bang-yan Feng and Nyaw Mee-kau, *Enriching Lives: A History of Insurance in Hong Kong, 1841–2010* (Hong Kong: Hong Kong University Press, 2010), 1–3; 116–26.

71. Steimer, "Jackie Chan Fan Survey," May 5, 2009; and Steimer, "Jackie Chan Fan Survey," November 15, 2015.

72. In this series the name of Chan's character, Chon Wang, is commonly mispronounced by Westerners as "John Wayne." The original film in the series is a western, and the series makes many lighthearted comparisons between Chan's character and the classical Hollywood action hero.

73. Monona Rossol, *The Health and Safety Guide for Film, TV, and Theater* (New York: Allworth, 2000), xx.

74. Ann Oldenburg, "Still Willing to Take the Fall," *USA Today*, June 6, 2003, http://www.usatoday.com/life/movies/news/2003-06-05-stunt_x.htm.

75. Two examples of nations with increasingly tighter health and safety regulations that produce many US films and television shows are Canada (Canadian Centre for Occupational Health and Safety) and Australia (Safe Work Australia).

Chapter 2: Hong Kong Action Cinema as Mode in Thai Action Stardom

1. *Crouching Tiger, Hidden Dragon* (*Wohu Canglong*; 卧虎藏龙), directed by Ang Lee, action choreography by Yuen Woo-ping (Beijing: China Film Co-Production Company, Columbia Pictures Film Production Asia, EDKO Film, Zoom Hunt International Productions, United China Vision, Asia Union Film and Entertainment; New York City: Sony Pictures Classics, Good Machine, 2000). *Crouching Tiger, Hidden Dragon* was a box office success in most markets with the major exceptions of Hong Kong and China. See Mark Landler, "Lee's 'Tiger,' Celebrated Everywhere but at Home," *New York Times*, February 27, 2001, https://www.nytimes.com/2001/02/27/movies/arts-abroad-lee-s-tiger-celebrated-everywhere-but-at-home.html.

2. Saskia Sassen, *Territory, Authority, Rights: From Medieval to Global Assemblages* (Princeton, NJ: Princeton University Press, 2008), 1.

3. The star's family name is Vismitananda, and her given name is Yanin, but her global stage name is Jeeja Yanin, as though Yanin were her surname. All future references to her here will use her stage name because it is how she is known to much of her transnational fan base.

4. Sassen, *Territory, Authority, Rights*, 4.

5. Salaheen Khan, Faridul Islam, and Syed Ahmed, "The Asian Crisis: An Economic Analysis of the Causes," *Journal of Developing Areas* 39, no. 1 (Fall 2005): 170. See also Pierre-Richard

Agénor, *The Asian Financial Crisis: Causes, Contagion and Consequences* (New York: Cambridge University Press, 1999); Morris Goldstein, *The Asian Financial Crisis: Causes, Cures, and Systemic Implications*, Policy Analyses in International Economics (Washington, DC: Institute for International Economics, 1998); and William Curt Hunter, George G. Kaufman, and Thomas H. Krueger, *The Asian Financial Crisis: Origins, Implications, and Solutions* (Chicago: Kluwer Academic, 1999).

6. Khan, Islam, and Ahmed, "Asian Crisis," 169–72.

7. Khan, Islam, and Ahmed, "Asian Crisis," 170–71. This argument is shared by many others, including Pierre-Richard Agénor, Joshua Aizenman, and Alexander W. Hoffmaister, "Contagion, Bank Lending Spreads and Output Fluctuations" (National Bureau of Economic Research Working Paper Series, no. w6850, Cambridge, MA, December 1998); and Reuven Glick and Andrew K. Rose, "Contagion and Trade: Why Are Currency Crises Regional?," *Journal of International Money and Finance* 18 (1999): 603–17.

8. Ubonrat Siriyuvasak, "The Ambiguity of the 'Emerging' Public Sphere and the Thai Media Industry," in *The New Communications Landscape: Demystifying Media Globalization*, ed. Georgette Wang, Jan Servaes, and Anura Goonasekera (New York: Routledge, 2000), 105–6.

9. Zhang Zhen, "Teahouse, Shadowplay, Bricolage: Laborer's Love and the Question of Early Chinese Cinema," in *Cinema and Urban Culture in Shanghai, 1922–1943*, ed. Yingjin Zhang (Stanford, CA: Stanford University Press, 1999), 27–50.

10. Scot Barmé, "Early Thai Cinema and Filmmaking: 1897–1922," *Film History* 11, no. 3 (1999): 312.

11. Barmé, "Early Thai Cinema," 317n31.

12. Annette Hamilton, "Rumors, Foul Calumnies and the Safety of the State: Mass Media and National Identity in Thailand," in *National Identity and Its Defenders: Thailand Today*, ed. Craig J. Reynolds (Chiang Mai, Thailand: Silkworm Books, 2002), 289.

13. Anchalee Chaiworaporn, "Thai Cinema since 1970," in *Film in South East Asia: Views from the Region*, ed. David Hanan (Hanoi: South East Asia-Pacific Audio Visual Archive Association, 2001), 141–62.

14. Dome Sukwong and Sawasdi Suwannapak, *A Century of Thai Cinema*, trans. Narisa Chakrabongse (London: Thames and Hudson, 2001), 25.

15. Boonrak Boonyakatmala, "The Rise and Fall of the Film Industry in Thailand, 1897–1992," *East-West Film Journal* 6, no. 2 (July 1992): 77.

16. Boonyakatmala, "Rise and Fall of the Film Industry," 77; and Adam Knee, "Thailand in the Hong Kong Cinematic Imagination," in *Hong Kong Film, Hollywood and the New Global Cinema: No Film Is an Island*, ed. Gina Marchetti and Tan See Kam (New York: Routledge, 2007), 77.

17. Siriyuvasak, "Ambiguity of the 'Emerging' Public Sphere," 105.

18. Anchalee Chaiworaporn and Adam Knee, "Thailand: Revival in an Age of Globalization," in *Contemporary Asian Cinema: Popular Culture in a Global Frame*, ed. Anne Tereska Ciecko (New York: Berg, 2002), 59.

19. Siriyuvasak, "Ambiguity of the 'Emerging' Public Sphere," 105–106.

20. Chaiworaporn and Adam Knee, "Thailand," 58.

21. Chaiworaporn and Knee, "Thailand," 58–60.

22. Sukwong and Suwannapak, *Century of Thai Cinema*, 8–9.

23. Knee, "Thailand," 77.

24. Alongkorn Klysorikhew, "Overview of Action Movies," in *Thai Cinema*, ed. Bastian Meiresonne (Lyon: Asiaexpo, 2006), 74.

25. Quoted in Klysorikhew, "Overview of Action Movies," 75.

26. Jaa was formerly known as Panom Yeerum.

27. "Tony Jaa Biography," Sahamongkol Film International, accessed February 4, 2010, http://www.iamtonyjaa.com/thai/biography.php.

28. *Born to Fight* (*Kerd ma Liu*; เกิดมาลุย), directed by Panna Rittikrai, action choreography by Panna Rittikrai and Banlu Srisaeng (Bangkok: Baa-Ram-Ewe and Sahamongkolfilm, 2004).

29. Interviewed in Anchalee Chaiworaporn, "Panna Rittikrai: The Man behind Ong Bak and Tony Jaa," Thaicinema.org, accessed February 4, 2010, http://www.thaicinema.org/interview15_pannae.asp.

30. Hans Gruber et al., "Persons in the Shadow: Assessing the Social Context of High Abilities," *Psychology Science Quarterly* 50, no. 2 (2008): 239.

31. *Ong Bak: Muay Thai Warrior* (องค์บาก), directed by Prachya Pinkaew, action choreography by Tony Jaa, Panna Rittikrai, and Seng Kawee (Thailand: Baa-Ram-Ewe and Sahamongkolfilm, 2003).

32. Lisa Purse, *Contemporary Action Cinema* (Edinburgh: Edinburgh University Press, 2011), 40; Yvonne Tasker, *Hollywood Action Adventure Film* (Malden, MA: Wiley Blackwell, 2015), 21; and Chris Holmlund, "Wham! Bam! Pam! Pam Grier as Hot Action Babe and Cool Action Mama," *Quarterly Review of Film and Video* 22, no. 2 (2005): 97.

33. Purse, *Contemporary Action Cinema*, 43.

34. Tasker, *Hollywood Action Adventure Film*, 21.

35. May Adadol Ingawanij, "*Nang Nak*: Thai Bourgeois Heritage Cinema," *Inter-Asia Cultural Studies* 8, no. 2 (May 2007): 180–81.

36. Lauren Steimer, "Tony Jaa Fan Survey" (online survey), January 15, 2010.

37. Steimer, "Tony Jaa Fan Survey," January 15, 2010.

38. *The Protector* (*Tom-Yum-Goong*; ต้มยำกุ้ง), directed by Prachya Pinkaew, action choreography by Tony Jaa and Panna Rittikrai (Bangkok: Sahamongkolfilm, Baa-Ram-Ewe, TF1 International, and Golden Network, 2005).

39. *Fong Sai-yuk* (方世玉; *Fang Shi Yu*), directed by Corey Yuen Kwai, action choreography by Corey Yuen Kwai, Kuo Hin-chui, Alien Sit, and Yuen Tak (Hong Kong: Eastern Productions, 1993).

40. Tom Gunning, "An Aesthetic of Astonishment: Early Film and the (In)Credulous Spectator," in *Viewing Positions: Ways of Seeing Film*, ed. Linda Williams (New Brunswick, NJ: Rutgers University Press, 1995), 116.

41. Gunning, "Aesthetic of Astonishment," 118.

42. Quoted in Leon Hunt, "*Ong-Bak*: New Thai Cinema, Hong Kong and the Cult of the 'Real,'" *New Cinemas: Journal of Contemporary Film* 3, no. 2 (2005): 77.

43. *The Matrix Reloaded*, directed by Lana and Lilly Wachowski, action choreography by Yuen Woo-ping (Los Angeles: Heineken Branded Entertainment, NPV Entertainment, Silver Pictures, Warner Bros; Melbourne: Village Roadshow Pictures, 2003).

44. Craig D. Reid, "Fighting without Fighting: Film Action Fight Choreography," *Film Quarterly* 47, no. 2 (Winter 1993–94): 32–35.

45. Thomas T. Chatkupt, Albert E. Sollod, and Sinth Sarobol, "Elephants in Thailand: Determinants of Health and Welfare in Working Populations," *Journal of Applied Animal Welfare Science* 2, no. 3 (1999): 187–89; Rita Ringis, *Elephants of Thailand in Myth, Art, and Reality* (Oxford: Oxford University Press, 1996), 1–32, 60–175; Prasob Tipprasert, "Elephants and Ecotourism in Thailand," in *Giants on Our Hands: Proceedings of the International Workshop on the Domesticated Asian Elephant*, ed. Iljas Baker and Masakazu Kashio (Bangkok: Food and Agriculture Organization of the United Nations, Regional Office for Asia and the Pacific, 2002), 157; and Roger Lohanan, "The Elephant Situation in Thailand and a Plea for Cooperation," in Baker and Kashio, *Giants on Our Hands*, 231.

46. *Ong Bak 2* (องค์บาก 2), directed by Tony Jaa and Panna Rittikrai, action choreography by Tony Jaa and Panna Rittikrai (Bangkok: Sahamongkolfilm International and Iyara Films, 2008).

47. *Ong Bak 3* (องค์บาก 3), directed by Tony Jaa and Panna Rittikrai, action choreography by Tony Jaa (Bangkok: Iyara Films, 2010).

48. ntsoopsip@gmail.com, "Tony Jaa Now Free to Pursue What's Left of His Dreams," *Nation* (Thailand), July 9, 2015, http://www.nationmultimedia.com/life/Tony-Jaa-now-free-to-pursue-whats-left-of-his-drea-30264041.html.

49. *Power Kids* (5 หัวใจฮีโร่; 5 Hawci Hiro), directed by Krissanapong Rachata, action choreography by Panna Rittikrai (Bangkok: Baa-Ram-Ewe, 2009).

50. Interviewed in Chaiworaporn, "Panna Rittikrai."

51. *Chocolate* (ช็อคโกแลต), directed by Prachya Pinkaew, action choreography by Panna Rittikrai (Bangkok: Sahamongkolfilm International and Baa-Ram-Ewe, 2008).

52. Yanin Vismitananda, "Q and A: Yanin Vismitananda," *BK Online*, January 30, 2008, accessed March 1, 2012, http://bkmagazine.com/feature/q-yanin-vismitananda.

53. *Raging Phoenix* (*Deu Suay Doo*; ดื้อ สวย ดุ), directed by Rashane Limtrakul, action choreography by Panna Rittikrai (Bangkok: Sahamongkolfilm and Baa-Ram-Ewe, 2009).

54. Thorsten Botz-Bornstein, "Wong Kar-Wai's Films and the Culture of the *Kawaii*," *SubStance: A Review of Theory and Literary Criticism* 37, no. 2 (2008): 95.

55. *The Kick* (더 킥), directed by Prachya Pinkaew, action choreography by Panna Rittikrai and Weerapon Poomatfon (Bangkok: Baa-Ram-Ewe, Bangkok Film Studio; Seoul: Kick Company, 2011).

56. *This Girl Is Bad Ass!!* (*Jukkalan*; จักกะแหล่น), directed by Petchtai Wongkamlao, martial arts choreography by Panna Rittikrai (Bangkok: Bam-Ram-Ewe, 2011).

Chapter 3: A Hong Kong Reservoir for *Xena*

1. Jacinda Read, "The Cult of Masculinity: From Fan-Boys to Academic Bad-Boys," in *Defining Cult Movies: The Cultural Politics of Oppositional Tastes*, ed. Mark Jancovich, Antonio Lazaro Reboli, Julian Stringer, and Andrew Willis (New York: Palgrave, 2003), 64.

2. *Xena: Warrior Princess*, created by Rob Tapert and John Schulian, action choreography by Peter Bell and Shane Dawson, aired September 15, 1995–June 18, 2001 (syndicated); *Double Dare*, directed by Amanda Micheli (San Francisco: Runaway Films; Atlanta, GA: Goodmovies Entertainment; Los Angeles: Map Point Pictures, 2005); *Kill Bill: Vol. 1*, directed by Quentin Tarantino, action choreography by Yuen Woo-ping, Sonny Chiba, Keith Adams, and Ku Huen-chiu (Los Angeles: A Band Apart, Super Cool ManChu; New York: Miramax Films, 2003); *Kill Bill: Vol. 2*, directed by Quentin Tarantino, action choreography by Yuen Woo-ping, Sonny Chiba, Keith Adams, and Ku Huen-chiu (Los Angeles: A Band Apart, Super Cool ManChu; New York: Miramax Films, 2004); *Death Proof*, directed by Quentin Tarantino, action choreography by Jeff Dashnaw (New York: Dimension Films, Weinstein Company; Austin: Troublemaker Studios, Rodriguez International Pictures, 2007); and *Catwoman*, directed by Pitof, action choreography by Kirk Caouette, Steve M. Davison, Mike Gunther, and Jacob Rupp (Los Angeles: Warner Bros Pictures, DiNovi Pictures, Maple Shade Films, Catwoman Films; Beverly Hills: Village Roadshow Pictures; Winnipeg: Frantic Films, 2004).

3. *Xena: Warrior Princess* was a first-run syndicated program in the United States, distributed by Universal Studios' television wing, MCA TV. The show was subsequently syndicated in Europe, Latin America, and Oceania by MCA TV International.

4. Peter Newmark, *Approaches to Translation* (Oxford: Pergamon, 1981), 39.

5. Peter Newmark, "Communicative and Semantic Translation," *Babel: International Journal of Translation* 23, no. 4 (1977): 163–80.

6. Linda Williams describes the "jerk reaction" as the physically jarring effects that on-screen action in slasher horror films (the "fear jerk"), women's weepies (the "tear jerk"), and pornography (the "jerk off") have on the spectator. See Williams, "Body Genres: Gender, Genre and Excess," in *Feminist Film Theory*, ed. Sue Thornham (New York: New York University Press, 1999), 269–71.

7. Liz Friedman, Doug Lefler, David Pollison, and Robert Tapert, "Xena's Hong Kong Origins," disc 7, *Xena: Warrior Princess*, Tenth Anniversary Collection, DVD (Beverly Hills: Anchor Bay Entertainment, 2005), at 00:08:42.

8. Angelika Foerst, "Subtext Matters: The Queered Curriculum behind the Warrior Princess and the Bard" (PhD diss., Arizona State University, 2008); Sara Gwenllian-Jones, "Histories, Fictions, and *Xena: Warrior Princess*," in *The Audience Studies Reader*, ed. Will Brooker and Deborah Jermyn (London: Routledge, 2003), 185–91; Sharon Marie Ross, "Super(Natural) Women: Female Heroes, Their Friends, and Their Fans" (PhD diss., University of Texas, 2004); Jeanne E. Hamming, "Whatever Turns You On: Becoming-Lesbian and the Production of Desire in the Xenaverse," *Genders* 34 (October 2001), https://www.colorado.edu/gendersarchive1998-2013/2001/10/01/whatever-turns-you-becoming-lesbian-and-production-desire-xenaverse; Elyce Rae Helford, "Feminism, Queer Studies, and the Sexual Politics of *Xena: Warrior Princess*," in *Fantasy Girls: Gender in the New Universe of Science Fiction and Fantasy Television*, ed. Elyce Rae Helford (Lanham, MD: Rowman and Littlefield, 2000), 135–62; and Joanne Morreale, "*Xena: Warrior Princess* as Feminist Camp," *Journal of Popular Culture* 32, no. 2 (1998): 79–86.

9. Historically, in China and Hong Kong, some actors performed their own stunts.

10. Rick Altman, "A Semantic/Syntactic Approach to Film Genre," *Cinema Journal* 23, no. 3 (Spring 1984): 10.

11. Jennifer M. Bean, "Technologies of Early Stardom and the Extraordinary Body," *Camera Obscura* 16, no. 3 (2001): 9–57; Miranda Janis Banks, "Bodies of Work: Rituals of Doubling and the Erasure of Film/TV Production Labor" (PhD diss., University of California, Los Angeles, 2006), 175–237; and Jacob Smith, "Seeing Double: Stunt Performers and Masculinity," *Journal of Film and Video* 56, no. 3 (Fall 2004): 35–53.

12. John Baxter, *Stunt: The Story of the Great Movie Stuntmen* (Garden City, NY: Doubleday, 1974); Yakima Canutt, *Stunt Man*, with Oliver Drake (Norman: University of Oklahoma Press, 1979); George Sullivan and Tim Sullivan, *Stunt People* (New York: Beaufort Books, 1983); and Kevin Conley, *The Full Burn: On the Set, at the Bar, behind the Wheel, and over the Edge with Hollywood Stuntmen* (New York: Bloomsbury, 2008).

13. David Bordwell, "Transcultural Spaces: Toward a Poetics of Chinese Film," *Post Script* 20, no. 2 (Winter–Spring 2001): 11.

14. Bordwell, "Transcultural Spaces," 11.

15. S. Gordon Redding, *The Spirit of Chinese Capitalism* (New York: Walter de Gruyter, 1993), 3.

16. Zoë Bell, in discussion with author, Irvine, CA, May 14, 2009.

17. Bordwell, "Transcultural Spaces," 10.

18. David Bordwell, *Planet Hong Kong: Popular Cinema and the Art of Entertainment* (Cambridge, MA: Harvard University Press, 2000), 221–31.

19. *Bride with White Hair* (*Bai Fa Mo Nu Zhuan*; 白髮魔女傳), directed by Ronny Yu, action choreography by Phillip Chung-fung Kwok (Hong Kong: Mandarin Films Distribution Co., 1993); *Heroic Trio* (*Dung Fong San Xia*; 東方三俠), directed by Johnny To, action choreography by Tony Ching Siu-tung (Hong Kong: China Entertainment Films Production and Paka Hill Productions, 1993); and *Dragon Inn* (*Xin Long Men Ke Zhan*; 新龍門客棧), directed by Raymond Lee, action choreography by Cheung Yiu-sing, Donnie Yen, and Yuen Bun (Hong

Kong: Film Workshop and Seasonal Film Corporation, 1992). The *Swordsman* series comprises *Swordsman* (*Xiao Ao Jiang Hu*; 笑傲江湖), directed by King Hu, Tony Ching Siu-tung, Ann Hui, Tsui Hark, Andrew Kam Yeung-wa, and Raymond Lee Wai-man, action choreography by Tony Ching Siu-tung, Lau Chi-ho, and Yuen Wah (Hong Kong: Film Workshop, 1990); *Swordsman II* (*Xiao Ao Jiang Hu II: Dong Fang Bu Bai*; 笑傲江湖II東方不敗), directed by Tony Ching Siu-tung, action choreography by Tony Ching Siu-tung, Yuen Bun, Cheung Yiu-sing, and Ma Yuk-sing (Hong Kong: Film Workshop, Long Shong Pictures, and Golden Princess Film Production), 1992); and *Swordsman III: The East Is Red* (*Dung Fang Bu Bai: Feng Yun Zai Qi*; 東方不敗—風雲再起), directed by Raymond Lee Wai-man and Tony Ching Siu-tung, action choreography by Tony Ching Siu-tung, Dion Lam Dik-on, and Ma Yuk-sing (Hong Kong: Film Workshop, Long Shong Pictures, and Golden Princess Film Production, 1993).

20. Zhang Zhen, "Bodies in the Air: The Magic of Science and the Fate of the Early 'Martial Arts' Film in China," *Post Script* 20, nos. 2–3 (Winter–Spring 2001): 44.

21. Stephen Teo, *Chinese Martial Arts Cinema: The Wuxia Tradition* (Edinburgh: Edinburgh University Press, 2009), 11.

22. Zhang Zhen, "Bodies in the Air," 51–55.

23. Robert Sklar, *Movie-Made America: A Cultural History of American Movies* (New York: Vintage Books, 1994), 289.

24. Some notable examples of high-dollar Hollywood productions of the 1960s that had a strong box office draw in Hong Kong and other parts of Asia were *Dr. No*, directed by Terence Young, action choreography by Bob Simmons (Santa Monica: Danjaq; London: Eon Productions, 1962); *From Russia with Love*, directed by Terence Young, action choreography by Peter Perkins (Santa Monica: Danjaq; London: Eon Productions, 1963); *Goldfinger*, directed by Guy Hamilton, action choreography by Bob Simmons (Santa Monica: Danjaq; London: Eon Productions, 1964); and *The Exorcist*, directed by William Friedkin (Los Angeles: Warner Brothers, Hoya Productions, 1973). See Sklar, *Movie-Made America*, 215–17.

25. The late 1960s were a turbulent time for Hong Kong. In 1967 a series of riots broke out in the colony. The government responded to the disturbances with new social welfare policies to foster a more amicable relationship between Hong Kong citizens and the police. Some scholars have suggested that the social unrest manifested itself on-screen in the form of martial arts violence, which was well received by Hong Kong audiences. See Kar Law, "Stars in a Landscape: A Glance at Cantonese Movies of the Sixties," in *The Restless Breed: Cantonese Stars of the Sixties*, ed. Kar Law (Hong Kong: Hong Kong Urban Council, 1996), 53–59.

26. I refer to the cables as "seemingly invisible" because they are more easily perceived in Shanghai and Hong Kong films from the 1920s, Mandarin high-budget productions of the 1960s, and Cantonese low-budget productions from the 1960s than in the new wuxia cycle in the late 1980s to 1990s, in which such wires were digitally erased. Using women with small frames allowed the thinnest possible wires to be used for support.

27. King Hu's film *A Touch of Zen* (*Xia Nu*; 俠女), directed by King Hu, action choreography by Han Ying-chieh and Pan Yao-kun (Hong Kong: Union Film Company, 1971), was pro-

duced in 1971, and in 1975 it was one of the earliest Chinese films to receive commendation at the Cannes Film Festival.

28. *The Jade Bow* (*Wan Hoi Yuk Gung Yuen*; 雲海玉弓緣), directed by Fu Chi and Cheung Sing-yim, action choreography by Lau Kar-leung and Tong Kai (Hong Kong: Great Wall Movie Enterprises Limited, 1966); *Tiger Boy* (*Hu Xia Jian Chou*; 虎俠殲仇), directed by Chang Che (Hong Kong: Shaw Brothers, 1966); *Come Drink with Me* (*Da Zui Xia*; 大醉俠), directed by King Hu, choreography by Han Ying-chieh and Poon Kin-kwan (Hong Kong: Shaw Brothers, 1966); *The Big Boss* (*Tang Shan Daxiong*; 唐山大兄), directed by Lo Wei, choreographed by Han Ying-chieh (Hong Kong: Golden Harvest, 1971); and Stephen Teo, *Hong Kong Cinema: The Extra Dimensions* (London: British Film Institute, 1997), 98.

29. Leon Hunt, *Kung Fu Cult Masters: From Bruce Lee to "Crouching Tiger"* (New York: Wallflower, 2003), 23.

30. Hunt, *Kung Fu Cult Masters*, 23–24.

31. The perceived division of Mandarin and Cantonese cinema along subgeneric lines held that wuxia films were Mandarin and kung fu films were Cantonese, but this is a misperception. See Teo, *Hong Kong Cinema*, 74, 98.

32. Cindy Hing-yuk Wong, "Cities, Cultures and Cassettes: Hong Kong Cinema and Transnational Audiences," *Post Script* 19, no. 1 (Fall 1999): 94–98.

33. Wong, "Cities, Cultures and Cassettes," 98–103.

34. Wong, "Cities, Cultures and Cassettes," 98.

35. *The Evil Dead*, directed by Sam Raimi, produced by Robert Tapert (New York: Renaissance Pictures, 1981); *Evil Dead II*, directed by Sam Raimi, produced by Robert Tapert, action choreography by Gary Jensen (Wilmington, NC: De Laurentiis Entertainment Group; New York: Renaissance Pictures, 1987); and *Army of Darkness*, directed by Sam Raimi, produced by Robert Tapert, action choreography by Chris Doyle (Wilmington, NC : Dino De Laurentiis Company, 1992).

36. Quoted in Craig Reid, "*Spider-Man 2*: On the Lam," *Kung Fu Magazine*, July 12, 2009, http://ezine.kungfumagazine.com/ezine/article.php?article=528.

37. Liz Friedman, Doug Lefler, David Pollison, and Robert Tapert, "Xena's Hong Kong Origins," disc 7, *Xena: Warrior Princess*, Tenth Anniversary Collection, DVD (Beverly Hills: Anchor Bay Entertainment, 2005).

38. *Chinese Ghost Story* (*Qian Nu You Hun*; 倩女幽魂), directed by Tony Ching Siu-tung, action choreography by Tony Ching Siu-tung, Alan Chung Shan-tsui, Lau Chi-ho, Tsu Kwok, Wu Chi-lung (Hong Kong: Cinema City, Film Productions, and Film Workshop, 1987); *Once Upon a Time in China* (*Huang Fei-hong*; 黃飛鴻), directed by Tsui Hark, action choreography by Yuen Cheung-yan, Yuen Sun-yi, and Lau Kar-wing (Hong Kong: Golden Harvest Company and Film Workshop, 1991); *Fong Sai Yuk* (*Fang Shi Yu*; 方世玉), directed by Corey Yuen Kwai, action choreography by Corey Yuen Kwai and Tak Yuen (Hong Kong: Eastern Productions, 1993) and *Ashes of Time* (*Dong Xie Xi Du*; 東邪西毒), directed by Wong Kar-wai, action choreography by Sammo Hung Kam-bo (Hong Kong: Beijing Film Studio, Jet Tone Production, Pony Canyon, and Scholar Productions, 1994).

39. Liz Friedman, Doug Lefler, David Pollison, and Robert Tapert, "Xena's Hong Kong Origins," disc 7, *Xena: Warrior Princess*, Tenth Anniversary Collection, DVD (Beverly Hills: Anchor Bay Entertainment, 2005), at 00:08:42.

40. Teo, *Chinese Martial Arts Cinema*, 88.

41. *Hercules: The Legendary Journeys*, created by Christian Williams, action choreography by Ben Cooke and Allan Poppleton, aired January 16, 1995–November 22, 1999 (syndicated).

42. Bruce Babington, *A History of the New Zealand Fiction Feature Film* (New York: Manchester University Press, 2007), 10.

43. Bell, discussion.

44. Liz Friedman, Doug Lefler, David Pollison, and Robert Tapert, "Xena's Hong Kong Origins," disc 7, *Xena: Warrior Princess*, Tenth Anniversary Collection, DVD (Beverly Hills: Anchor Bay Entertainment, 2005), at 00:41:45.

45. Babington, *History of the New Zealand Fiction Feature*, 184–85.

46. *Lord of the Rings: Fellowship of the Ring*, directed by Peter Jackson, action choreography by George Marshall Ruge (New York: New Line Cinema; Wellington: WingNut Films, 2001); *Lord of the Rings: The Two Towers*, directed by Peter Jackson, action choreography by George Marshall Ruge (New York: New Line Cinema; Wellington: WingNut Films, 2002); and *Lord of the Rings: Return of the King*, directed by Peter Jackson, action choreography by George Marshall Ruge (New York: New Line Cinema; Wellington: WingNut Films, 2003).

47. I am indebted to studio companion animal labor scholar Kelly Wolf for this insight, gained in a conversation about her archival research in the Hedda Hopper Special Collection at the Herrick Library. See Rudd Weatherwax, interview by Hedda Hopper, November 19, 1957, Hedda Hopper Collection, Margaret Herrick Library, Academy of Motion Picture Arts and Sciences, Beverly Hills, CA; *Lassie Come Home*, directed by Fred M. Wilcox, animal wrangler Rudd Weatherwax (United States: Loew's/MGM, 1943); *Goldeneye*, directed by Martin Campbell, action choreography by Simon Crane (London: Eon Productions; Los Angeles: United Artists, 1995); *The Matrix Reloaded*, directed by Lana and Lilly Wachowski, action choreography by Yuen Woo-ping (Los Angeles: Heineken Branded Entertainment, NPV Entertainment, Silver Pictures, Warner Bros; Melbourne: Village Roadshow Pictures, 2003).

48. In point of fact, Bell mentioned to me that she was learning to skateboard, a pleasurable activity for the average person new to the sport that could become, for Bell, a valuable addition to her résumé. Bell, discussion.

49. Barry King, "Articulating Stardom," in *Stardom: Industry of Desire*, ed. Christine Gledhill (New York: Routledge, 1991), 171.

50. Bell, discussion; and *Xena: Warrior Princess*, season 6, episode 16, "Send in the Clones," directed by Charlie Haskell, action choreography by Allan Poppleton, aired April 23, 2001 (syndicated).

51. *Amazon High*, directed by Michael Hurst, action choreography by Jonathan Costelloe (New York: Renaissance Pictures, Unaired Pilot, 1997).

52. The stunt team was run by Peter Bell.

53. Jennifer M. Bean, "Technologies of Early Stardom and the Extraordinary Body," *Camera Obscura* 16, no. 3 (2001): 9–57.

54. Zhang Zhen, "Bodies in the Air," 51.

55. *Xena: Warrior Princess*, season 6, episode 22, "A Friend in Need, Part 2," directed by Robert Tapert, action choreography by Mark Rounthwaite, aired June 18, 2001 (syndicated).

56. Richard Allen has identified a similar tendency in the work of Alfred Hitchcock, in which bold color motifs bring objects to the attention of the audience. See Richard Allen, "Hitchcock's Color Designs," in *Color: The Film Reader*, ed. Angela Dalle Vacche and Brian Price (New York: Routledge, 2006), 137–39.

57. *Xena: Warrior Princess*, season 6, episode 21, "A Friend in Need, Part 1," directed by Robert Tapert, action choreography by Allan Poppleton, aired June 11, 2001 (syndicated).

58. Zoë Bell and Lucy Lawless, "Seeing Double," disc 7, *Xena: Warrior Princess*, Tenth Anniversary Collection, DVD (Beverly Hills: Anchor Bay Entertainment, 2005), at 00:07:37.

59. Sean Collier, "Interview: Zoë Bell," *Verbicide* 25 (Spring 2009): 18.

60. Bell, discussion.

61. Joanna R. Sofaer, *The Body as Material Culture: A Theoretical Osteoarchaeology* (New York: Cambridge University Press, 2006), 72–73.

62. I do not mean to suggest that either *Xena* or the *Kill Bill* series is limited to Hong Kong action films in their aesthetic, generic, and narrative influences. *Xena* has an obvious debt to 1970s television heroines like Wonder Woman and the Bionic Woman, and Tarantino's series betrays a wide array of influences and intertextual references: the *chambara* films, the spaghetti western, Ozploitation horror (*Patrick*, directed by Richard Franklin [Melbourne: Filmways Australasia, 1978]), and even a Swedish rape-revenge exploitation film, *They Call Her One Eye* (*Thriller—en grym film*), directed by Bo Arne Vibenius, action choreography by Jan Kreigsman (Stockholm: BAV Film and United Producers, 1973).

63. Richard Schechner, *Between Theater and Anthropology* (Philadelphia: University of Pennsylvania Press, 1985), 35–38.

64. Lauren Steimer, "Zoë Bell Fan Survey" (online survey), August 5, 2009.

65. *Wonder Woman*, produced by Douglas S. Cramer, aired November 7, 1975–September 11, 1979, on ABC and CBS.

66. This dual role is unique because *Death Proof* is a contemporary American film. In the 1910s, stunting stars were more common in the United States.

67. Bell, discussion.

68. Conley, *Full Burn*, 120.

69. Lauren Steimer, "Zoë Bell Fan Survey" (online survey), June 3, 2009; and Steimer, "Zoë Bell Fan Survey," August 5, 2009.

70. Of forty-five people, thirteen were introduced to Bell as a stunting star in *Double Dare*, and twenty-seven first came to know her as a star in *Death Proof*. Steimer, "Zoë Bell Fan Survey," June 3, 2009; and Steimer, "Zoë Bell Fan Survey," August 5, 2009.

71. Bell, discussion.

72. Bean, "Technologies of Early Stardom."

73. Jacob Smith has also addressed this issue. See Smith, "Seeing Double," 37.

74. Tom Gunning, "The Cinema of Attractions: Early Film, Its Spectator and the Avant-Garde," in *Early Cinema: Space, Frame, Narrative*, ed. Thomas Elsaesser and Adam Barker (London: British Film Institute, 1990), 56–62.

75. Smith, "Seeing Double," 35–36, 38–43.

76. As Bean, Smith, and Conley have alluded to, not all of the silent-era stars really performed their own stunts.

77. The special relationship that some viewers have to the material function of nonstunting stars can be lived out in various ways, but the most common articulation of this aspect of fandom is participation in a production-site tour. The fan will visit the location of a film or television show's production to gain further knowledge of the text's construction and to feel a physical proximity to the star/character. In some instances, production-site tours can be prompted by fascination with the narrative universe of a text and not simply with individual actors. While there are many reasons that tourists attend the *Sex and the City* tour in New York or the *Lord of the Rings* tour in New Zealand, the desire to gain a material connection to a diegetic universe or a character/star is common.

78. *Shall We Dance*, directed by Mark Sandrich (Los Angeles: RKO Radio Pictures, 1937).

79. Williams, "Body Genres," 268–71.

80. Quoted in Kate Kyriacou, "A Feisty Kiwi's Proof Positive," *Sunday Telegraph* (Sydney), November 4, 2007.

Chapter 4: Hong Kong Action In Transit

1. Lisa Odham Stokes and Michael Hoover, *City on Fire: Hong Kong Cinema* (New York: Verso, 1999), 19.

2. *Ash vs Evil Dead*, produced by Robert Tapert, stunt coordination by Stuart Thorpe, Dayna Grant, and Tim Wong, aired October 31, 2015–April 29, 2018, on Starz.

3. David Bordwell, *Planet Hong Kong: Popular Cinema and the Art of Entertainment* (Cambridge, MA: Harvard University Press, 2000); Esther Ching-mei Yau, *At Full Speed: Hong Kong Cinema in a Borderless World* (Minneapolis: University of Minnesota Press, 2001); and Meaghan Morris, Siu Leung Li, and Stephen Chan Ching-kiu, eds., *Hong Kong Connections: Transnational Imagination in Action Cinema* (Durham, NC: Duke University Press; Hong Kong: Hong Kong University Press, 2005).

4. Bordwell, *Planet Hong Kong*, xi–xii.

5. Yau, *At Full Speed*, 1.

6. Meaghan Morris, "Introduction: Hong Kong Connections," in *Hong Kong Connections: Transnational Imagination in Action Cinema*, ed. Meaghan Morris, Siu Leung Li, and Stephen Chan Ching-kiu (Durham, NC: Duke University Press; Hong Kong: Hong Kong University Press, 2005), 3.

7. Hamid Naficy, *An Accented Cinema: Exilic and Diasporic Filmmaking* (Princeton, NJ: Princeton University Press, 2001).

8. Toby Miller et al., *Global Hollywood* (London: British Film Institute, 2001), 40–42, 44–82.

9. Daya Kishan Thussu, "Introduction," in *Media on the Move: Global Flow and Contra-Flow*, ed. Daya Kishan Thussu (New York: Routledge, 2007), 3.

10. Sheldon Hsiao-peng Lu, ed., "Historical Introduction Chinese Cinemas (1896–1996) and Transnational Film Studies," in *Transnational Chinese Cinemas: Identity, Nationhood, Gender*, ed. Sheldon Hsiao-peng Lu (Honolulu: University of Hawaii Press, 1997), 10–11.

11. Stephen J. Collier and Aihwa Ong, "Global Assemblages, Anthropological Problems," in *Global Assemblages: Technology, Politics, and Ethics as Anthropological Problems*, ed. Aihwa Ong and Stephen J. Collier (Hoboken, NJ: Wiley-Blackwell, 2004), 4.

12. Nitin Govil, "Wind(fall) from the East," *Television and New Media* 10, no. 1 (January 2009): 63–65.

13. Sylvia J. Martin, *Haunted: An Ethnography of the Hollywood and Hong Kong Media Industries* (New York: Oxford University Press, 2017), 37.

14. Linda Hutcheon, Djelal Kadir, and Mario J. Valdes, "Collaborative Historiography: A Comparative Literary History of Latin America," *American Council of Learned Societies Occasional Paper*, no. 35 (1996): 2, quoted in Ying-jin Zhang, "National Cinema as Translocal Practice: Reflections on Chinese Film Historiography," in *The Chinese Cinema Book*, ed. Songhwee Lim and Julian Ward (London: British Film Institute, 2011), 21.

15. Poshek Fu and David Desser, quoted in Morris, "Introduction," 10.

16. Martin, *Haunted*, 51–52.

17. Bryan Chang, "Sculptures in Motion: The Mind, Body and Spirit of Hong Kong Action Cinema," trans. Ranchos Cong, in *A Tribute to Action Choreographers: A 30th Hong Kong International Film Festival Programme*, ed. Li Cheuk-to (Hong Kong: Hong Kong International Film Festival Society, 2006), 16.

18. Yung Sai-shing, "Moving Body: The Interactions between Chinese Opera and Action Cinema," in Morris, Li, and Chan, *Hong Kong Connections*, 28–31.

19. Yung, "Moving Body," 26–27.

20. Chang, "Sculptures in Motion," 17–18.

21. Craig D. Reid, "Fighting without Fighting: Film Action Fight Choreography," *Film Quarterly* 47, no. 2 (Winter 1993–94): 33.

22. *Game of Thrones*, created by David Benioff and D. B. Weiss, aired April 17, 2011–May 19, 2019, on HBO; and Rowley Irlam, "Game Revealed: Season 7 Episode 4: Warrior Women (HBO)," Game of Thrones: Behind the Scenes, September 18, 2017, https://www.facebook.com/GameOfThrones/posts/10155173241602734.

23. *The Matrix*, directed by Lana and Lilly Wachowski, action choreography by Yuen Woo-ping (Los Angeles: Silver Pictures, Groucho II Film Partnership, and Warner Brothers; Melbourne: Village Roadshow Pictures, 1999).

24. *Les tribulations d'un Chinois et Chine* (*Chinese Adventures in China*), directed by Philippe de Broca (Paris: Les Films Ariane, Les Productions Aristes Associés, and Vides Cinematograg-ica, 1965). See Bryan Chang, "The Boys of the Sand Pebbles," trans. Davina To, in Li, *Tribute to Action Choreographers*, 151.

25. Quoted in Chang, "Boys of the Sand Pebbles," 151. In Hong Kong the preferred nomenclature for some action designers or stunt coordinators is *action director*. It is a title some assumed because they felt it awarded them similar cultural and industrial status to first-unit directors.

26. *The Sand Pebbles*, directed by Robert Wise (Los Angeles: Argyle Enterprises, Robert Wise Productions, Solar Productions, and Twentieth Century Fox, 1966).

27. Stephen Tung Wai, "Interview with Stephen Tung Wai: Keeping It Real," interview by Cheung Chi-sing, Li Cheuk-to, Pang Chi-ming, Bryan Chang, and Wong Ching, trans. Bede Chang, in Li, *Tribute to Action Choreographers*, 107.

28. Tong Kai, "Interview with Tong Kai, the Invincible Master of Weapons," interview by Donna Chu, trans. Piera Chen, in Li, *Tribute to Action Choreographers*, 49.

29. Toby Miller et al., *Global Hollywood* (London: British Film Institute, 2001), 52–55.

30. *Superman*, directed by Richard Donner, stunt coordination by Vic Armstrong (Los Angeles: Dovemead Films, Film Export, and International Film Production, 1978).

31. Fung Hak-on, "The Bearable Lightness of Wire: A Milestone for the Wire," collated by Keith Chan, trans. Maggie Lee, in Li, *Tribute to Action Choreographers*, 141.

32. Lee Kwan-lung, "The Bearable Lightness of Wire: Interview with Lee Kwan-lung," collated by Keith Chan, trans. Maggie Lee, in Li, *Tribute to Action Choreographers*, 143.

33. Martin, *Haunted*, 51.

34. Martin, *Haunted*, 51.

35. Martin, *Haunted*, 49.

36. Yuen Woo-ping, "Conquering the West, One Kick at a Time," collated by Keith Chan, trans. Davina To, in Li Cheuk-to, *Tribute to Action Choreographers*, 157; *The Matrix*; *Kill Bill: Vol. 1*, directed by Quentin Tarantino, action choreography by Yuen Woo-ping, Sonny Chiba, Keith Adams, and Ku Huen-chiu (Los Angeles: A Band Apart, Super Cool ManChu; New York: Miramax Films, 2003); and *Kill Bill: Vol. 2*, directed by Quentin Tarantino, action choreography by Yuen Woo-ping, Sonny Chiba, Keith Adams, and Ku Huen-chiu (Los Angeles: A Band Apart, Super Cool ManChu; New York: Miramax Films, 2004).

37. Stephen Tung Wai, "Conquering the West, One Kick at a Time," collated by Keith Chan, trans. Davina To, in Li, *Tribute to Action Choreographers*, 157.

38. Mark Banks, "Craft Labour and Creative Industries," *International Journal of Cultural Policy* 16, no. 3 (2010): 305.

39. Richard de Cordova, "Genre and Performance: An Overview," in *Film Genre Reader IV*, ed. Barry Keith Grant (Austin: University of Texas Press, 2012), 148.

40. Mark Banks, "Craft Labour and Creative Industries," 305.

41. Mark Banks, "Craft Labour and Creative Industries," 307; and Richard Sennett, *The Craftsman* (New Haven, CT: Yale University Press, 2008), 60.

42. Mark Banks, *The Politics of Cultural Work* (New York: Palgrave Macmillan, 2007), 29.

43. Michael Curtin and Kevin Sanson, "Listening to Labor," in *Voices of Labor: Creativity, Craft, and Conflict in Global Hollywood*, ed. Michael Curtin and Kevin Sanson (Berkeley: University of California Press, 2017), 5.

44. Sennett, *Craftsman*, 27.

45. Curtin and Sanson, "Listening to Labor," 5.

46. Maureen Guirdham, *Work Communication: Mediated and Face-to-Face Practices* (New York: Palgrave, 2015), 275.

47. Jean Lave and Etienne Wenger, *Situated Learning: Legitimate Peripheral Participation* (Cambridge: Cambridge University Press, 1991); and Etienne Wenger, *Communities of Practice: Learning, Meaning, and Identity* (New York: Cambridge University Press, 2003).

48. See the discussion of the selective raced and gendered admissions policies of the original Hollywood Stuntmen's Association of Motion Pictures in Miranda Janis Banks and Lauren Steimer, "The Heroic Body: Toughness, Femininity, and the Stunt Double," in *Gender and Creative Labor*, ed. Bridget Conor, Rosalind Gill, and Stephanie Taylor, Sociological Review Monograph Series (Hoboken, NJ: Wiley-Blackwell, 2015), 144–57.

49. Christopher Cram, "Digital Cinema: The Role of the Visual Effects Supervisor," *Film History: An International Journal* 24, no. 2 (2012): 176.

50. Cram, "Digital Cinema," 176.

51. Cale Schultz, in discussion with the author, Los Angeles, June 7, 2016.

52. Schultz, discussion.

53. Reid, "Fighting without Fighting," 35.

54. Martin, *Haunted*, 50.

55. *Serenity*, directed by Joss Whedon, stunt coordination by Chad Stahelski (Universal City: Universal Pictures; Los Angeles: Barry Mendel Productions, 2005).

56. *John Wick*, directed by Chad Stahelski and David Leitch, stunt coordination by Darrin Prescott (Santa Monica: Thunder Road Pictures; Los Angeles: 87eleven, MJW Films, and DefyNite Films, 2014); and *Atomic Blonde*, directed by David Leitch, stunt coordination by

Sam Hargrave (Los Angeles: 87eleven, Closed on Mondays Entertainment, and Denver and Delilah Productions, 2017).

57. *Mad Max: Fury Road*, directed by George Miller, stunt coordination by Glen Suter and Steve Griffin (Los Angeles: Warner Bros. Pictures; Melbourne: Village Roadshow Pictures, and Kennedy Miller Productions, 2015); *The Chronicles of Narnia: The Lion, the Witch and the Wardrobe*, directed by Andrew Adamson, stunt coordination by Allan Poppleton and Stuart Thorpe (Los Angeles: Walt Disney Pictures and Walden Media, 2005); and *Underworld: Rise of the Lycans*, directed by Patrick Tatopoulos, stunt coordination by Allan Poppleton and Paul Shapcott (Beverly Hills: Lakeshore Entertainment; Culver City: Screen Gems; Los Angeles: Sketch Films, and UW3 Film Productions, 2009).

58. Dayna Grant, in discussion with the author, Auckland, New Zealand, May 9, 2017.

59. Grant, discussion.

60. Grant, discussion.

61. Lucy Lawless, in discussion with the author, Auckland, New Zealand, May 9, 2017.

62. *Ash vs Evil Dead*, season 3, episode 6, "Tales from the Rift," directed by Regan Hall, written by Aaron Lam, stunt coordination by Stuart Thorpe, Dayna Grant, and Tim Wong, aired April 1, 2018, on Starz.

63. *A Chinese Ghost Story* (*Qian Nu You Hun*; 倩女幽魂), directed by Tony Ching Siu-tung, produced by Tsui Hark, action choreography by Tony Ching Siu-tung, Alan Chung Shan-tsui, Lau Chi-ho, Tsu Kwok, and Wu Chi-lung (Hong Kong: Cinema City Film Productions and Film Workshop, 1987).

64. Grant, discussion; Lawless, discussion.

65. Grant, discussion; Lawless, discussion.

66. Grant, discussion.

67. Eimear O'Grady, in discussion with the author, Wicklow, Ireland, March 8, 2017.

68. Michelene T. H. Chi, "Two Approaches to the Study of Experts' Characteristics," in *The Cambridge Handbook of Expertise and Expert Performance*, ed. K. Anders Ericsson, Neil Charness, Paul J. Feltovich, and Robert R. Hoffman (New York: Cambridge University Press, 2007), 24.

69. Curtin and Sanson, "Listening to Labor," 3.

Conclusion

1. *Beijing 2008 Olympic Opening Ceremony*, directed by Zhang Yimou, action choreography by Tony Ching Siu-tung, aired August 8, 2008, on China Central Television and NBC.

2. Thomas Clayburn, "Some Beijing Olympic Fireworks Faked," *Information Week*, August 11, 2008, https://www.informationweek.com/some-beijing-olympic-fireworks-faked/d/d-id /1070881.

3. Quoted in Brian Lowry, "XXIX Summer Olympics Opening Ceremony," *Variety*, August 9, 2008, http://variety.com/2008/scene/markets-festivals/xxix-summer-olympics-opening-ceremony-1200507863/.

4. Winifred R. Poster, Marion Crain, and Miriam A. Cherry, "Introduction: Conceptualizing Invisible Labor," in *Invisible Labor: Hidden Work in the Contemporary World*, ed. Marion Crain, Winifred R. Poster, and Miriam A. Cherry (Berkeley: University of California Press, 2016), 6.

5. A literal translation is "skill man."

6. See Jonathan Franks, "'Furious 7': Stunt Crew Members Reportedly Left Out of Credits," *Inquisitr*, April 22, 2015, https://www.inquisitr.com/2034260/furious-7-stunt-crew-out-of-credits/.

7. Poster, Crain, and Cherry, "Introduction," 11.

8. *Daredevil*, created by Drew Goddard, action choreography by Chris Brewster and Philip J. Silvera, written by Bill Everett, streamed April 10, 2015–October 19, 2018, on Netflix; and *Luke Cage*, written by Cheo Hodari Coker, action choreography by James Lew, Alvin Hsing, Guy Fernandez, and Matt Mullins, streamed September 30, 2016–June 22, 2018, on Netflix.

9. *Agents of S.H.I.E.L.D.*, season 2, episode 4, "Face My Enemy," fight choreography by Matt Mullins, directed by Kevin Tancharoen, aired October 14, 2014, on ABC.

10. Poster, Crain, and Cherry, "Introduction," 9.

11. Roland Barthes, "The Face of Garbo," in *Film Theory and Criticism: Introductory Readings*, ed. Leo Braudy and Marshall Cohen (New York: Oxford University Press, 2004), 590.

12. K. Anders Ericsson, "An Introduction to Cambridge Handbook of Expertise and Expert Performance: Its Development, Organization, and Content," in *The Cambridge Handbook of Expertise and Expert Performance*, ed. K. Anders Ericsson, Neil Charness, Paul Feltovich, and Robert R. Hoffman (New York: Cambridge University Press, 2006), 10.

13. Andrea Towers, "Behind the Scenes of the 'Agents of SHIELD' May vs May Fight," *Entertainment Weekly*, December 18, 2014, http://ew.com/article/2014/12/18/agents-of-shield-may-fight/.

14. Quoted in Towers, "Behind the Scenes."

15. A key part of this system that I do not have time to discuss but that is worthy of acknowledgment is the degree to which this process is structured by repeated failure and injury, such that extended deliberate practice in martial arts or intersectional bodily disciplines produces trained experts who readily accept pain, failure, and repetition as normal to their work process—that is, ideal stunt workers.

16. Three projects that directly engage with stunt workers include Miranda Janis Banks, "Bodies of Work: Rituals of Doubling and the Erasure of Film/TV Production Labor" (PhD diss., University of California, Los Angeles, 2006), 175–237; Miranda Janis Banks and Lauren Steimer, "The Heroic Body: Toughness, Femininity, and the Stunt Double," in *Gender and Creative Labor*, ed. Bridget Conor, Rosalind Gill, and Stephanie Taylor, Sociological Review Monograph Series (Hoboken, NJ: Wiley-Blackwell, 2015), 144–57; and Sylvia J. Martin,

Haunted: An Ethnography of the Hollywood and Hong Kong Media Industries (New York: Oxford University Press, 2017).

17. Paul Willemen, "Action Cinema, Labour Power and the Video Market," in *Hong Kong Connections: Transnational Imagination in Action Cinema*, ed. Meaghan Morris, Siu Leung Li, and Stephen Chan Ching-kiu (Durham, NC: Duke University Press; Hong Kong: Hong Kong University Press, 2005), 223–47.

Agénor, Pierre-Richard. *The Asian Financial Crisis: Causes, Contagion and Consequences*. New York: Cambridge University Press, 1999.

Agénor, Pierre-Richard, Joshua Aizenman, and Alexander W. Hoffmaister. "Contagion, Bank Lending Spreads and Output Fluctuations." National Bureau of Economic Research Working Paper Series, no. w6850, Cambridge, MA, December 1998.

Allen, Richard. "Hitchcock's Color Designs." In *Color: The Film Reader*, edited by Angela Dalle Vacche and Brian Price, 131–44. New York: Routledge, 2006.

Altman, Rick. "A Semantic/Syntactic Approach to Film Genre." *Cinema Journal* 23, no. 3 (Spring 1984): 6–18.

Anderson, Aaron. "Violent Dances in the Martial Arts Film." *Jump Cut: A Review of Contemporary Media* 44 (Fall 2001). http://www.ejumpcut.org/archive/jc44.2001/aarona/aaron1.html.

Babington, Bruce. *A History of the New Zealand Fiction Feature Film*. New York: Manchester University Press, 2007.

Banks, Mark. "Craft Labour and Creative Industries." *International Journal of Cultural Policy* 16, no. 3 (2010): 305–21.

Banks, Mark. *The Politics of Cultural Work*. New York: Palgrave Macmillan, 2007.

Banks, Miranda Janis. "Bodies of Work: Rituals of Doubling and the Erasure of Film/TV Production Labor." PhD diss., University of California, Los Angeles, 2006.

Banks, Miranda Janis, and Lauren Steimer. "The Heroic Body: Toughness, Femininity, and the Stunt Double." In *Gender and Creative Labor*, edited by Bridget Conor, Rosalind Gill, and Stephanie Taylor, 144–57. Sociological Review Monograph Series. Hoboken, NJ: Wiley-Blackwell, 2015.

Barmé, Scot. "Early Thai Cinema and Filmmaking: 1897–1922." *Film History* 11, no. 3 (1999): 308–18.

Barthes, Roland. "The Face of Garbo." In *Film Theory and Criticism: Introductory Readings*, edited by Leo Braudy and Marshall Cohen, 589–91. New York: Oxford University Press, 2004.

Baxter, John. *Stunt: The Story of the Great Movie Stuntmen*. Garden City, NY: Doubleday, 1974.

Bean, Jennifer M. "Technologies of Early Stardom and the Extraordinary Body." *Camera Obscura* 16, no. 3 (2001): 9–57.

Berry, Chris, and Mary Farquhar. *China on Screen*. New York: Columbia University Press, 2006.

Bloom, Benjamin Samuel. "Generalizations about Talent Development." In *Developing Talent in Young People*, edited by Benjamin Samuel Bloom, 507–49. New York: Ballantine Books, 1985.

Boonyakatmala, Boonrak. "The Rise and Fall of the Film Industry in Thailand, 1897–1992." *East-West Film Journal* 6, no. 2 (July 1992): 62–98.

Bordwell, David. *Planet Hong Kong: Popular Cinema and the Art of Entertainment*. Cambridge, MA: Harvard University Press, 2000.

Bordwell, David. "Transcultural Spaces: Toward a Poetics of Chinese Film." *Post Script* 20, no. 2 (Winter–Spring 2001): 9–24.

Botz-Bornstein, Thorsten. "Wong Kar-Wai's Films and the Culture of the *Kawaii*." *SubStance: A Review of Theory and Literary Criticism* 37, no. 2 (2008): 94–109.

Bourdieu, Pierre. *Distinction: A Social Critique of the Judgment of Taste*. Translated by Richard Nice. Cambridge, MA: Harvard University Press, 1984.

Bryan, William Lowe, and Noble Harter. "Studies on the Telegraphic Language: The Acquisition of a Hierarchy of Habits." *Psychological Review* 6 (1899): 345–75.

Canutt, Yakima. *Stunt Man*. With Oliver Drake. Norman: University of Oklahoma Press, 1979.

Chaiworaporn, Anchalee. "Panna Rittikrai: The Man behind Ong Bak and Tony Jaa." Thai cinema.org. Accessed February 4, 2010. http://www.thaicinema.org/interview15 _pannae.asp.

Chaiworaporn, Anchalee. "Thai Cinema since 1970." In *Film in South East Asia: Views from the Region*, edited by David Hanan, 141–62. Hanoi: South East Asia-Pacific Audio Visual Archive Association, 2001.

Chaiworaporn, Anchalee, and Adam Knee. "Thailand: Revival in an Age of Globalization." In *Contemporary Asian Cinema: Popular Culture in a Global Frame*, edited by Anne Tereska Ciecko, 58–70. New York: Berg, 2002.

Chan, Jackie. *I Am Jackie Chan: My Life in Action*. With Jeff Yang. New York: Ballantine Books, 1998.

Chang, Bryan. "The Boys of the Sand Pebbles." Translated by Davina To. In *A Tribute to Action Choreographers: A 30th Hong Kong International Film Festival Programme*, edited by Li Cheuk-to, 150–51. Hong Kong: Hong Kong International Film Festival Society, 2006.

Chang, Bryan. "Sculptures in Motion: The Mind, Body and Spirit of Hong Kong Action Cinema." Translated by Ranchos Cong. In *A Tribute to Action Choreographers: A 30th Hong Kong International Film Festival Programme*, edited by Li Cheuk-to, 15–21. Hong Kong: Hong Kong International Film Festival Society, 2006.

Chase, William G., and Herbert A. Simon. "Perception in Chess." *Cognitive Psychology* 4 (1973): 55–81.

Chatkupt, Thomas T., Albert E. Sollod, and Sinth Sarobol. "Elephants in Thailand: Determinants of Health and Welfare in Working Populations." *Journal of Applied Animal Welfare Science* 2, no. 3 (1999): 187–89.

Chi, Michelene T. H. "Two Approaches to the Study of Experts' Characteristics." In *The Cambridge Handbook of Expertise and Expert Performance*, edited by K. Anders Ericsson, Neil Charness, Paul J. Feltovich, and Robert R. Hoffman, 21–30. New York: Cambridge University Press, 2007.

Clayburn, Thomas. "Some Beijing Olympic Fireworks Faked." *Information Week*, August 11, 2008. https://www.informationweek.com/some-beijing-olympic-fireworks-faked /d/d-id/1070881.

Collier, Sean. "Interview: Zoë Bell." *Verbicide* 25 (Spring 2009): 17–19. https://www .verbicidemagazine.com/2009/03/10/interview-zoe-bell/.

Collier, Stephen J., and Aihwa Ong. "Global Assemblages, Anthropological Problems." In *Global Assemblages: Technology, Politics, and Ethics as Anthropological Problems*, edited by Aihwa Ong and Stephen J. Collier, 3–21. Hoboken, NJ: Wiley-Blackwell, 2004.

Conley, Kevin. *The Full Burn: On the Set, at the Bar, behind the Wheel, and over the Edge with Hollywood Stuntmen*. New York: Bloomsbury, 2008.

Cram, Christopher. "Digital Cinema: The Role of the Visual Effects Supervisor." *Film History: An International Journal* 24, no. 2 (2012): 169–86.

Cui, Meng-yang. "Hong Kong Cinema and the 1997 Return of the Colony to Mainland China: The Tensions and the Consequences." Master's thesis, University of Bedfordshire, 2007.

Curtin, Michael, and Kevin Sanson. "Listening to Labor." In *Voices of Labor: Creativity, Craft, and Conflict in Global Hollywood*, edited by Michael Curtin and Kevin Sanson, 1–17. Berkeley: University of California Press, 2017.

de Cordova, Richard. "Genre and Performance: An Overview." In *Film Genre Reader IV*, edited by Barry Keith Grant, 148–58. Austin: University of Texas Press, 2012.

Degner, Stefan, and Hans Gruber. "Persons in the Shadow: How Guidance Works in the Acquisition of Expertise." In *The Politics of Empathy: New Interdisciplinary Perspectives on an Ancient Phenomenon*, edited by Barbara Weber, 103–16. Berlin: Lit, 2011.

Ericsson, K. Anders. "The Acquisition of Expert Performance: An Introduction to Some of the Issues." In *The Road to Excellence: The Acquisition of Expert Performance in the Arts and Sciences, Sports, and Games*, edited by K. Anders Ericsson, 1–50. Mahwah, NJ: Erlbaum, 1996.

Ericsson, K. Anders. "An Introduction to Cambridge Handbook of Expertise and Expert Performance: Its Development, Organization, and Content." In *The Cambridge Handbook of Expertise and Expert Performance*, edited by K. Anders Ericsson, Neil Charness, Paul Feltovich, and Robert R. Hoffman, 3–20. New York: Cambridge University Press, 2006.

Ericsson, K. Anders, Ralf T. Krampe, and Clemens Tesch-Römer. "The Role of Deliberate Practice in the Acquisition of Expert Performance." *Psychological Review* 100, no. 3 (1993): 363–406.

Farquhar, Mary. "Jackie Chan: A New Dragon for a New Generation." *Journal of Chinese Cinemas* 2, no. 2 (2008): 137–46.

Feng Bang-yan, and Nyaw Mee-kau. *Enriching Lives: A History of Insurance in Hong Kong, 1841–2010*. Hong Kong: Hong Kong University Press, 2010.

Foerst, Angelika. "Subtext Matters: The Queered Curriculum behind the Warrior Princess and the Bard." PhD diss., Arizona State University, 2008.

Fore, Stephen. "Jackie Chan and the Cultural Dynamics of Global Entertainment." In *Transnational Chinese Cinemas*, edited by Sheldon Hsiao-peng Lu, 239–62. Honolulu: University of Hawai'i Press, 1997.

Franks, Jonathan. "'Furious 7': Stunt Crew Members Reportedly Left Out of Credits."

Inquisitr, April 22, 2015. https://www.inquisitr.com/2034260/furious-7-stunt-crew-out-of-credits/.

Fu Poshek, and David Desser. Introduction to *The Cinema of Hong Kong: History, Arts Identity*, edited by Poshek Fu and David Desser, 1–16. Cambridge: Cambridge University Press, 1990.

Fung Hak-on. "The Bearable Lightness of Wire: A Milestone for the Wire." Collated by Keith Chan. Translated by Maggie Lee. In *A Tribute to Action Choreographers: A 30th Hong Kong International Film Festival Programme*, edited by Li Cheuk-to, 140–41. Hong Kong: Hong Kong International Film Festival Society, 2006.

Glick, Reuven, and Andrew K. Rose. "Contagion and Trade: Why Are Currency Crises Regional?" *Journal of International Money and Finance* 18 (1999): 603–17.

Goldstein, Joshua. *Drama Kings: Players and Publics in the Re-creation of Peking Opera, 1870–1937*. Berkeley: University of California Press, 2007.

Goldstein, Morris. *The Asian Financial Crisis: Causes, Cures, and Systemic Implications*. Policy Analyses in International Economics. Washington, DC: Institute for International Economics, 1998.

Govil, Nitin. "Wind(fall) from the East." *Television and New Media* 10, no. 1 (January 2009): 63–65.

Gruber, Hans, Erno Lehtinen, Tuire Palonen, and Stefan Degner. "Persons in the Shadow: Assessing the Social Context of High Abilities." *Psychology Science Quarterly* 50, no. 2 (2008): 237–58.

Guirdham, Maureen. *Work Communication: Mediated and Face-to-Face Practices*. New York: Palgrave, 2015.

Gunning, Tom. "An Aesthetic of Astonishment: Early Film and the (In)Credulous Spectator." In *Viewing Positions: Ways of Seeing Film*, edited by Linda Williams, 114–33. New Brunswick, NJ: Rutgers University Press, 1995.

Gunning, Tom. "The Cinema of Attractions: Early Film, Its Spectator and the Avant-Garde." In *Early Cinema: Space, Frame, Narrative*, edited by Thomas Elsaesser and Adam Barker, 56–62. London: British Film Institute, 1990.

Gwenllian-Jones, Sara. "Histories, Fictions, and *Xena: Warrior Princess*." In *The Audience Studies Reader*, edited by Will Brooker and Deborah Jermyn, 185–91. London: Routledge, 2003.

Halson, Elizabeth. *Peking Opera*. New York: Oxford University Press, 1966.

Hamera, Judith. "The Romance of Monsters: Theorizing the Virtuoso Body." *Theatre Topics* 10, no. 2 (September 2000): 144–53.

Hamilton, Annette. "Rumors, Foul Calumnies and the Safety of the State: Mass Media and National Identity in Thailand." In *National Identity and Its Defenders: Thailand Today*, edited by Craig J. Reynolds, 277–307. Chiang Mai, Thailand: Silkworm Books, 2002.

Hamming, Jeanne E. "Whatever Turns You On: Becoming-Lesbian and the Production of Desire in the Xenaverse." *Genders* 34 (October 2001). https://www.colorado.edu/gendersarchive1998-2013/2001/10/01/whatever-turns-you-becoming-lesbian-and-production-desire-xenaverse.

Hartwig, Eugene. "New Directives in Collective Bargaining." In *American Labor Policy: A*

Critical Appraisal of the National Labor Relations Act, edited by Charles J. Morris, 258–62. Washington, DC: Bureau of National Affairs, 1987.

Helford, Elyce Rae. "Feminism, Queer Studies, and the Sexual Politics of *Xena: Warrior Princess*." In *Fantasy Girls: Gender in the New Universe of Science Fiction and Fantasy Television*, edited by Elyce Rae Helford, 135–62. Lanham, MD: Rowman and Littlefield, 2000.

Hilmes, Michele. *Network Nations: A Transnational History of British and American Broadcasting*. New York: Routledge, 2011.

Hodgson, James D. "Enactment of OSHA Required Ingenious Compromises and Strategies." *Monthly Labor Review* 111 (1988): 41–43.

Holmlund, Chris. "Wham! Bam! Pam! Pam Grier as Hot Action Babe and Cool Action Mama." *Quarterly Review of Film and Video* 22, no. 2 (2005): 97–112.

Hunt, Leon. *Kung Fu Cult Masters: From Bruce Lee to "Crouching Tiger."* New York: Wallflower, 2003.

Hunt, Leon. "*Ong-Bak*: New Thai Cinema, Hong Kong and the Cult of the 'Real.'" *New Cinemas: Journal of Contemporary Film* 3, no. 2 (2005): 69–82.

Hunter, William Curt, George G. Kaufman, and Thomas H. Krueger. *The Asian Financial Crisis: Origins, Implications, and Solutions*. Chicago: Kluwer Academic, 1999.

Ingawanij, May Adadol. "*Nang Nak*: Thai Bourgeois Heritage Cinema." *Inter-Asia Cultural Studies* 8, no. 2 (May 2007): 180–93.

Irlam, Rowley. "Game Revealed: Season 7 Episode 4: Warrior Women (HBO)." Game of Thrones: Behind the Scenes, September 18, 2017. https://www.facebook.com/GameOfThrones/posts/10155173241602734.

Jarvie, I. C. *Window on Hong Kong: A Sociological Study of the Hong Kong Film Industry and Its Audience*. Hong Kong: University of Hong Kong Press, 1977.

Khan, Salaheen, Faridul Islam, and Syed Ahmed. "The Asian Crisis: An Economic Analysis of the Causes." *Journal of Developing Areas* 39, no. 1 (Fall 2005): 169–90.

King, Barry. "Articulating Stardom." In *Stardom: Industry of Desire*, edited by Christine Gledhill, 167–82. New York: Routledge, 1991.

Klysorikhew, Alongkorn. "Overview of Action Movies." In *Thai Cinema*, edited by Bastian Meiresonne, 70–81. Lyon: Asiaexpo, 2006.

Knee, Adam. "Thailand in the Hong Kong Cinematic Imagination." In *Hong Kong Film, Hollywood and the New Global Cinema: No Film Is an Island*, edited by Gina Marchetti and Tan See Kam, 77–90. New York: Routledge, 2007.

Kyriacou, Kate. "A Feisty Kiwi's Proof Positive." *Sunday Telegraph* (Sydney), November 4, 2007.

Landler, Mark. "Lee's 'Tiger,' Celebrated Everywhere but at Home." *New York Times*, February 27, 2001. https://www.nytimes.com/2001/02/27/movies/arts-abroad-lee-s-tiger-celebrated-everywhere-but-at-home.html.

Lave, Jean, and Etienne Wenger. *Situated Learning: Legitimate Peripheral Participation*. Cambridge: Cambridge University Press, 1991.

Law, Kar. "Stars in a Landscape: A Glance at Cantonese Movies of the Sixties." In *The Restless Breed: Cantonese Stars of the Sixties*, edited by Kar Law, 53–62. Hong Kong: Hong Kong Urban Council, 1996.

Lee, Bruce. *Tao of Jeet Kune Do*. Burbank, CA: Ohara, 1975.

Lee, Kwan-lung. "The Bearable Lightness of Wire: Interview with Lee Kwan-lung." Collated by Keith Chan. Translated by Maggie Lee. In *A Tribute to Action Choreographers: A 30th Hong Kong International Film Festival Programme,* edited by Li Cheuk-to, 140–43. Hong Kong: Hong Kong International Film Festival Society, 2006.

Li Ruru. *The Soul of Beijing Opera.* Hong Kong: Hong Kong University Press, 2010.

Lim, Bliss. *Translating Time: Cinema, the Fantastic, and Temporal Critique.* Durham, NC: Duke University Press, 2009.

Locke, Edwin A., and Gary P. Latham. *A Theory of Goal Setting and Task Performance.* Englewood Cliffs, NJ: Prentice Hall, 1990.

Logan, Bey. *Hong Kong Action Cinema.* New York: Overlook, 1996.

Lohanan, Roger. "The Elephant Situation in Thailand and a Plea for Co-operation." In *Giants on Our Hands: Proceedings of the International Workshop on the Domesticated Asian Elephant,* edited by Iljas Baker and Masakazu Kashio, 231–38. Bangkok: Food and Agriculture Organization of the United Nations, Regional Office for Asia and the Pacific, 2002.

Lowry, Brian. "XXIX Summer Olympics Opening Ceremony." *Variety,* August 9, 2008. http://variety.com/2008/scene/markets-festivals/xxix-summer-olympics-opening -ceremony-1200507863/.

Lu, Sheldon Hsiao-peng. "Historical Introduction: Chinese Cinemas (1896–1996) and Transnational Film Studies." In *Transnational Chinese Cinemas: Identity, Nationhood, Gender,* edited by Sheldon Hsiao-peng Lu, 1–32. Honolulu: University of Hawaii Press, 1997.

Mackerras, Colin. *Peking Opera.* New York: Oxford University Press, 1997.

Martin, Sylvia J. *Haunted: An Ethnography of the Hollywood and Hong Kong Media Industries.* New York: Oxford University Press, 2017.

Mendeloff, John. *Regulating Safety: An Economic and Political Analysis of Safety and Health Policy.* Cambridge, MA: MIT Press, 1979.

Metzner, Paul. *Crescendo of the Virtuoso: Spectacle, Skill, and Self-Promotion in Paris during the Age of Revolution.* Berkeley: University of California Press, 1998.

Miller, George. "The Magical Number Seven, Plus or Minus Two: Some Limits on Our Capacity for Processing Information." *Psychological Review* 63 (1956): 81–97.

Miller, Toby, Nitin Govil, John McMurria, and Richard Maxwell. *Global Hollywood.* London: British Film Institute, 2001.

Mintz, Benjamin W. *OSHA: History, Law, and Policy.* Washington, DC: Bureau of National Affairs, 1984.

Morreale, Joanne. "*Xena: Warrior Princess* as Feminist Camp." *Journal of Popular Culture* 32, no. 2 (1998): 79–86.

Morris, Meaghan. "Introduction: Hong Kong Connections." In *Hong Kong Connections: Transnational Imagination in Action Cinema,* edited by Meaghan Morris, Siu Leung Li, and Stephen Chan Ching-kiu, 1–18. Durham, NC: Duke University Press; Hong Kong: Hong Kong University Press, 2005.

Morris, Meaghan, Siu Leung Li, and Stephen Chan Ching-kiu, eds. *Hong Kong Connections: Transnational Imagination in Action Cinema.* Durham, NC: Duke University Press; Hong Kong: Hong Kong University Press, 2005.

Naficy, Hamid. *An Accented Cinema: Exilic and Diasporic Filmmaking*. Princeton, NJ: Princeton University Press, 2001.

Newmark, Peter. *Approaches to Translation*. Oxford: Pergamon, 1981.

Newmark, Peter. "Communicative and Semantic Translation." *Babel: International Journal of Translation* 23, no. 4 (1977): 163–80.

ntsoopsip@gmail.com. "Tony Jaa Now Free to Pursue What's Left of His Dreams." *Nation* (Thailand), July 9, 2015. http://www.nationmultimedia.com/life/Tony-Jaa-now-free-to-pursue-whats-left-of-his-drea-30264041.html.

Oldenburg, Ann. "Still Willing to Take the Fall." *USA Today*, June 6, 2003. http://www.usatoday.com/life/movies/news/2003-06-05-stunt_x.htm.

Poster, Winifred R., Marion Crain, and Miriam A. Cherry. "Introduction: Conceptualizing Invisible Labor." In *Invisible Labor: Hidden Work in the Contemporary World*, edited by Marion Crain, Winifred R. Poster, and Miriam A. Cherry, 3–27. Berkeley: University of California Press, 2016.

Purse, Lisa. *Contemporary Action Cinema*. Edinburgh: Edinburgh University Press, 2011.

Read, Jacinda. "The Cult of Masculinity: From Fan-Boys to Academic Bad-Boys." In *Defining Cult Movies: The Cultural Politics of Oppositional Tastes*, edited by Mark Jancovich, Antonio Lazaro Reboli, Julian Stringer, and Andrew Willis, 54–70. New York: Palgrave, 2003.

Redding, S. Gordon. *The Spirit of Chinese Capitalism*. New York: Walter de Gruyter, 1993.

Reid, Craig D. "Fighting without Fighting: Film Action Fight Choreography." *Film Quarterly* 47, no. 2 (Winter 1993–94): 30–35.

Reid, Craig. "*Spider-Man 2*: On the Lam." *Kung Fu Magazine*, July 12, 2009. http://ezine.kungfumagazine.com/ezine/article.php?article=528.

Ringis, Rita. *Elephants of Thailand in Myth, Art, and Reality*. Oxford: Oxford University Press, 1996.

Rodriguez, Hector. "Hong Kong Popular Culture as an Interpretive Arena: The Huang Feihong Film Series." *Screen* 38, no. 1 (Spring 1997): 1–24.

Ross, Sharon Marie. "Super(Natural) Women: Female Heroes, Their Friends, and Their Fans." PhD diss., University of Texas, 2004.

Rossol, Monona. *The Health and Safety Guide for Film, TV, and Theater*. New York: Allworth, 2000.

Sahamongkol Film International. "Tony Jaa Biography." Accessed February 4, 2010. http://www.iamtonyjaa.com/thai/biography.php.

Salthouse, Timothy A. "Effects of Age and Skill in Typing." *Journal of Experimental Psychology: General* 113, no. 3 (1984): 345–71.

Sassen, Saskia. *Territory, Authority, Rights: From Medieval to Global Assemblages*. Princeton, NJ: Princeton University Press, 2008.

Schechner, Richard. *Between Theater and Anthropology*. Philadelphia: University of Pennsylvania Press, 1985.

Sennett, Richard. *The Craftsman*. New Haven, CT: Yale University Press, 2008.

Shilling, Chris. "Physical Capital and Situated Action: A New Direction for Corporeal Sociology." *British Journal of Sociology of Education* 25, no. 4 (2004): 473–87.

Singh, Julietta. *Unthinking Mastery: Dehumanism and Decolonial Entanglements.* Durham, NC: Duke University Press, 2018.

Siriyuvasak, Ubonrat. "The Ambiguity of the 'Emerging' Public Sphere and the Thai Media Industry." In *The New Communications Landscape: Demystifying Media Globalization,* edited by Georgette Wang, Jan Servaes, and Anura Goonasekera, 97–123. New York: Routledge, 2000.

Sklar, Robert. *Movie-Made America: A Cultural History of American Movies.* New York: Vintage Books, 1994.

Smith, Jacob. "Seeing Double: Stunt Performers and Masculinity." *Journal of Film and Video* 56, no. 3 (Fall 2004): 35–53.

Sobchack, Vivian. *Carnal Thoughts: Embodiment and Moving Image Culture.* Berkeley: University of California Press, 2004.

Sofaer, Joanna R. *The Body as Material Culture: A Theoretical Osteoarchaeology.* New York: Cambridge University Press, 2006.

Stam, Robert. "Introduction: The Theory and Practice of Adaptation." In *Literature and Film: A Guide to the Theory and Practice of Film Adaptation,* edited by Robert Stam and Alessandra Raengo, 1–52. Malden, MA: Blackwell, 2005.

Starkes, Janet L., Janice M. Deakin, Fran Allard, Nicola J. Hodges, and April Hayes. "Deliberate Practice in Sports: What Is It Anyway?" In *The Road to Excellence: The Acquisition of Expert Performance in the Arts and Sciences, Sports and Games,* edited by K. Anders Ericsson, 81–106. New York: Psychology Press, 2014.

Steimer, Lauren. "Jackie Chan Fan Survey." Online survey. May 5, 2009.

Steimer, Lauren. "Jackie Chan Fan Survey." Online survey. October 3, 2009.

Steimer, Lauren. "Jackie Chan Fan Survey." Online survey. November 15, 2015.

Steimer, Lauren. "Tony Jaa Fan Survey." Online survey. January 15, 2010.

Steimer, Lauren. "Zoë Bell Fan Survey." Online survey. June 3, 2009.

Steimer, Lauren. "Zoë Bell Fan Survey." Online survey. August 5, 2009.

Stokes, Lisa Odham, and Michael Hoover. *City on Fire: Hong Kong Cinema.* New York: Verso, 1999.

Sukwong, Dome, and Sawasdi Suwannapak. *A Century of Thai Cinema.* Translated by Narisa Chakrabongse. London: Thames and Hudson, 2001.

Sullivan, George, and Tim Sullivan. *Stunt People.* New York: Beaufort Books, 1983.

Tasker, Yvonne. *Hollywood Action Adventure Film.* Malden, MA: Wiley Blackwell, 2015.

Teo, Stephen. *Chinese Martial Arts Cinema: The Wuxia Tradition.* Edinburgh: Edinburgh University Press, 2009.

Teo, Stephen. *Hong Kong Cinema: The Extra Dimensions.* London: British Film Institute, 1997.

Thussu, Daya Kishan. Introduction to *Media on the Move: Global Flow and Contra-Flow,* edited by Daya Kishan Thussu, 1–8. New York: Routledge, 2007.

Tipprasert, Prasob. "Elephants and Ecotourism in Thailand." In *Giants on Our Hands: Proceedings of the International Workshop on the Domesticated Asian Elephant,* edited by Iljas Baker and Masakazu Kashio, 157–72. Bangkok: Regional Office for Asia and the Pacific, 2002.

Tong Kai. "Interview with Tong Kai, the Invincible Master of Weapons." Interview by Donna Chu. Translated by Piera Chen. In *A Tribute to Action Choreographers: A 30th Hong Kong*

International Film Festival Programme, edited by Li Cheuk-to, 48–51. Hong Kong: Hong Kong International Film Festival Society, 2006.

Towers, Andrea. "Behind the Scenes of the 'Agents of SHIELD' May vs May Fight." *Entertainment Weekly*, December 18, 2014. http://ew.com/article/2014/12/18/agents-of-shield-may-fight/.

Tung, Stephen Wai. "Conquering the West, One Kick at a Time." Collated by Keith Chan. Translated by Davina To. In *A Tribute to Action Choreographers: A 30th Hong Kong International Film Festival Programme*, edited by Li Cheuk-to, 156–59. Hong Kong: Hong Kong International Film Festival Society, 2006.

Tung, Stephen Wai. "Interview with Stephen Tung Wai: Keeping It Real." Interview by Cheung Chi-sing, Li Cheuk-to, Pang Chi-ming, Bryan Chang, and Wong Ching. Translated by Bede Chang. In *A Tribute to Action Choreographers: A 30th Hong Kong International Film Festival Programme*, edited by Li Cheuk-to, 103–7. Hong Kong: Hong Kong International Film Festival Society, 2006.

US Department of Labor, Occupational Safety and Health Administration. "Duty to Have Fall Protection and Falling Object Protection." *Occupational Safety and Health Standards*. 1910.28. Accessed June 19, 2020. https://www.osha.gov/laws-regs/regulations/standardnumber/1910/1910.28.

US Department of Labor, Occupational Safety and Health Administration. "Walking-Working Surfaces." *Occupational Safety and Health Standards*. 1910:28. Accessed June 19, 2020. https://www.osha.gov/laws-regs/regulations/standardnumber/1910/1910.28.

Vismitananda, Yanin. "Q and A: Yanin Vismitananda." *BK Online*, January 30, 2008. Accessed March 1, 2012. http://bkmagazine.com/feature/q-yanin-vismitananda.

Wasko, Janet. "Financing and Production: Creating the Hollywood Film Commodity." In *The Contemporary Hollywood Film Industry*, edited by Paul McDonald and Janet Wasko, 43–62. Malden, MA: Blackwell, 2008.

Weatherwax, Rudd. Interview by Hedda Hopper. November 19, 1957. Hedda Hopper Collection. Margaret Herrick Library, Academy of Motion Picture Arts and Sciences, Beverly Hills, CA.

Weil, David. "If OSHA is So Bad, Why is Compliance So Good?" *RAND Journal of Economics* 27, no. 3 (Autumn 1996): 618–40.

Wenger, Etienne. *Communities of Practice: Learning, Meaning, and Identity*. New York: Cambridge University Press, 2003.

Willemen, Paul. "Action Cinema, Labour Power and the Video Market." In *Hong Kong Connections: Transnational Imagination in Action Cinema*, edited by Meaghan Morris, Siu Leung Li, and Stephen Chan Ching-kiu, 223–47. Durham, NC: Duke University Press; Hong Kong: Hong Kong University Press, 2005.

Williams, Linda. "Body Genres: Gender, Genre and Excess." In *Feminist Film Theory*, edited by Sue Thornham, 267–81. New York: New York University Press, 1999.

Wong, Cindy Hing-yuk. "Cities, Cultures and Cassettes: Hong Kong Cinema and Transnational Audiences." *Post Script* 19, no. 1 (Fall 1999): 87–106.

Yao, Hai-shing. "Martial-Acrobatic Arts in Peking Opera." *Journal of Asian Martial Arts* 10, no. 1 (2001): 18–35.

Yau, Esther Ching-mei, ed. *At Full Speed: Hong Kong Cinema in a Borderless World*. Minneapolis: University of Minnesota Press, 2001.

Yau, Esther Ching-mei, ed. "Introduction: Hong Kong Cinema in a Borderless World." In *At Full Speed: Hong Kong Cinema in a Borderless World*, edited by Esther Ching-mei Yau, 1–3. Minneapolis: University of Minnesota Press, 2001.

Yuen Woo-ping. "Conquering the West, One Kick at a Time." Collated by Keith Chan. Translated by Davina To. In *A Tribute to Action Choreographers: A 30th Hong Kong International Film Festival Programme*, edited by Li Cheuk-to, 156–59. Hong Kong: Hong Kong International Film Festival Society, 2006.

Yung Sai-shing. "Moving Body: The Interactions between Chinese Opera and Action Cinema." In *Hong Kong Connections: Transnational Imagination in Action Cinema*, edited by Meaghan Morris, Siu Leung Li, and Stephen Chan Ching-kiu, 21–34. Durham, NC: Duke University Press; Hong Kong: Hong Kong University Press, 2005.

Zarrilli, Phillip B. "What Does It Mean to 'Become the Character': Power, Presence, and Transcendence in Asian In-Body Disciplines of Practice." In *By Means of Performance: Intercultural Studies of Theatre and Ritual*, edited by Richard Schechner and Willa Appel, 131–48. Cambridge: Cambridge University Press, 1990.

Zhang, Ying-jin. "National Cinema as Translocal Practice: Reflections on Chinese Film Historiography." In *The Chinese Cinema Book*, edited by Song-hwee Lim and Julian Ward, 17–25. London: British Film Institute, 2011.

Zhang Zhen. *An Amorous History of the Silver Screen: Shanghai Cinema, 1896–1937*. Chicago: University of Chicago Press, 2005.

Zhang Zhen. "Bodies in the Air: The Magic of Science and the Fate of the Early 'Martial Arts' Film in China." *Post Script* 20, nos. 2–3 (Winter–Spring 2001): 43–60.

Zhang Zhen. "Teahouse, Shadowplay, Bricolage: Laborer's Love and the Question of Early Chinese Cinema." In *Cinema and Urban Culture in Shanghai, 1922–1943*, edited by Ying-jin Zhang, 27–50. Stanford, CA: Stanford University Press, 1999.

Zhao, Yue-zhi. "Whose *Hero*? The 'Spirit' and 'Structure' of a Made-in-China Global Blockbuster." In *Reorienting Global Communication: Indian and Chinese Media beyond Borders*, edited by Michael Curtin and Hemant Shaw, 161–82. Urbana: University of Illinois Press, 2010.

Filmography

Armstrong, Vic, stunt coordinator. *Superman*. Directed by Richard Donner. Los Angeles: Dovemead Films, Film Export, and International Film Production, 1978.

Bell, Peter, and Shane Dawson, action choreographers. *Xena: Warrior Princess*. Created by Rob Tapert and John Schulian. Aired September 15, 1995–June 18, 2001. United States and New Zealand: Renaissance Pictures and Universal Television (syndicated).

Bell, Zoë, and Lucy Lawless. "Seeing Double." Disc 7. *Xena: Warrior Princess*. Tenth Anniversary Collection. Beverly Hills: Anchor Bay Entertainment, 2005.

Benioff, David, and D. B. Weiss, creators. *Game of Thrones.* Aired April 17, 2011–May 19, 2019, on HBO.

Brewster, Chris, and Philip J. Silvera, action choreographers. *Daredevil.* Created by Drew Goddard. Written by Bill Everett. Streamed April 10, 2015–October 19, 2018, on Netflix. United States: ABC Studios, DeKnight Productions, Goddard Textiles, Marvel Entertainment, and The Walt Disney Company.

Caouette, Kirk, Steve M. Davison, Mike Gunther, and Jacob Rupp, action choreographers. *Catwoman.* Directed by Pitof. Los Angeles: Warner Bros Pictures, DiNovi Pictures, Maple Shade Films, Catwoman Films; Beverly Hills: Village Roadshow Pictures; Winnipeg: Frantic Films, 2004.

Chan, Jackie, dir. *Jackie Chan: My Stunts* (*Cheng Long: Wo De Te Ji*; 成龍:我的特技). Hong Kong: Jackie Chan Group and Media Asia Films, 1999.

Chan, Jackie, action choreographer. *Who Am I* (*Wo Shi Shei*; 我是誰). Directed by Benny Chan and Jackie Chan. Hong Kong: Golden Harvest Entertainment Company, 1998.

Chan, Jackie, Bradley James Allan, Eddie Braun, Philippe Guegan, Michel Julienne, and Conrad Palmisano, action choreographers. *Rush Hour 3.* Directed by Brett Ratner. New York: New Line Cinema; Los Angeles: Roger Birnbaum Productions, 2007.

Chan, Jackie, Bradley James Allan, Steve M. Davison, Chung Chi-li, and Jaroslav Peterka, action choreographers. *Shanghai Knights.* Directed by David Dobkin. Burbank, CA: Touchstone Pictures; Los Angeles: Spyglass Entertainment, Birnbaum/Barber Productions, All Knight Productions; Hong Kong: Jackie Chan Films, 2003.

Chan, Jackie, Danny Chow Yun-gin, Benny Lai Keung-kuen, Fung Hak-on, Mars, Paul Wong Kwan, and Chris Lee Kin-sang, action choreographers. *Police Story* (*Jingcha Gushi*; 警察故事). Directed by Jackie Chan. Hong Kong: Golden Harvest, 1985.

Chan, Jackie, Muhammed Ali Kesici, Terry Leonard, Chung Chi-li, and Sam Wong Ming-sing, action choreographers. *Rush Hour.* Directed by Brett Ratner. New York: New Line Cinema; Los Angeles: Roger Birnbaum Productions, 1998.

Chan, Jackie, Muhammed Ali Kesici, Ed McDermott II, Conrad E. Palmisano, and Scott Richards, action choreographers. *Rush Hour 2.* Directed by Brett Ratner. New York: New Line Cinema; Los Angeles: Roger Birnbaum Productions, 2001.

Chang, Che, dir. *Tiger Boy* (*Hu Xia Jian Chou*; 虎俠殲仇). Hong Kong: Shaw Brothers, 1966.

Cheung Yiu-sing, Donnie Yen, and Yuen Bun, action choreographers. *Dragon Inn* (*Xin Long Men Ke Zhan*; 新龍門客棧). Directed by Raymond Lee. Hong Kong: Film Workshop and Seasonal Film Corporation, 1992.

Ching, Tony Siu-tung, action choreographer. *Beijing 2008 Olympic Opening Ceremony*. Directed by Zhang Yi-mou. Aired August 8, 2008, on China Central Television and NBC.

Ching, Tony Siu-tung, action choreographer. *Heroic Trio* (*Dung Fong San Xia*; 東方三俠). Directed by Johnny To. Hong Kong: China Entertainment Films Production and Paka Hill Productions, 1993.

Ching, Tony Siu-tung, Dion Lam Dik-on, and Ma Yuk-sing, action choreographers. *Swordsman III: The East Is Red* (*Dong Fang Bu Bai: Feng Yun Zai Qi*; 東方不敗一風雲再起). Directed by Raymond Lee Wai-man and Tony Ching Siu-tung. Hong Kong: Film Workshop, Long Shong Pictures, and Golden Princess Film Production, 1993..

Ching, Tony Siu-tung, Lau Chi-ho, and Yuen Wah, action choreographers. *Swordsman* (*Xiao Ao Jiang Hu*; 笑傲江湖). Directed by King Hu, Tony Ching Siu-tung, Ann Hui, Tsui Hark, Andrew Kam Yeung-wa, and Raymond Lee Wai-man. Hong Kong: Film Workshop, 1990.

Ching, Tony Siu-tung, Alan Chung Shan-tsui, Lau Chi-ho, Tsu Kwok, and Wu Chi-lung, action choreographers. *Chinese Ghost Story* (*Qian Nu You Hun*; 倩女幽魂). Directed by Tony Ching Siu-tung. Produced by Tsui Hark. Hong Kong: Cinema City Film Productions and Film Workshop, 1987..

Ching, Tony Siu-tung, Yuen Bun, Cheung Yiu-sing, and Ma Yuk-sing, action choreographers. *Swordsman II* (*Xiao Ao Jiang Hu II: Dong Fang Bu Bai*; 笑傲江湖 II 東方不敗). Directed by Tony Ching Siu-tung. Hong Kong: Film Workshop, Long Shong Pictures, and Golden Princess Film Production, 1992.

Cooke, Ben, and Kyle Gardiner, stunt coordinators. *Thor: Ragnarok*. Directed by Taika Waititi. Los Angeles: Marvel Studios and Walt Disney Pictures, 2017.

Cooke, Ben, and Allan Poppleton, action choreographers. *Hercules: The Legendary Journeys*. Created by Christian Williams. Aired January 16, 1995–November 22, 1999 (syndicated).

Costelloe, Jonathan, action choreographer. *Amazon High*. Directed by Michael Hurst. New York: Renaissance Pictures, 1997. Unaired pilot.

Cramer, Douglas S., producer. *Wonder Woman*. Aired November 7, 1975–September 11, 1979, on ABC and CBS.

Crane, Simon, action choreographer. *Goldeneye*. Directed by Martin Campbell. London: Eon Productions; Los Angeles: United Artists, 1995.

Dashnaw, Jeff, action choreographer. *Death Proof*. Directed by Quentin Tarantino. New York: Dimension Films, Weinstein Company; Austin: Troublemaker Studios, Rodriguez International Pictures, 2007.

de Broca, Philippe, dir. *Les Tribulations d'un Chinois et Chine* (*Chinese Adventures in China*). Paris: Les Films Ariane, Les Productions Aristes Associés, and Vides Cinematogragica, 1965.

Doyle, Chris, action choreographer. *Army of Darkness*. Directed by Sam Raimi. Wilmington, NC : Dino De Laurentiis Company, 1992.

Franklin, Richard, dir. *Patrick*. Melbourne: Filmways Australasia, 1978.

Friedkin, William, dir. *The Exorcist*. Los Angeles: Warner Brothers, Hoya Productions, 1973.

Friedman, Liz, Doug Lefler, David Pollison, and Robert Tapert. "Xena's Hong Kong Origins." Disc 7. *Xena: Warrior Princess*. Tenth Anniversary Collection. Beverly Hills: Anchor Bay Entertainment, 2005.

Geerlings, Evan, producer. *Xena's Hong Kong Origins*. West Hollywood: Davis-Panzer Productions, 2005.

Han, Ying-chieh, action choreographer. *The Big Boss* (*Tang Shan Daxiong*; 唐山大兄). Directed by Lo Wei. Hong Kong: Golden Harvest, 1971.

Han, Ying-chieh, and Poon Kin-kwan, action choreographers. *Come Drink with Me* (*Da Zui Xia*; 大醉俠). Directed by King Hu. Hong Kong: Shaw Brothers, 1966.

Han Ying-chieh, and Pan Yao-kun, action choreographers. *A Touch of Zen* (*Xia Nu*; 俠女). Directed by King Hu. Hong Kong: Union Film Company, 1971.

Hargrave, Sam, stunt coordinator. *Atomic Blonde*. Directed by David Leitch. Los Angeles: 87eleven, Closed on Mondays Entertainment, and Denver and Delilah Productions, 2017.

Hung, Sammo Kam-bo, action choreographer. *Ashes of Time* (*Dong Xie Xi Du*; 東邪西). Directed by Wong Kar-wai. Hong Kong: Beijing Film Studio, Jet Tone Production, Pony Canyon, and Scholar Productions, 1994.

Hung, Sammo Kam-bo, action choreographer. *Enter the Dragon*. Directed by Robert Clouse. Hong Kong: Golden Harvest and Concord Productions; Los Angeles: Sequoia Productions, and Warner Brothers Pictures, 1973.

Hung, Sammo Kam-bo, action choreographer. *Painted Faces* (*Qi Xiao Fu*; 七小福). Directed by Alex Law. Hong Kong: Golden Harvest and Shaw Brothers, 1988.

Hung, Sammo Kam-bo, and Jackie Chan, action choreographers. *Project A* (*'A' Ji Hua*; A 計劃). Directed by Jackie Chan. Hong Kong: Paragon Films, 1983.

Jaa, Tony, action choreographer. *Ong Bak 3* (องค์บาก 3). Directed by Tony Jaa and Panna Rittikrai. Bangkok: Iyara Films, 2010.

Jaa, Tony, and Panna Rittikrai, action choreographers. *Ong Bak 2* (องค์บาก 2). Directed by Tony Jaa and Panna Rittikrai. Bangkok: Sahamongkolfilm International and Iyara Films, 2008.

Jaa, Tony, and Panna Rittikrai, action choreographers. *The Protector* (*Tom-Yum-Goong*; ต้มยำกุ้ง). Directed by Prachya Pinkaew. Bangkok: Sahamongkolfilm, Baa-Ram-Ewe, TF1 International, and Golden Network, 2005.

Jaa, Tony, Panna Rittikrai, and Seng Kawee, action choreographers. *Ong Bak: Muay Thai Warrior* (องค์บาก). Directed by Prachya Pinkaew. Bangkok: Baa-Ram-Ewe and Sahamongkolfilm, 2003.

Jensen, Gary, action choreographer. *Evil Dead II*. Directed by Sam Raimi. Wilmington, NC: De Laurentiis Entertainment Group; New York, NY: Renaissance Pictures, 1987.

Kreigsman, Jan, action choreographer. *They Call Her One Eye* (*Thriller—en grym film*). Directed by Bo Arne Vibenius. Stockholm: BAV Film, United Producers, 1973.

Kwok, Phillip Chung-fung, action choreographer. *Bride with White Hair* (*Bai Fa Mo Nu Zhuan*; 白髮魔女傳). Directed by Ronny Yu. Hong Kong: Mandarin Films Distribution Co., 1993.

Lau Kar-leung and Jackie Chan, action choreographers. *Drunken Master II* (*Zui Quan Er*; 醉拳二). Directed by Lau Kar-leung and Jackie Chan. Hong Kong: Golden Harvest, Hong Kong Stuntman Association, and Paragon Films, 1994.

Lau Kar-leung and Tong Kai, action choreographers. *The Jade Bow* (*Wan Hoi Yuk Gung Yuen*; 雲海玉弓緣). Directed by Fu Chi and Cheung Sing-yim. Hong Kong: Great Wall Movie Enterprises Limited, 1966.

Lee, Bruce, martial arts dir. *The Way of the Dragon* (*Meng Long Guo Jiang*; 猛龍過江). Directed by Bruce Lee. Hong Kong: Golden Harvest and Concord Production, 1972.

Lee, Bruce, and Sammo Hung Kam-bo, action choreographers. *Game of Death*. Directed by Robert Clouse and Bruce Lee. Hong Kong: Golden Harvest; Los Angeles: Columbia Pictures, 1978.

Lew, James, Alvin Hsing, Guy Fernandez, and Matt Mullins, action choreographers. *Luke Cage*. Written by Cheo Hodari Coker. Streamed September 30, 2016–June 22, 2018, on

Netflix. Burbank, CA: Disney-ABC Domestic Television, Marvel Television, and Walt
Disney Television; Los Gatos, CA: Netflix.

Liu Kar-wing, action choreographer. *Armour of God* (*Long Xiong Hu Di*; 龙兄虎弟). Directed
by Jackie Chan and Eric Tsang. Hong Kong: Golden Harvest, 1987

Mak Wai-cheung, Dang Tak-wing, Hi Hon-chau, Chan Man-ching, Sam Wong Ming-sing,
Stanley Tong Gwai-lai, and Ailen Sit Chun-wai, action choreographers. *Police Story 3:
Supercop* (*Jingcha Gushi 3: Chao Ji Jing Cha*; 警察故事 3: 超級警察). Directed by Stanley
Tong Gwai-lai. Hong Kong: Golden Harvest Company and Golden Way Films, 1992.

Micheli, Amanda, dir. *Double Dare*. San Francisco: Runaway Films; Atlanta, GA: Goodmovies
Entertainment; Los Angeles: Map Point Pictures, 2005.

Mullins, Matt, fight choreographer. *Agents of S.H.I.E.L.D.* Season 2, episode 4, "Face My Enemy." Directed by Kevin Tancharoen. Aired October 14, 2014, on ABC.

Newmeyer, Fred, and Sam Taylor, dirs. *Safety Last*. Culver City: Hal Roach Studios, 1923.

Perkins, Peter, action choreographer. *From Russia with Love*. Directed by Terence Young.
Santa Monica: Danjaq; London: Eon Productions, 1963.

Poppleton, Allan, action choreographer. *Xena: Warrior Princess*. Season 6, episode 16, "Send in
the Clones." Directed by Charlie Haskell. Aired April 23, 2001 (syndicated).

Poppleton, Allan, action choreographer. *Xena: Warrior Princess*. Season 6, episode 21, "A
Friend in Need, Part 1." Directed by Robert Tapert. Aired June 11, 2001 (syndicated).

Poppleton, Allan, and Paul Shapcott, stunt coordinators. *Underworld: Rise of the Lycans*. Directed by Patrick Tatopoulos. Beverly Hills: Lakeshore Entertainment; Culver City:
Screen Gems; Los Angeles: Sketch Films and UW3 Film Productions, 2009.

Poppleton, Allan, and Stuart Thorpe, stunt coordinators. *The Chronicles of Narnia: The Lion,
the Witch, and the Wardrobe*. Los Angeles: Walt Disney Pictures and Walden Media,
2005.

Prescott, Darrin, stunt coordinator. *John Wick*. Directed by Chad Stahelski and David Leitch.
Santa Monica: Thunder Road Pictures; Los Angeles: 87eleven, MJW Films, and
DefyNite Films, 2014.

Raimi, Sam, dir. *The Evil Dead*. New York: Renaissance Pictures, 1981.

Rittikrai, Panna, action choreographer. *Chocolate* (ช็อคโกแลต). Directed by Prachya Pinkaew.
Bangkok: Sahamongkolfilm International and Baa-Ram-Ewe, 2008.

Rittikrai, Panna, action choreographer. *Power Kids* (5 หัวใจฮีโร่; *5 Hawci Hiro*). Directed by Krissanapong Rachata. Bangkok: Baa-Ram-Ewe, 2009.

Rittikrai, Panna, action choreographer. *Raging Phoenix* (*Deu Suay Doo*; ดึอ สวย ดุ). Directed by
Rashane Limtrakul. Bangkok: Sahamongkolfilm and Baa-Ram-Ewe, 2009.

Rittikrai, Panna, martial arts choreographer. *This Girl Is Bad Ass!!* (*Jukkalan*; จิกกะแหลน). Directed by Petchtai Wongkamlao. Bangkok: Bam-Ram-Ewe, 2011.

Rittikrai, Panna, and Banlu Srisaeng, action choreographers. *Born to Fight* (*Kerd ma Lui*; เกิดมา
ลุย). Directed by Panna Rittikrai. Bangkok: Baa-Ram-Ewe and Sahamongkolfilm, 2004.

Rittikrai, Panna, and Weerapon Poomatfon, action choreographers. *The Kick* (더 킥; *Deo Kig*).
Directed by Prachya Pinkaew. Bangkok: Baa-Ram-Ewe, Bangkok Film Studio; Seoul:
Kick Company, 2011.

Rounthwaite, Mark, action choreographer. *Xena: Warrior Princess*. Season 6, episode 22, "A

Friend in Need, Part 2." Directed by Robert Tapert. Aired June 18, 2001 (syndicated). United States and New Zealand: Renaissance Pictures Limited and Universal Television.

Ruge, George Marshall, action choreographer. *Lord of the Rings: Fellowship of the Ring*. Directed by Peter Jackson. New York: New Line Cinema; Wellington: WingNut Films, 2001.

Ruge, George Marshall, action choreographer. *Lord of the Rings: Return of the King*. Directed by Peter Jackson. New York: New Line Cinema; Wellington: WingNut Films, 2003.

Ruge, George Marshall, action choreographer. *Lord of the Rings: The Two Towers*. Directed by Peter Jackson. New York: New Line Cinema; Wellington: WingNut Films, 2002.

Sandrich, Mark, dir. *Shall We Dance*. Los Angeles: RKO Radio Pictures, 1937.

Simmons, Bob, action choreographer. *Dr. No*. Directed by Terence Young. Santa Monica: Danjaq; London: Eon Productions, 1962.

Simmons, Bob, action choreographer. *Goldfinger*. Directed by Guy Hamilton. Santa Monica: Danjaq; London: Eon Productions, 1964.

Stahelski, Chad, stunt coordinator. *Serenity*. Directed by Joss Whedon. Universal City: Universal Pictures; Los Angeles: Barry Mendel Productions, 2005.

Suter, Glen, and Steve Griffin, stunt coordinators. *Mad Max: Fury Road*. Directed by George Miller. Los Angeles: Warner Bros. Pictures; Melbourne: Village Roadshow Pictures; Sydney: Kennedy Miller Productions, 2015.

Thorpe, Stuart, Dayna Grant, and Tim Wong, stunt coordinators. *Ash vs Evil Dead*. Produced by Robert Tapert. Aired October 31, 2015–April 29, 2018, on Starz. United States and New Zealand: Renaissance Pictures and Starz!

Thorpe, Stuart, Dayna Grant, and Tim Wong, stunt coordinators. *Ash vs Evil Dead*. Season 3, episode 6, "Tales from the Rift." Directed by Regan Hall. Written by Aaron Lam. Aired April 1, 2018, on Starz.

Tong, Stanley Gwai-lai, and Jackie Chan, action choreographers. *Police Story 4: First Strike* (*Jingcha Gushi 4: Zhi Jian Dan Ren Wu*; 警察故事 4:之簡單任務). Directed by Stanley Tong Gwai-lai. Hong Kong: Golden Harvest Company, New Line Cinema, Paragon Films, and Raymond Chow, 1996.

Tong, Stanley Gwai-lai, and Jackie Chan, action choreographers. *Rumble in the Bronx* (*Hung Fan Ou*; 紅番區). Directed by Stanley Tong Gwai-lai. Hong Kong: Golden Harvest Productions, 1995.

Weatherwax, Rudd, animal wrangler. *Lassie Come Home*. Directed by Fred M. Wilcox. Beverly Hills, CA: Loew's/MGM, 1943.

Wise, Robert, dir. *The Sand Pebbles*. Los Angeles: Argyle Enterprises, Robert Wise Productions, Solar Productions, and Twentieth Century Fox, 1966.

Yuen Biao, stunt choreographer. *Shanghai Noon*. Directed by Tom Dey. Burbank, CA: Touchstone Pictures; Los Angeles: Spyglass Entertainment, Birnbaum/Barber Productions; Hong Kong: Jackie Chan Films, 2000.

Yuen Cheung-yan, Yuen Sun-yi, and Lau Kar-wing, action choreographers. *Once upon a Time in China* (*Huang Fei-hong*; 黃飛鴻). Directed by Tsui Hark. Hong Kong: Golden Harvest Company and Film Workshop, 1991.

Yuen, Corey Kwai, Kuo Hin-chui, Alien Sit, and Yuen Tak, action choreographers. *Fong Sai-*

yuk (方世玉; *Fang Shi Yu*). Directed by Corey Yuen Kwai. Hong Kong: Eastern Productions, 1993.

Yuen Woo-ping, action choreographer. *Crouching Tiger, Hidden Dragon* (*Wohu Canglong*; 卧虎藏龙). Directed by Ang Lee. Beijing: China Film Co-Production Company, Columbia Pictures Film Production Asia, EDKO Film, Zoom Hunt International Productions, United China Vision, and Asia Union Film and Entertainment; New York City: Sony Pictures Classics and Good Machine, 2000.

Yuen Woo-ping, action choreographer. *The Matrix*. Directed by Lana and Lilly Wachowski. Los Angeles: Silver Pictures, Groucho II Film Partnership, and Warner Brothers; Melbourne: Village Roadshow Pictures, 1999.

Yuen Woo-ping, action choreographer. *The Matrix Reloaded*. Directed by Lana and Lilly Wachowski. Los Angeles: Heineken Branded Entertainment, NPV Entertainment, Silver Pictures, and Warner Bros; Melbourne: Village Roadshow Pictures, 2003.

Yuen Woo-ping, and Hsu Hsia, action choreographers. *Drunken Master*, directed by Yuen Woo-ping. Hong Kong: Golden Harvest and Seasonal Film Corporation, 1978.

Yuen Woo-ping, Sonny Chiba, Keith Adams, and Ku Huen-chiu, action choreographers. *Kill Bill: Vol. 1*. Directed by Quentin Tarantino. Los Angeles: A Band Apart and Super Cool ManChu; New York: Miramax Films, 2003.

Yuen Woo-ping, Sonny Chiba, Keith Adams, and Ku Huen-chiu, action choreographers. *Kill Bill: Vol. 2*. Directed by Quentin Tarantino. Los Angeles: A Band Apart and Super Cool ManChu; New York: Miramax Films, 2004.

Index

Page numbers in italics refer to figures.

Stunt Team; *Xena: Warrior Princess*; Yuen Woo-ping Stunt Team

stunting, 4, 13, 31, 60, 93, 103, 105, 141, 143, 169; as craftwork, 123, 140; communities of practice, 22, 122, 128, 132, 135–36, 138–39, 144, 159, 161; in Hollywood, 5, 20; in Hong Kong-style action, 121; as spectacular feats, 20–21, 37, 56, 71, 72, 77, 83, 118; and team-work, 5, 34, 40, 42, 44, 46, 53, 55, 78, 80–82, 101, 123, 133, 136–37, 140–41, 150–51, 157, 160, 161, 165. *See also* 87eleven Action Design team; *Jackie Chan: My Stunts*; Jackie Chan Stunt Team; Muay Thai Stunt Team; stunting stars

stunting stars, 2, 4, 19, 22, 118–19, 171; and bodily peril, 20, 26, 36, 42, 49, 53, 67, 81; expertise of, 57, 61, 70, 91, 115, 116; in Holly-wood, 2, 191n66; in Hong Kong cinema, 2, 85, 87; labor of, 4, 13, 46, 87, 103, 105, 117, 163; and spectators, 46, 119, 192n77; and training, 5, 69, 104; and virtuosity, 14, 21. *See also* Bell, Zoë; body spectacle; Chan, Jackie; Jaa, Tony; Lee, Bruce; Vismita-nanda, Yanin "Jeeja"

Sui-tien, Yuen, 26

Supercop, 44

Superman, 132, 133

superstition, 94

Swinton, Tilda, 148

swordplay films, 26, 28, 94

Swordsman series, 94, 100

symmetrical organization of perspectival relations, 25

tae kwon do, 7, 80, 87, 89, 104, 106–7, 109, 111, 161

taichi quan (flowing energy fist), 42

Tak-hing, Kwan, 27, 94

Tancharoen, Kevin, 169

tanzi gong (mat/rug work), 30

Tapert, Robert, 98, 99

Tarantino, Quentin, 109, 115

Tasker, Yvonne, 69, 70

Tat-chiu, Lee, 144, *145*, *146*

Television Broadcasts Limited (TVB), 26

Teo, Stephen, 95, 96, 100

Tesch-Römer, Clemens, 29

Thai Motion Picture Producers Associa-tion, 63

theater ownership, 62

Theron, Charlize, 148

This Girl Is Bad Ass!!, 84

Thorpe, Stuart, 148, 155

Thurman, Uma, 110, 112, *113*

Thussu, Daya Kishan, 126

Tiger Boy, 96

Tong Kai, 132

tourism, 78

training. *See* Bell, Zoë: training; Chan, Jackie: training; deliberate practice; Grant, Dayna: training; Jaa, Tony: train-ing; Lee, Bruce: training; Peking opera: training; Vismitananda, Yanin "Jeeja": training

trampolines/minitramps, 28, 89, 91, 93, 94, 97, 107

translocal/translocality, 5, 19, 125, 127, 128, 131, 136, 173

transnational Chinese cinemas, 95, 125, 126

transnational labor, 7, 126

transnational media studies, 16, 17, 22, 122, 123, 125, 127, 128, 139, 140, 156, 160, 172–73

transnational media, 17, 22, 123, 123, 125, 127, 128, 139, 140, 156, 160, 172, 173

Triads. *See* Hong Kong cinema: Triad control of; Organized Crime and Triad Ordinance (Hong Kong)

Triple O (One On One), 33

Tung, Stephen Wai, 134

Underworld: Rise of the Lichens, 149

Union Odeon Company, 64

US Occupational Safety and Health Adminis-tration (OSHA), 49, 50, 53, 54

virtuoso reception context, 13–16, 21, 24, 35–37, 45–46, 52, 57, 58, 59, 61, 72, 73, 89, 105, 116, 120, 130, 173